Foundations of Software Measurement

Martin Shepperd

Prentice Hall

London New York Toronto Singapore Tokyo
Madrid Mexico City Munich

First published 1995 by
Prentice Hall International (UK) Limited
Campus 400, Maylands Avenue
Hemel Hempstead
Hertfordshire, HP2 7EZ
A division of
Simon & Schuster International Group

Typeset in 10pt Times
by Mathematical Composition Setters, Salisbury Wiltshire.

Printed and bound in Great Britain by
T J Press (Padstow) Ltd.

Library of Congress Cataloging-in-Publication Data

Shepperd, Martin, 1959-
Foundations of software measurement/Martin Shepperd.
p. cm.
Includes bibliographical references and index.
ISBN 0-13-336199-3
1. Computer software–Quality control. I. Title.
QA76.76.Q35S53 1995 95-6634
005.1′068′5-dc20 CIP

British Library Cataloguing in Publication Data

A catalogue record for this book is available from the British Library

ISBN 0-13-336199-3

1 2 3 4 5 99 98 97 96 95

To Linda

Contents

Preface

Over recent years there has been a growing awareness of the relationship between engineering and measurement: that if software engineering as a concept is to be taken seriously, then consideration must be given to the role of measurement. Despite this awareness, the translation of theory into practice has at best been painstaking, and frequently imperceptible. Why should this be so? There is a variety of reasons but perhaps most important are the naïve and highly *ad hoc* approaches that are typically brought to bear. Software systems, and the processes to build them, can be amongst the most complex of human endeavours, yet the majority of workers in the field have paid insufficient attention to the development of sound models and the underlying theory of their measurements. As a result, software engineering measures, or metrics as they are often termed, can end up as grotesque simplifications and meaningless caricatures of the systems and processes they purport to represent. Moreover, they are frequently collected with no coherent view of how to use them;

This book has as its aim the better integration of measurement into the practice of software engineering. In order to accomplish this, the reader is provided with sufficient theoretical background to understand, develop and apply metrics to software engineering projects. Consequently, the book covers a range of topics, including measurement theory, statistics and experimental design. A particular concern is the use of measurement within the context of models. It is strongly argued that modelling is a powerful aid for understanding what is to be measured, together with the meaning of the measurement, and that without some form of model, measurement can degenerate into an aimless collection of numbers.

It is intended that the book will provide a self contained introduction to the field of software engineering metrics. It is unusual in that it seeks to combine *modern* metrics research with a practical treatment of the industrial application of these metrics. However, it is not aimed to be an exhaustive treatise on all published metrics, about many of which the author has serious reservations concerning either their formal foundations or their utility. Rather, the emphasis is upon general methods and techniques – illustrated by specific examples – which equip the reader to develop and apply metrics to his or her own specific situation. There are no universal solutions. Useful software engineering measurement requires effort.

Audience

This book is written for an audience with some background knowledge in software engineering or software development, although no prior knowledge of software metrics is assumed. It is anticipated that it will be of particular interest to final year computer science undergraduates, post-graduates and researchers in the field of software engineering. The emphasis upon applying research results should also make it relevant to the needs of project managers and anybody establishing a software metrics programme within an organization.

Structure

Chapters 1–5 form the necessary foundations for the development and evaluation of software metrics. The subsequent chapters offer more advanced material upon specific topics that the reader can access if, when, and in what order, required. For example, a reader already well versed in statistics and experimental design might omit Chapter 7, whilst other readers with an implacable hatred of mathematics would do well to omit Chapter 6!

Acknowledgements

Many people have contributed to this book. Ian Bray provided the soft touch systems example used in Chapter 5 and Liguang Chen the role activity diagram in Chapter 8. Thank you. Thanks are due to the many people who commented on early drafts: Norman Fenton, Paul Goodman, Darrel Ince, Chris Kemerer, Barbara Kitchenham, Andrew Khan, David Knight, Keith Phalp and Steve Webster. Finally, my gratitude goes (again) to Jacqui Harbor of Prentice Hall who has had the patience and professionalism to steer this project from a wild idea to a completed manuscript.

Martin Shepperd
School of Computing and Cognition
Bournemouth University

Part 1

Foundations

Chapter 1

Introducting software measurement

Synopsis

Measurement is becoming an increasingly accepted part of software engineering, but it is not always a well-understood one. A distinction is made between measures as representations of observable attributes of objects or processes and prediction systems that combine measurements and parameters in order to make quantitative predictions. This is an important distinction when validating measures. By recourse to measurement theory it can be determined whether the measure is proper in the sense of representing the attribute adequately. However, empirical validation of the engineering usefulness of a measure requires an explicit prediction system.

1.1 What is measurement?

This book concerns measurement. It is therefore appropriate to consider briefly what we mean by measurement. It is such an everyday activity that we take it for granted. Measurement is defined as:

the process of assigning symbols, usually numbers, to represent an attribute of the entity of interest, by rule.

There are a number of points to note from this definition. First, the *entity* that we wish to measure can either be an object, for example a person or a computer program, or it could be a process, for example travelling from Bournemouth to London or debugging some code. Second, there must be some distinct *attribute* that we wish to measure; examples are: height, length, duration and cost. Third, typically, although not necessarily,[1] we use numbers to *represent* the attribute being measured. The length of a program could be represented by the number 315 or the letter 'Q' or the vector $\langle 1, 9, -0.2 \rangle$. At present we will postpone the issue of scale and units, so it will remain unclear whether the program length is 315 lines of code (LOC) or bytes or something else. Last, and certainly not least, is the requirement that the assignment of numbers, or whatever, must be according to some explicit *rule*. In other words, we must know how to choose which symbol should represent the attribute. Without this caveat, we wouldn't be able to discriminate between measurement and the random assignment of numbers. This requirement for explicit rules provides a basis for objectivity in the measurement process. If we can't tell why the attribute being measured is represented by a given number, it makes the process impossible to reproduce, or, at the very least, vulnerable to bias from the person carrying out the process. The more carefully the rules are defined the more scope there is for objectivity. Of course, we can have unambiguous rules and still suffer from measurement error. This type of 'noise' is overcome either by improving the data collection methods or by a statistical treatment of the data, where it is assumed that errors will follow a recognizable distribution.

1.2 Why measure?

Why measure? We measure in order to answer questions. How large? How maintainable? Does technique A yield more productivity gains than technique B? What characterizes error-prone programs? How long will it take? So, if we have no questions, we have no need of measurement. Measurement informs our analysis and hones our critical faculties, it helps us to overcome subjectivity and provides a level of precision not otherwise possible. This is not to say that measurement is a panacea – misuse is all too possible – however, it has the potential to underpin computing as an observational science and software development as an engineering activity.

From this it should be possible to appreciate that the potential diversity of software engineering related measures, generally termed 'software metrics', is vast. This is best shown by briefly considering a few examples, although, of course, the entire book is devoted to this theme!

A major concern of managers is determining staffing requirements early on in a project. Project effort estimation is underpinned by quantitative understanding of the

[1] Note that we are not limited to using numbers to represent attributes. Alternatives include labels and other mathematical objects such as vectors. We will discuss the implications of measuring without numbers in Section 1.3.

productivity of software engineers. At its simplest, if it has been observed that under certain conditions an engineer can produce twenty-five lines of debugged and documented code per day, and if we can estimate the size of the product in terms of lines of code (LOC), then we can predict required project engineering effort as (estimated-LOC/25) person days. Chapter 4 addresses this topic in depth.

Another application of measurement is to monitor software reliability over time. Is it improving? If so, at what rate? Again, without counting defects this is a difficult question to answer with any kind of accuracy. One is reduced to the purely anecdotal level. Measuring quality characteristics also helps us to understand productivity measures better. Modest gains in productivity, but at the expense of a large loss in reliability, could well be regarded as unattractive.

Yet another use of measurement could be to assess the maintainability of ageing software systems and to direct re-engineering or re-structuring activities. A well-known phenomenon of software systems is the decay in structure and the corresponding increase in difficulty in making changes or adaptations with each successive maintenance change. In order to counteract this process, maintenance staff can measure the number and distribution of connections between system components. Those components most tightly connected are potentially the most troublesome. Measurement can be used to assess the impact of a maintenance change before it is made. It can also be applied to identify the most difficult to maintain components – often referred to as 'hot spots'. This can enable engineers to perform highly targeted re-engineering work and reap much of the benefit of re-building the entire system at a fraction of the cost.[2]

A fourth example of software engineers applying measurement is early identification of a project going off course. For instance, unusually high levels of defects at design time could indicate the presence of incipient problems. The advantage with this type of approach is that there is scope for the project manager to take investigative and corrective action. Again, without measurement it would be difficult to determine typical defect levels for a project at a design stage.

The idea of using measurement as part of software development is not new. Right from the pioneering days of computers, people have been concerned with questions such as how long will a program take to execute and how much memory will it occupy? One of the earliest papers to consider measurement of the amount of effort consumed by each stage of a software project was by Benington in 1956 [1]. This paper also contains the first – known to the author – reference to measuring program complexity. In the early-1970s, as the scale of software started to increase dramatically from merely automating algorithms to constructing systems of many programs, so researchers became more concerned with the complexity of software, and how to measure it. The reasoning was: it was complexity that made programs difficult to write, understand and change and that the more complex the software the more error-prone these processes. If only we could measure complexity we would

[2] This is an example of exploiting the so-called 80 : 20 'rule', where benefits are not in linear proportion to costs.

begin to be in a position to control it and consequently improve the quality of the software we produced.

Amongst the first workers in the field to develop a coherent model of software complexity was Halstead. This was known as software science. Halstead proposed a set of relationships which he believed to be analogous to 'natural laws' and these were codified into a system of equations. These equations were based upon a few simple counts derived from the source code of a computer program, and included the number of unique operands (variables and constants) and unique operators (function calls, arithmetic functions and so forth). Figure 1.1 shows a very simple example of the type of calculations involved.

Halstead claimed that, by means of software science, it was possible to predict a wide range of software quality characteristics. More recent work has shown software science to be flawed but it has proved influential in at least two respects. First, it encouraged people to regard software as a product that could be measured and analyzed like other more tangible artefacts. Second, it reinforced the focus on complexity measurement.[3]

Work on code measurement blossomed, with many complexity measures being proposed through the 1970s and on into the early-1980s. Perhaps the best known, and most enduring, was McCabe's cyclomatic complexity measure, `v(G)` [11]. This was derived from an analysis of the control flow of software. McCabe recommended that if the number of decisions in a piece of code exceeded nine,[4] then the programmer should consider subdividing it into smaller, and therefore more easily testable, units since more decisions lead to more execution paths through the code. Following on from this initial idea there have been many attempts to use `v(G)` to predict a wide range of software attributes such as development effort, defect levels, understandability and ease of making a subsequent maintenance change. Although early reports claimed strong empirical support for this type of predictive application of McCabe's measure, more recent work has cast considerable doubt over both experimental procedures and statistical analysis of a number of these empirical studies. The moral is: empirical investigation requires a great deal of care in order to generate meaningful results.

```
X := Y + 1
IF X = Z THEN WRITELN (X);
```

Unique operands (n_1): X, Y, 1, Z	=4
Operand count (N_1): X, Y, 1, X, Z, X	=6
Unique operators (n_2): :=, +, IF ... THEN, =, WRITELN, ()	=6
Operator count (N_2): :=, +, IF ... THEN, =, WRITELN, ()	=6

Figure 1.1 Deriving software science measures from code

[3] Strictly speaking, Halstead proposed a measure of effort, `E` and program level, `L` (most workers have used its inverse, that is, difficulty `D`, where `D = 1/L`). For a fuller account of software science see [7].

[4] McCabe actually suggested a value of `v(G) = 10`; however, since `v(G)` equates to the decision count plus 1, this gives a suggested upper limit of nine decisions.

Measurement work in the 1980s was characterized by exploration of other intermediate products to measure, most notably, designs and specifications. This was a reflection of a shift in emphasis, within the software engineering community as a whole, to the earlier stages of a software project. The vital role of design upon maintainability and re-use became better understood. Likewise, specifying and validating software requirements was seen as fundamental. What purpose was there in building high quality code that didn't accomplish what the user wanted? As a consequence, these intermediate products, were seen as candidates for measurement in much the same way that code was in the 1970s. Again, typically the aim was to measure design complexity with a view to being able to predict quality characteristics earlier on in the project (Chapter 2 gives a detailed account of some of these design or system architecture measures). Specifications were measured with the objective of predicting project development effort, the major contributor to cost. The best known of these measures is Function Points (FP), which attempts to capture the functionality contained within a specification by counting the different inputs, outputs, interfaces, internal files and enquiries (a full definition can be found in Chapter 4). By determining appropriate productivity values, that is, effort per FP, for the local measurement environment,[5] it is possible to make effort predictions at a relatively early stage in a project.

During the early-1990s attention has turned to process. The measures described so far have all been of software engineering products. However, the processes that led to the creation of these products are also very important. Many people argue that a quality process will lead to a quality product. Moreover, many applications of product measures involve processes. For instance, these measures can form feedback into a process (e.g. if McCabe's measure is unacceptably high, one could choose to re-design the software). Product measures can also help to evaluate a process (e.g. obtain quantitative evidence that use of formal methods does actually reduce defect incidence under given conditions). Indeed, the mere acts of collecting and interpreting a measure are processes in themselves and so we should not see measurement as an activity isolated from the rest of software engineering but, rather as being highly integrated in terms of process (see Chapter 8).

The other trend worthy of note, is the growing interest in classical measurement theory, that software engineers are not the only people to conduct measurement and that much can be learnt from returning to basics. This is, in part, fuelled by dissatisfaction in the very *ad hoc* approaches of much of the preceding measurement work, coupled with an appreciation that successful measurement is an altogether more complex activity than has been previously supposed (a brief overview of measurement theory can be found in the next section).

In summary, software measurement is, as a field of study, at least thirty-five years old. It is characterized by diversity in the range of products and processes that are being measured and yet there is still far to go. Measurement is not as commonplace

[5] This is known as calibration, an important but all too often neglected aspect of software measurement (see Chapter 4).

as one might expect for an engineering activity, and problems have arisen from both the lack of theoretical underpinning and suspect empirical methodology. The next section goes on to look at the first of these concerns, measurement theory.

1.3 Measurement theory

There is a tendency amongst some software engineers to assume that measurement is unique to their field. This section comprises a brief account of measurement theory to enable us to provide a more rigorous treatment for valid measures, scale and meaningful statements. For a detailed description of the application of this theory to software engineering measures, see Fenton [5].

We have already seen that measurement is concerned with representing empirically observable properties, that is, attributes, of objects or processes by symbols. These observations can be modelled as relations.[6] Suppose that we are interested in the modularity of software; we observe that programs X and Y are equally modular, and likewise programs V and W. This can be shown by a set of binary relations (with infix notation for readability):

$$X \sim Y$$
$$V \sim W$$

where ~ is empirical equivalence. If, empirically, all we are able to do is to observe that attributes are equal, or not equal, then we can do little more than classify or measure on a *nominal* scale. A simple example of classifying software systems is by the type of programming language they are implemented in, such as C++, Fortran, a 4GL or a hybrid. In addition, however, it would be desirable to rank the programs for modularity so as to construct a weak order. To do this we need a more-modular-than relation, so that we can say that X is more-modular-than Y, Y is more-modular-than Z and so forth. This can be depicted by a set of binary relations:

$$X > Y$$
$$Y > Z$$

where > is more-modular-than. With these two relations we could measure on an *ordinal* scale. This enables us to measure the amount or level of an attribute that the entity possesses and to determine that the programs can be ranked X, Y, Z in terms of decreasing modularity.

[6] A relation is a means of mathematically describing relationships between objects from specified sets. For example, we could have the set of all databases and wish to record that database d_1 has been updated more recently than database d_2. This can be depicted as (_more-recently-updated-than_) where the underscores are the argument place holders, so we have (d_1 more-recently-updated-than d_2). In this case, all the objects within the relation are drawn from the same set, that is, databases, but this need not be so. Note also that, although infix notation has been used for this example, we could equally well have had (more-recently-updated-than__,__).

Another empirical observation concerns the size of the intervals between pairs of observations, and leads to a quaternary relation equivalent-interval. For instance, if we know that the difference in modularity between programs X and Y is the same as the difference between Y and Z, then we have:

$$(X, Y) \sim (Y, Z)$$

Likewise, if we observe that the difference in modularity between program X and Z is greater than Y and W, then we can use another quaternary relation:

$$(X, Z) > (Y, W)$$

The ability to distinguish between intervals, in other words to ask how much more, forms the empirical basis for *interval* and *ratio* scales. The difference between the interval and ratio scale lies in the fact that for the latter absolute zero is always implied; in other words the object or process can possess none of the attribute. This leads to a final type of empirical observation based upon equality of ratio. Informally, we observe that program X is twice as modular as program Y, which in turn is twice as modular as Z; hence:

$$(X/Y) \sim (Y/Z)$$

The basic empirical relations for each scale are summarized in Table 1.1.

So far we have dealt with the empirical relation structure of the attribute being measured. There are, however, two other components to a measurement system: the numerical relation system[7] into which we measure and the actual measurement function itself, which maps from the empirical into the number system. Within the number system we need a set of relations to mirror those from the empirical system. Summarizing from Finkelstein and Leaning [6] the empirical relation system is denoted:

$$\langle Q, \{R_1, R_2, \ldots, R_n\} \rangle$$

where Q is the set of all observations of the attribute and $R_1, R_2, \ldots, R_n$ is the set of

Table 1.1 Basic empirical operations by scale

Scale	*Empirical relations*
Nominal	equality (~)
Ordinal	equality, more-than (~, >)
Interval	equality, more-than, equality of intervals (~, >, (X, Y ~ V, W))
Ratio	equality, more-than equality of intervals and ratios (~, >, (X, Y ~ VW), (X/Y ~ V/W))

[7] Strictly speaking, we are not restricted to numbers, although this is normal practice and simplifies the following discussion.

all relations, such as ~, on Q. The numerical relation system is given as:

$$\langle N, \{P_1, P_2, \ldots, P_n\}\rangle$$

where N is the set of real numbers, and $P_1, P_2, \ldots, P_n$ is the set of relations on N. From this we have the measurement function as:

$$M: Q \rightarrow N$$

Clearly, in order for M to be a valid measuring operation there are restrictions on the way it maps from empirical observations to numbers. We consider these now. First and foremost, M must map in such a way as to preserve the empirical relations as equivalent relations in the number system. This is best illustrated by an example. Suppose we have the following empirical relation system for modularity:

$$\langle\{X, Y\}, \{\sim\}\rangle$$

and a number system

$$\langle N, \{=\}\rangle$$

Suppose we observe the empirical relation $A \sim B$, that is, A and B are equally modular. Suppose, also, that the measurement function M maps:

$$A \mapsto 20;\ B \mapsto 20$$

then we have relation $20 = 20$ and therefore the two structures are homomorphic and M is a valid measurement function; it represents the attribute modularity in such a way that the equality relation holds in both systems.

Clearly, there are many other valid mappings for M, such as:

$$A \mapsto 28;\ B \mapsto 28$$

or:

$$A \mapsto 2.09;\ B \mapsto 2.09$$

which are equally valid. On the other hand:

$$A \mapsto 3;\ B \mapsto 4$$

is not a proper representation since the relation $3 = 4$ does not hold whilst $A \sim B$ does.

This concept of the numbers representing the empirical world is shown graphically in Figure 1.2. As well as programs A and B we introduce a third program C, which we observe is less modular than either A or B. Our modularity measurement function is acceptable because it maps program C to a number value which is less than the values for A and B.

The above example of program modularity is generalized as the Representation Theorem, which must be true for any proper measure. This theorem states that the relations between the empirical observations must also hold for the number system relations. This does not necessarily impose many restrictions upon the measurement

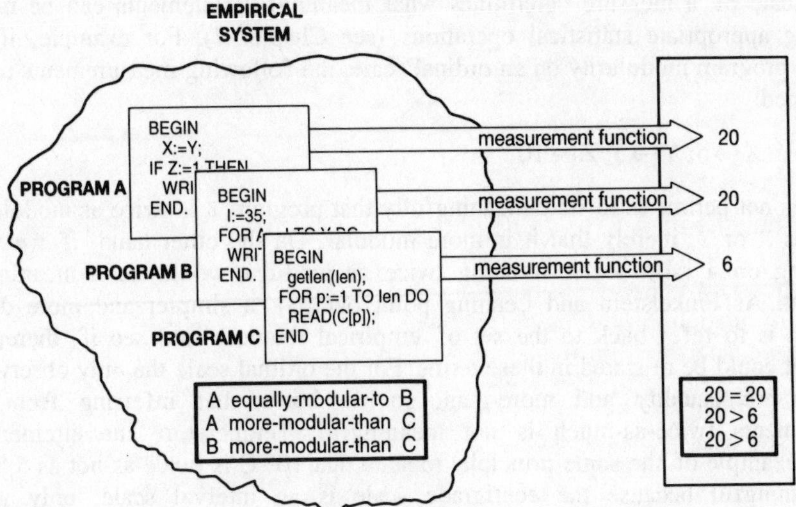

Figure 1.2 The representation condition for measurement systems

function, and it is this observation that enables us to formally distinguish between scale types.

This defining property for scales is known as the uniqueness condition. Table 1.2 (based on Stevens [13]) shows the allowable transformations on `M` which still leave us with values that satisfy the representation condition. The set of allowable transformations for each scale becomes increasingly limited. For the nominal scale, any one-to-one transformation can be made without violating the representation condition; in other words we can permute all the `3`s to `47`s without it mattering. In other words, it doesn't make any difference whether the measurement function `M` assigns `3` or `47` for all observationally equivalent programs. On the other hand, for the absolute scale, that is, counting, no transformations can be made. If we count that there are seventeen modules, this cannot be altered without a loss of representation.

Table 1.2 Allowable transformations defining scale

Scale	*Allowable transformations on M that preserve the representation condition*
Nominal	permutation group: $M' = f(M)$
Ordinal	isotonic group: $M' = f(M)$ where $f(M)$ is any monotonic increasing function
Interval	general linear group: $M' = \alpha M + \beta$ where $\alpha > 0$
Ratio	similarity group: $M' = \alpha M$ where $\alpha > 0$
Absolute	$M' = M$

The scale of a measure determines what meaningful statements can be made, including appropriate statistical operations (see Chapter 7). For example, if we measure program modularity on an ordinal scale, the following measurements might be obtained:

$$X \mapsto 5;\ Y \mapsto 5;\ Z \mapsto 10$$

This does not permit us to state meaningfully that program `Z` is twice as modular as programs `X` or `Y`, merely that it is more modular. On the other hand, if we were measuring on a ratio scale, `Z` being twice as modular would be a meaningful statement. As Finkelstein and Leaning point out [6], a simpler and more direct approach is to refer back to the set of empirical relations and see if, there, the statement could be re-stated in these terms. For the ordinal scale the only observable relations are equality and more-than, so we know that inferring from the measurements twice-as-much is not meaningful. Temperature measurement is another example of the same principle: to state that 10 °C is twice-as-hot as 5 °C is not meaningful because the centigrade scale is an interval scale: only when measuring temperature using degrees Kelvin (based on absolute zero and therefore a ratio scale) does such a statement become meaningful.

How is this useful? Returning to the definition of measurement it becomes clear that the nub of the matter is the set of empirical observations and these demand that we share some common understanding of the attribute to be measured. A difficulty with some of the more transcendental attributes, such as complexity and quality, is that we do not have this shared understanding; it would be difficult to obtain sufficient agreement over the empirical relations – that module `A` is more complex than module `B`, and so on. A second, related, difficulty is that whilst researchers might state that they have a complexity measure, the attribute that they are actually capturing is often distinct, and usually rather more specific. For this reason, it is often helpful to explicitly state the attribute or property that it is the target of measurement. Third, we need a rule for determining the measurement values, that is, defining the function `M`. For complexity this can be quite difficult, as indicated by the ironic description from Curtis [3] that complexity is 'a not-so-warm feeling in the tummy'!

As an example of applying some of the principles discussed above, consider the following modularity measure:

`MEASURE:`	Martin's Example Measure
`ENTITY:`	source code
`ATTRIBUTE:`	modularity
`RULE:`	1: low modularity – few, very large procedural units 2: intermediate – procedural units reflecting basic functionality 3: high – functional decomposition, use of abstract data types
`SCALE:`	ordinal

That modularity may be measured on the ordinal scale is predicated upon the existence of two observable empirical relations about program modularity – these are (i) equally-modular and (ii) more-modular-than. Without this, we cannot set up the necessary empirical relation system and demonstrate that the representation condition holds and that the numbers reflect the observed program modularity relations. The rule for measuring appears somewhat suspect as there is considerable scope for individual interpretation and hence a loss of objectivity. However, pragmatic reasons might encourage us to use this measure despite this lack of precision. Any analysis of the results would need to be tempered by our awareness of the lack of objectivity. Ideally, we would take steps to refine the measurement rule. The other application of measurement theory is to assess what meaningful statements can be made concerning the measurements. As has already been noted, statements such as half-as-modular are not admissable for an ordinal scale.

This has only been a brief summary of measurement theory. One area that we have chosen to ignore is uncertainty and error. Methods of dealing with this are either based upon a probabilistic treatment (see e.g. Kyburg [9]) or additional relations such as just-noticeable-difference to construct semi-orders [10].

1.4 Measurement and prediction systems

Having examined some of the basics of measurement theory and how we can establish whether we have a proper measure, we now turn to determining whether we have a useful measure. A major use of measures is to use them to predict or anticipate events. In order to do this we need to combine measures into models or systems.

But, first, it will be helpful to examine Fenton's distinction between internal and external attributes measurement [5]. An *internal attribute* is one that can be measured independently of other entities. Examples are the size of a test suite and the depth of a module calling hierarchy. These attributes can be measured in isolation, whereas an *external attribute* can only be determined in conjunction with internal attribute measurements. Examples are the maintainability of a user guide (since the answer depends upon the person carrying out the maintenance task and also upon the precise nature of the maintenance change) and the reliability of a software system (since it also depends upon the type of usage).

It is important to keep this distinction in mind, because it underlines the difference between a measurement and a prediction system. A prediction system is a model that takes quantitative inputs and yields one, or occasionally more than one, quantitative output. These systems have particular importance because they enable us to anticipate events before they happen. An example is the software project effort system described earlier in this chapter. Here it would be far more useful to know the effort required to develop a software system *before* the project commences rather than after the project has been completed. This is to assist in tendering, budgeting

and for logistical purposes. Another, example is reliability. Certifying authorities often demand reliability levels of less than one defect per 10^9 operating hours of safety critical software. Unfortunately, we simply cannot observe this level of reliability by direct measurement: life is too short! So, again, we need some sort of prediction system.

Figure 1.3 illustrates the basic structure of a prediction system. Prediction systems must have at least three components. These are (i) a set of one or more input measures ($M_{1...n}$), (ii) the output measure (M_{pred}), which is the quantity being predicted, and (iii) the prediction system itself which will be a system of equations that enable us to derive a value for M_{pred} from $M_{1...n}$. In addition, the prediction system can be parameterized in order to adapt it to different measurement environments. For instance, Figure 1.4 shows a simple system to predict the number of defects contained in a software system.

In this prediction system the number of software defects is determined by measuring the length of the program in terms of LOC. Here the system is parameterized by a to reflect differences between defect rates from differing application types: real-time systems are treated as more defect-prone than management information systems.

The question as to whether the defect prediction system is useful or not can only be determined via empirical study. Note, however, that it is the prediction system that is validated and not the measure LOC. The observation that the above prediction system is found to perform very poorly does not necessarily imply that LOC is a 'bad metric'. From Section 1.3 we saw that for LOC to be a valid measure of the attribute software length requires us, amongst other things, to demonstrate that the relations on the number system properly represent the empirical relations. This is

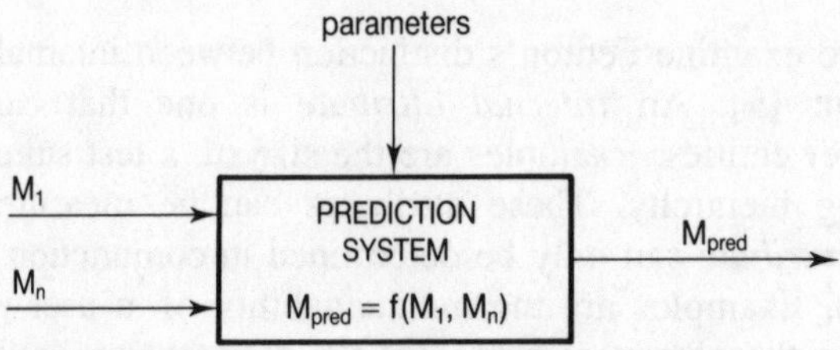

Figure 1.3 The structure of prediction systems

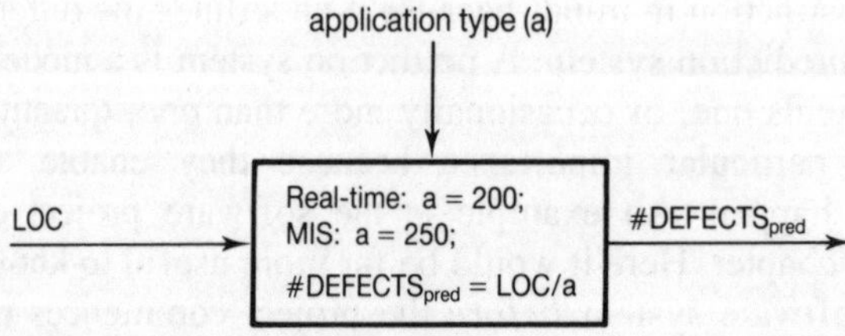

Figure 1.4 A defect prediction system

quite distinct from whether or not we can use LOC as a useful input for a defect prediction system. On the other hand, the absence of any prediction system will render LOC substantially less interesting to the software engineer.

1.5 Validating 'metrics'

Having established the foundations we can now explore how some of the popular metrics fit into this framework and where some of the difficulties lie.

Consider the influential McCabe's cyclomatic complexity `v(G)` measure [11]. Recall that this measure is derived from an analysis of the control flow of a piece of procedural code. Although McCabe gives a derivation of the measure in terms of graph theory – where executable statements correspond to nodes and transfers of control to directed edges (see Figure 1.5) – the calculation reduces to a count of decisions plus one per module (in Figure 1.5 this gives a value of `v(G) = 3`). The initial step in applying our measurement framework is to separate our view of `v(G)` as a measure from its use as a predictor of various software quality characteristics.

First, then, `v(G)` as a measure. McCabe states that the 'overall strategy will be to measure the complexity of a program by computing the number of linearly independent paths `v(G)` ...'. Clearly, the target of measurement is the program source code, and the attribute being measured is complexity. Recall that the measure can be obtained as the number of decisions plus one, so this suggests that

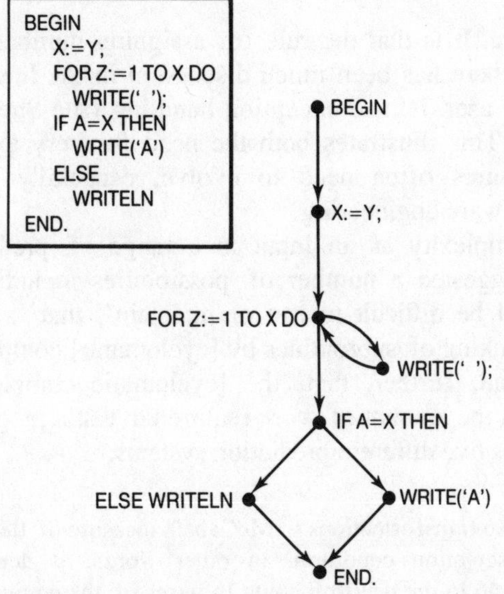

Figure 1.5 Deriving McCabe's `a(G)` measure from code

we have a measure based on an interval scale rather than a ratio scale [15].[8] So we have:

`MEASURE:`	McCabe's cyclomatic complexity
`ENTITY:`	source code
`ATTRIBUTE:`	complexity
`RULE:`	decision count plus one
`SCALE:`	interval

This leads to certain difficulties. The first problem is with the attribute complexity, since it is not at all clear what is intended by this attribute. In the past, researchers have distinguished between cognitive and computational complexity. Here it is unclear what type of complexity is being measured. Moreover, different people can have quite different perspectives upon complexity. For example, I might find data structures based upon linked lists incomprehensible whilst colleagues could find them trivial. In other words, complexity is what Fenton would describe as an external attribute that requires measures of other attributes in order to be meaningful. It is difficult to validate `v(G)` as a measure of complexity because it is difficult to construct a set of empirical relations concerning the agreed complexities of a set of programs. The problem is that the complexity also depends upon *who* is carrying out *what* task under *which* circumstances. Yet, without the empirical relations we cannot determine whether the measure satisfies the representation condition of a proper measure. It is interesting to see that, elsewhere, McCabe is more specific concerning the attribute being measured, for example he states that there should be some 'correlation between the complexity numbers and our intuitive notion of control flow complexity'. None the less, our arguments concerning the external nature complexity as an attribute still pertain.

The second problem is less severe. It is that the rule for assigning numbers can often be ambiguous. For example, there has been much discussion in the literature of how to treat `CASE` statements or user defined exception handling (see Shepperd [12] for a more detailed account). This illustrates both the need for very explicit measurement rules and how measures often need to evolve, especially for a relatively new discipline such as software engineering.

Second, we view cyclomatic complexity as an input to a range of prediction systems. McCabe [11], himself suggested a number of possibilities including to 'identify software modules that will be difficult to test or maintain', that 'a close correlation was found between the ranking of subroutines by [cyclomatic] complexity and a ranking by reliability ...' and, further, that 'the [cyclomatic complexity] measure should correlate closely with the amount of work required to test a program'. These are summarized in Figure 1.6 as five different prediction systems.

[8] Informally, that is because we can make transformations to McCabe's measure of the form $M' = \alpha M + \beta$ which preserve the representation condition. In other words, it does not particularly matter whether we add 1 or 46 to the decision count in terms of the equivalence between the empirical and numerical relational systems.

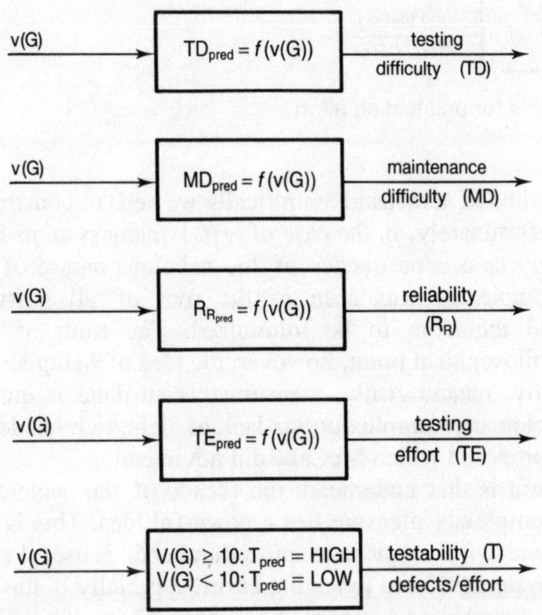

Figure 1.6 Prediction systems for McCabes' cyclomatic measure

Note that testing effort and testing difficulty are not the same and that testing and maintenance difficulty are external attributes suggesting that these prediction systems are, at least in certain respects, incomplete. This can be inferred from the fact that in order to measure the attribute meaningfully we need to measure other attributes such as the maintenance task and the ability of the engineer performing it. This is not to say that such prediction systems are incapable of yielding useful approximations, but it does highlight areas of simplification. The final system to predict testability (i.e. defects uncovered per unit effort) highlights a number of features. McCabe suggested the use of `v(G)` to provide a recommended upper limit for the number of decisions within a piece of code, in other words a quality control application, this is an implied prediction system: software components that exceed this threshold will be less testable than those that do not. The other observation is that the commodity being predicted, testability, is in fact a synthetic measure derived from two other attributes, defects detected and testing effort.

Figure 1.6 illustrates five systems that McCabe implicitly assumes. However, many researchers, in attempting to validate the measure empirically, actually generated and evaluated yet other prediction systems ranging from design effort [14] to program recall [4] and many more beside.

So what does this tell us of the validity of McCabe's measure? First, to be a proper measure it must satisfy a number of obligations derived from measurement theory. In this case, we have major concerns about the attribute complexity and some minor ones relating to the measurement rules and the choice of scale. Second, to be

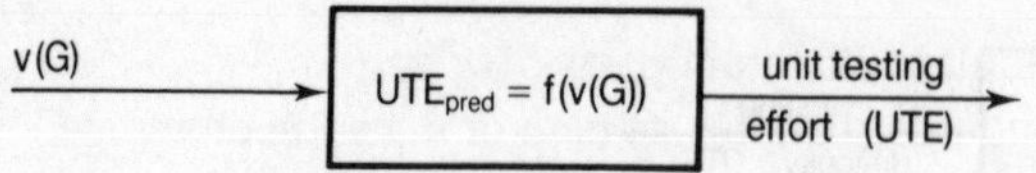

Figure 1.7 Prediction systems for unit testing effort

able to validate the predictive claims of a measure empirically we need to construct a prediction system explicitly. Unfortunately, in the case of `v(G)` many systems have been proposed implicitly, largely as a consequence of the nebulous nature of the attribute complexity where complexity was seen as the root of all software engineering unpleasantness and therefore to be minimized. The truth of this proposition is something of a philosophical point, however; the idea of being able to accurately and, more importantly, meaningfully, measure this attribute is quite a different matter. In terms of cyclomatic complexity this lack of definition has led to many prediction systems being proposed which McCabe did not intend.

The positive lesson to be learnt is that underneath the facade of the cyclomatic number as a general program complexity measure lies a powerful idea. This is that measuring the number of decisions within a piece of procedural code is useful since it can form input to prediction systems related to testing effort, especially if the unit testing is based on such glass box strategies as decision coverage. From our analysis this would lead to the following re-definition:

`MEASURE:`	McCabe's cyclomatic complexity (Mk II)
`ENTITY:`	source code
`ATTRIBUTE:`	control flow branching
`RULE:`	decision count
`SCALE:`	absolute

and the yet to be validated prediction system in Figure 1.7. Although this is rather more modest than some of the prediction systems proposed, it is far more attainable and is therefore of vastly greater value to the software engineering community.

1.6 Summary

In this chapter we have introduced measurement and the range of measures possible within software engineering. Measurement can either be of a product such as a user guide, requirements specification, data model or source code, or it can be of a process such as integration testing, debugging or maintaining software. Such measurements are useful for a wide range of activities, including the following:

- comparing the effect of a new technology over current practice;
- assessing productivity trends over a period of time;
- predicting project development effort;
- identifying good and bad practice;

- identifying the most difficult to maintain parts of a system;
- setting minimum test standards, perhaps as path or decision coverage.

Next we have more formally characterized measurement as systems of empirical and number relations and a mapping function from the domain of empirical observations to numbers. We have seen that, for this to be a proper measure, the mapping must preserve 'real world' or empirical relations as equivalent relations in the number system (i.e. satisfy the representation condition). We have distinguished between scale types in terms of observable relations and also allowable transformations on the number system which still preserve the representation condition. Scales enable us to determine what meaningful statements may be made concerning measurements.

We have drawn a distinction between measures and prediction systems. The former are validated by reference to measurement theory; the latter are validated by reference to empirical observation. This means that in order to validate a measure empirically we must understand what it is intended to be used for. We cannot state that LOC is a 'bad measure' on the basis that it does not enable us to predict maintenance effort accurately; it is both a valid measure of the attribute length of a program and a component of a poor prediction system of maintenance effort.

Finally, we conclude that the emergence of measures of attributes is an incremental and sometimes protracted process and that the starting point is an intuitive or informal understanding of the attribute in question. As Finkelstein and Leaning put it:

> In the development of scales of measurement for particular [attributes], it is common to start with a qualitative, verbally described concept of the [attribute]. The aim of measurement is to give the description of the [attribute] objectivity, an empirical basis, precision and conciseness.' (Finkelstein and Leaning. [6])

1.7 Exercises and further reading

1. Apply the measurement framework described in this chapter to identify (i) the entity, (ii) the attribute, (iii) the scale and (iv) the measurement rules for the executable lines of code (ELOC) in a C program.
2. To what extent do you consider it possible to measure transcendental qualities such as the style of a program? One attempt to quantify such an attribute is the Berry–Meekings 'style metric' [2, 8]. Do you consider this to be a valid measure of style? Explain your answer in terms of measurement theory.

Fenton, N.E., *Software Metrics: A Rigorous Approach*, Chapman & Hall, London, 1991.

An excellent text on software measurement that endeavours to apply many of the concepts of measurement theory to the problems of software measurement. Chapters 2 and 3 are particularly relevant to this introduction.

Fenton, N.E. and B.A. Kitchenham, 'Validating software measures', *Journal of Software Testing, Verification and Reliability*, **1**(2), 27–42, 1991.

This article makes the distinction between measures and prediction systems and the implications this has upon validation. It also examines the use of measurement theory to validate that a candidate measure is indeed a proper measure and the demands of statistically meaningful empirical validation. Highly recommended reading.

Finkelstein, L. and M.S. Leaning, 'A review of the fundamental concepts of measurement', *Measurement*, **2**(1) 25–34, 1984.

As the title suggests a concise review of measurement theory including representation, uniqueness, scale and measurement uncertainty. It is also a taster for …

Krantz, D.H., R.D. Luce, P. Suppes and A. Tversky, *Foundations of Measurement*, Volume 1, Academic Press, London, 1971.

This monumental work is still a definitive text on measurement theory and is valuable reading for anyone wishing to pursue this topic further.

Shepperd, M.J., 'An evaluation of software product metrics', *Information and Softw. Tech.*, **30**(3), 177–88, 1988.

Although slightly dated, this survey paper provides a reasonably compact account of the range of software product measurement work that has been undertaken. It makes the important observation that, unfortunately, much of this work is unsubstantiated by empirical work.

References

[1] Benington, H.D., 'Production of large computer programs', in *Proc. Symp. on Advanced Computer Programs for Digital Computers*. Washington, DC.: Office of Naval Research, 1956.

[2] Berry, R.E. and B.A.E. Meekings, 'A style analysis of C programs', *CACM*, **28**(1), 80–88, 1985.

[3] Curtis, B., 'In search of software complexity', in *Proc. Workshop on Quant. Softw. Complexity Models*, 1979.

[4] Curtis, B. *et al.*, 'Measuring the psychological complexity of software maintenance tasks with the Halstead and McCabe metrics', *IEEE Trans. on Softw. Eng.*, **5**(2), 96–104, 1979.

[5] Fenton, N.E., *Software Metrics: A rigorous approach*. Chapman & Hall: London, 1991.

[6] Finkelstein, L. and M.S. Leaning, 'A review of the fundamental concepts of measurement', *Measurement*, **2**(1), 25–34, 1984.

[7] Halstead, M.H., 'Advances in software science', in *Advances in Computers*, M. Yovits, ed., Academic Press: NY, 1979.

[8] Harrison, W. and C.R. Cook, 'A note on the Berry-Meekings style metric', *CACM*, **29**(2), 123–5, 1986.

[9] Kyburg, H.E., *Theory and Measurement*. Cambridge Univ. Press: Cambridge, England, 1984.

[10] Luce, R.D., 'Semi-orders and a theory of utility discrimination', *Econometrica*, 24, 178–91, 1956.

[11] McCabe, T.J., 'A complexity measure', *IEEE Trans. on Softw. Eng.*, **2**(4), 308–20, 1976.

[12] Shepperd, M.J., 'A critique of cyclomatic complexity as a software metric', *Softw. Eng. J.*, **3**(2), 1–8, 1988.

[13] Stevens, S.S., 'On the theory of scales of measurement', *Science*, **103**, 677–80, 1946.

[14] Sunohara, T. *et al.*, 'Program complexity measure for software development management', in *Proc. 5th IEEE Intl. Conf. on Softw. Eng.* Computer Society Press, 1981.

[15] Zuse, H. and P. Bollmann, 'Software metrics: using measurement theory to describe the properties and scales of static complexity metrics', *ACM SIGPLAN Not.*, **24**(8), 23–33, 1989.

Chapter 2

The architecture of software

Synopsis

Architectural design – be it the decomposition of a system into interacting constituent parts, or the choice of data structures – is an activity that is fundamental to software engineering. It has far-reaching consequences, both in terms of the quality and the cost of the software delivered. Current quantitative methods of functional design, such as information flow metrics, are presented by means of specific examples of software design. There follows a discussion concerning the limitations of models based upon a single dimension, and a more sophisticated multi-dimensional model of software architecture is introduced. The chapter concludes by considering how the lessons drawn from system architecture might be more generally applied to software engineering measurement.

2.1 Software design

From the 1970s onwards, there has been a growing appreciation of the huge impact that architecture can have upon the quality of a software system. A poor architecture can lead to a system that is difficult to implement, understand, maintain or re-use and can even have a deleterious impact upon performance. The design of software systems is generally divided into high and low level design. High level design is the process of making decisions about the software architecture, whereas low level design deals with the details of algorithms and control flow. This chapter is solely concerned with high level or architectural design.

What is software architecture? Architecture is concerned with the form and structure of a system; in the case of software this includes the choice of components and their interfaces. Components include both functional units and storage or data structures, and interface design addresses how the components are combined, normally meaning the types of calling or access mechanism, together with data flows across the interface.

Making these important design decisions is a skilled process that demands considerable judgement and experience on the part of a software engineer. For any given set of software requirements, one could theoretically generate an extremely large number of architectures that could, in some sense, be made to 'work', that is, they could be implemented with varying degrees of effort. However, these architectures would not all be equivalent in terms of the different quality characteristics of the resultant software. One architecture might lead to a more maintainable system than another, one architecture might be easier to unit test than another and so forth. So high level design is about selecting one architecture from a set of one or more candidates. Design is not easily amenable to mechanization because we unfortunately do not have an exact set of rules, so the problem becomes one of how best to support software designers in their decision making. This chapter will show how measurement can make a large contribution.

Design is not a process unique to software engineering. Indeed, some invaluable insights have come from the architect Christopher Alexander, who, in 1964, published a work [1] that, amongst other things, described the layout of an ideal Third World village. In the discussion, Alexander suggested two design objectives: to aim for units with a singleness of purpose and to have as simple as possible interfaces with their environment. Recalling that design is about making choices, it will be apparent that Alexander's work offers the basis for being able to compare candidate architectures. We have two design evaluation criteria.

Returning to software, the 1970s were characterized by a number of new software design methods, including the work of Stevens *et al.* on structured design [40]. Apart from proposing the use of data flow diagrams (DFDs) and module hierarchy charts, structured design develops Alexander's ideas and applies them to software systems. They proposed two design evaluation criteria, which they called module coupling and module cohesion.[1] These criteria have proved to be highly influential

[1] Other workers have proposed similar sets of design evaluation criteria. For example, Parnas [30] describes his principle of information hiding; however, this leads to a reduction in module coupling and so is not fundamentally distinct as a criterion. Meyer [27] in his book on object-oriented software development proposes five criteria with which to evaluate system architecture. These are module decomposability, composability, understandability, continuity and protection. However, with the exception of module protection – which relates to how locally an abnormal condition is handled – the other criteria are all consequences of module coupling and cohesion.

upon design methods and are applicable to almost any design method, not merely structured design. For these reasons, this chapter will examine coupling and cohesion in some detail. Before this is possible, however, we need to consider a notation to describe software architecture.

2.1.1 Preliminaries

Rather than present the detailed design notation of a particular design method, we will use a generalized and fairly abstract method to describe system architecture. Additional detail will be added later in the chapter as required.

There are five basic constructs, as follows:

- modules;[2]
- module calls;
- parameters (imports or exports);
- data structures;
- data structure accesses (update, retrieve, update and retrieve).

The notation is shown in Figure 2.1.

Figure 2.2 presents a simple architecture comprising three modules `A`, `B` and `C` and a single data structure `DS`. Module `A` is the parent or top level module. It has two subordinate modules `B` and `C`. When module `B` is invoked it imports `x`, and after elaboration module `C` exports `y`. Module `B` can be seen to update the data structure `DS` and module `C` to retrieve from `DS`. It is important to appreciate that module hierarchy diagrams convey no control flow or timing information. We cannot, for

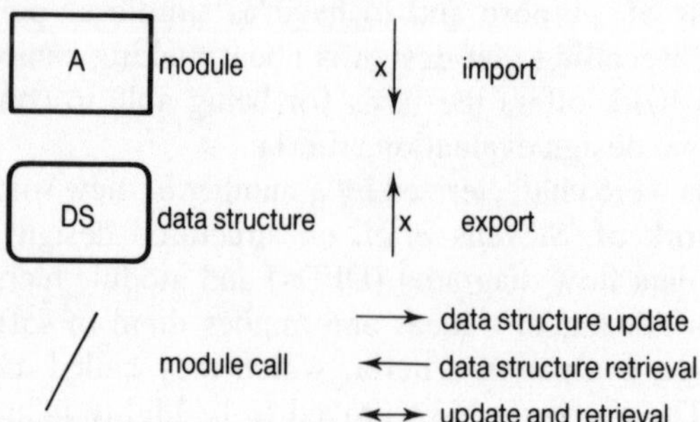

Figure 2.1 Key to module hierarchy diagram notation

[2] Since we will be using the term 'module' frequently in this chapter, we need to consider a definition. A module is a functional system component or unit that has the following two properties. It can be invoked by name from other parts of the system, and it returns execution to the point of call after execution. The precise details of how a module is realized are obviously language dependent. For example, a module in COBOL might be a paragraph or section, and a function in C. This, however, is not an important issue since our primary concern is system architecture.

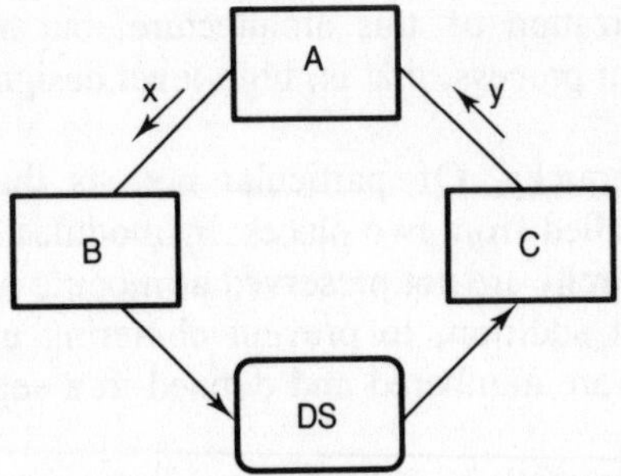

Figure 2.2 An example module hierarchy diagram

example, state that module B will be invoked prior to module C, if indeed it will be invoked at all. The call of module B may be dependent upon a particular set of conditions which may not always be fulfilled. Nor does the notation differentiate between different types of call. We cannot distinguish between sequential and concurrent calling structures. A possible implementation of this architecture in the programming language Pascal is given below.

```
program example (input, output);
...

vars
  x,y : integer;
  ds: data_structure;

procedure b (x: integer);
begin
  ds := x;
end; {b}

procedure c (var y: integer);
begin
  y:=ds;
end; {c}

begin { a }
  b(x);
  c(y)
end {a}.
```

This is not the only possible code realization of this architecture, but at this comparatively early stage in the development process, that is, high-level design, this is not a major concern.

Figure 2.3 shows a second module hierarchy. Of particular note is that the structure is not a pure tree[3] as module `C` is called from two places: by modules `A` and `B`. Moreover, even the strict levels of a hierarchy are not preserved as module `A` calls `C` directly and indirectly via module `B`. In addition, to prevent cluttering up the diagram with arrows the module interfaces are numbered and defined in a separate table below the module hierarchy diagram.

Although this notation may appear highly simplistic, it has the twin advantages of not being tied to any particular design method and it enables us to focus upon the basic structure of a software system without getting bogged down with too many details of control flow or implementation. There are also domain limitations. The notation is not good at describing system architectures which are dominated by complex relationships between data items, such as management information systems. Even more problematic is using the notation for non-procedural paradigms, such as rule based systems. The final section attempts some answers to these problems but the whole area remains an unsolved research problem.

2.1.2 Module coupling and cohesion

We now return to the design evaluation criteria of Stevens *et al.* [40]. Like Alexander, they suggested that the simplest and most adaptable systems were those made up of components that have:

- a single specific function;
- a simple interface with the rest of the system.

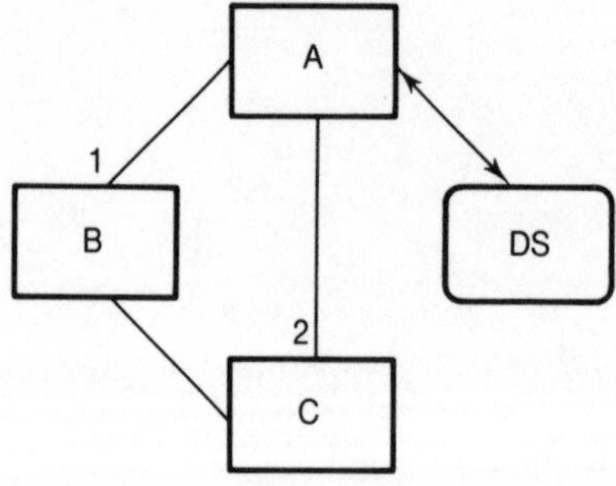

Interface	Imports	Exports
1	x, y	–
2	x	x

Figure 2.3 A system architecture showing re-use

[3] The hierarchy or graph is not a pure tree because there exists more than one path from the top level module or root node to a bottom level module or leaf node.

To assess architectures for these characteristics, Stevens *et al.* proposed two indicators, namely: module coupling and module cohesion.

Module cohesion is the singleness of purpose or function of a module. A module that validates a transaction and provides a horoscope analysis has low cohesion because it performs two functions that are completely unrelated. This is generally considered to be an undesirable property of a module, since it will result in the module being more difficult to understand, more difficult to modify and unsuitable for re-use.

Module coupling is, in many ways, the corollary of cohesion. It is the degree of independence of one module from another. Minimizing connections between modules makes them easier to understand, update and replace. This characteristic will naturally arise from modules that have high cohesion, whilst high coupling is often the consequence of a module that fails to perform a single well-defined function:

> *The designer should seek to maximize module cohesion and minimize module coupling.*

These design evaluation criteria are of particular interest because they can be applied independently of any one design method. We can use them when using MASCOT to develop the real-time software for a satellite tracking system, or equally when using the celebrated back of an envelope for some trivial housekeeping program. How do we assess a design against these two criteria? Stevens *et al.* [40] and Myers [28] provide detailed guidance which we will now examine more thoroughly.

Module cohesion is the strength of the relationship between the elements within a module. Structured Design identifies a number of different types, or strengths, of cohesion which can be summarized as five categories, as follows:

```
1. Functional                     strongest
2. Communicational                    ↑
3. Temporal                           |
4. Logical                            ↓
5. Coincidental                    weakest
```

1. Functional cohesion occurs when all the module elements combine to accomplish a 'single specific objective' [40]. Examples are as follows:

    - validate an account number;
    - retrieve a customer record;
    - fetch the next sensor reading.

    This is the most desirable form of module cohesion because highly functional modules aid comprehension: there are no extraneous elements. Each statement in the module `validate_account_number` will support that single function, thereby saving the reader from having to differentiate between statements implementing the validation function and, say, the horoscope function! One means of identifying a functional level of cohesion is to describe the purpose of the module as one short sentence. A single verb indicates a highly functional module. Consider the following two sentences:

> Fetch a command.
> Fetch a command, validate it and update the audit file.

The first description contains a single verb, whilst the second contains three verbs and a conjunction, revealing the lack of functional cohesion.

2. Communicational cohesion is the next strongest form of module cohesion. In this case all the elements of the module reference the same data structure, for example using the same transaction data to update a master file and maintain an audit file within one module. This becomes undesirable should the designer wish to re-use only the master file update part of the module. The alternatives are either to duplicate this part of the module – with the attendant maintenance 'time bomb'[4] this implies – or to modify the module so that the audit file is optionally updated depending upon the value of a control flag. This will complicate the interface, making the module more difficult to understand and test.
3. Temporal cohesion is defined to be present when the elements of a module have nothing in common other than the fact that they are executed at the same time, such as in an initialization module. As with communicational cohesion, this type of module is more difficult to re-use. It can also lead to a lack of data isolation and therefore an increase in module coupling. Furthermore, if many functions are grouped together, such modules can be difficult to understand because the reader must distinguish between the elements contributing to the many different tasks.
4. Logical cohesion occurs when a module contains several distinct functions that are logically related, typically using the same verb, such as 'edit'. Usually, the first part of such a module is a case structure or multi-way switch. There is a presumed advantage of possibly sharing some code but at the cost of being complex, more difficult to change and more difficult to re-use. Consider, the following module `edit_queue`:

```
procedure edit_queue (edit_cmnd: edit_cmnd_type);
begin
  case edit_cmnd of
  insert: begin
            if not full(q) then ...
        end;
  front: begin
            if not empty(q) then ...
        end;
  end; {case}
end; {edit_queue}
```

[4] The term 'time bomb' is used to describe this kind of design decision since it is frequently exposed at a later date when changes to the master file are not consistently applied throughout the system, with potentially catastrophic results.

At first sight the module `edit_queue` might appear harmless, but the immediate difficulty is that it would be impossible to re-use the queue insert part of the module without the front function. A better solution, and one that increases module cohesion, would be to have separate modules for insert and front.

5. Coincidental cohesion is the least desirable form of cohesion and indicates no meaningful relationship between the internal module components. This was more common in the past, often in order to save limited memory via segmentation or by eliminating repeated sequences of instructions. Problems arising from this type of module include the fact that changes needed by one caller may not be required by others, leading to a proliferation of control flags to determine the needs of the caller. The module will be more difficult to understand and, since the likelihood of anyone requiring the exact same set of functions is low, the probability of re-use is correspondingly low. An example is:

```
P100-COINCIDENTAL-MODULE.
    DISPLAY "Hello Helen".
    COMPUTE M=H+C.
    WRITE MASTER-REC.
```

Module coupling is the strength of association between a module and its calling environment. Again Stevens *et al.* [40], amongst others, identify various strengths or levels of coupling, based upon three aspects of these connections. These are as follows:

- The type of invocation. (Coupling will be minimized when the module call refers to the whole module and not to any internal part.)
- The type of information connection. (Coupling will be minimized when imports and exports are parameterized rather than communicated via non-local data access.[5])
- The size of connection. (The fewer the number of distinct data objects communicated, the lower the coupling.)
- The type of information communicated. (The less control flags communicated, the lower the coupling.)

The identification of the different levels of module cohesion and coupling is not an exact classification scheme. Rather, its purpose is to help direct the software designer towards the problem of assessing and comparing different software architectures. Even so, assessing module coupling and cohesion remains a subjective and skilful process.[6]

[5] Steven's view on the benefits of parameterized communication have not been substantiated by empirical evidence and can lead to lengthy and therefore clumsy parameter lists.

[6] The author's experience has been that the basic concepts of module cohesion and coupling are easily learnt in principle, but – without considerable experience – difficult to apply in practice.

It is also important to stress that there are other factors which a designer ought to take into account when evaluating an architecture, though these may vary from problem to problem. These include the following:

- Ensuring that the structure of the design matches the structure of the problem.[7]
- Restricting the span of control, that is, the number of subordinate modules. Various upper limits have been advocated, nine modules being a common value, although adherence to the first factor will impose some flexibility; a command or transaction processor would normally have one subordinate per command or transaction type.
- Data and device isolation.
- Taking advantage of machine and operating system specific features when demanded by system performance requirements.

None the less, coupling and cohesion have proved to be useful, if slightly elusive, concepts with which to analyze software architecture. They have also been highly influential for workers with design metrics, as will become apparent throughout this chapter. We conclude this section with a small case study.

2.1.3 Evaluating an example software architecture

Consider the architecture of the software for a highly simplified reactor control system. There are the following requirements.

> Prior to initiating the reaction process, the operator must advise the system of the maximum safe operating temperature, which will vary according to the process. The system polls a number of sensors that monitor the temperature of the reactor vessel. In the event of the temperature exceeding the pre-defined level, the reactor will be automatically closed down. Each sensor will identify itself. Should a sensor fail, the software will detect which sensor is not reporting and the operator will be alerted. In addition, the operator may initiate a reactor shut down at any time, for example in response to a sensor failure or at the end of a process.

Figure 2.4 presents one possible solution to the above set of requirements for the reactor control software. Communication between the modules is by a combination of parameterized interfaces, as shown by the interface table, and shared data structures, such as the reactor-status variable. Each module is described in turn.

> `REACTOR SYSTEM` is the top level module which has two subordinate modules. Its purpose is the overall scheduling of the system.

[7] Matching problem and solution structures is similar to the ideas of Jackson, as expressed in the low level design method JSP [20]. A claimed advantage is that such architectures are more resilient to changes in system requirements.

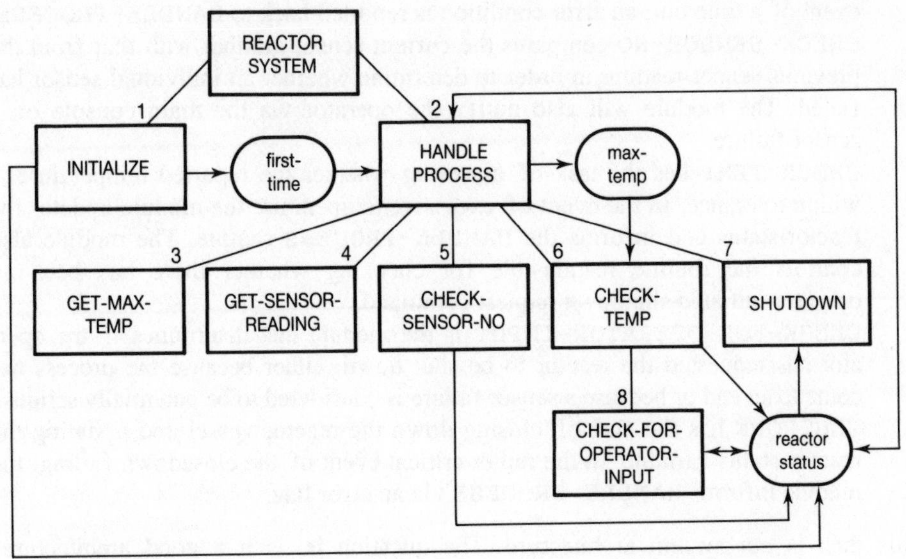

Interface table

Interface	Imports	Exports
1	—	—
2	—	—
3	—	max-temp
4	—	sensor-no., temp, err-f
5	sensor-no., last sensor-no.	err-f
6	sensor-no., temp	err-f, op-shutdown-f
7	—	err-f
8	—	op-shutdown-f

Figure 2.4 Reactor control system

`INITIALIZE`, as the name suggests, is called once at the commencement of reactor operation to set various flags and the reactor-status variable to an initial value.

`HANDLE-PROCESS` is responsible for all the other system functions. If the first-time flag is set it must invoke the `GET-MAX-TEMP` module. In addition it coordinates polling the sensors, checking the sensor readings, checking for any dangerous reactor condition or for an operator shutdown command and managing the shutdown of the reactor. Finally, in the event of a reactor shutdown failure the module displays a suitably worded warning message!

`GET-MAX-TEMP` is the module that obtains the maximum safe temperature for a particular process, from the operator.

`GET-SENSOR-READING` fetches the next available sensor reading. In the event of a time out, an error condition is reported back to HANDLE-PROCESS. CHECK-SENSOR-NO compares the current sensor number with that from the previous sensor reading in order to determine whether an individual sensor has failed. The module will also notify the operator via the main console of a sensor failure.

CHECK-TEMP has the task of assessing whether the reported temperature is within tolerance. In the event of excessive temperature the module updates the reactor-status and informs the HANDLE-PROCESS routine. The module also controls the routine responsible for checking whether there has been an operator initiated shutdown request command.

CHECK-FOR-OPERATOR-INPUT is the module that determines if the operator has requested the reactor to be shut down, either because the process has come to an end or because a sensor failure is considered to be potentially serious.

SHUTDOWN has the task of closing down the reactor vessel and updating the reactor-status variable. In the rather critical event of the closedown failing, the module informs HANDLE-PROCESS via an error flag.

This then is our system architecture. The question is: is it a good architecture? Applying the criteria of module cohesion and coupling we have some basis for evaluation.

REACTOR SYSTEM would seem to exhibit functional cohesion, in that, it performs a single function, that is, to provide a reactor control system. Incidentally, functional cohesion is almost inevitable for top level modules because they subsume the functionality of the entire system. Coupling is low since the module neither imports nor exports variables with any subordinate module and, furthermore, the module does not access any global data structure.

INITIALIZE shows temporal cohesion – as one might expect from this type of module, where there are no primitive units for each initialization function. The only coupling is via global data structures, although, due to the fact that reactor-status is heavily used, this in fact results in couplings with three other modules.

HANDLE-PROCESS on first sight would seem to be fairly cohesive since it controls the actual running of the reaction process. Closer inspection reveals that it is something of a ragbag: functions, apart from controlling the process, include obtaining user input and shutdown. This module must therefore be classified as showing coincidental cohesion. Coupling is little better. The module accesses all three global data structures and imports or exports variables to all five subordinate modules.

CHECK-TEMP is another possible cause for concern with low cohesion due to the subordinate module CHECK-FOR-OPERATOR-INPUT, which carries out an entirely unrelated function. Coupling is also higher than one might expect due to the data structures' reactor-status and max-temp.

Excepting the above four modules, the remaining modules appear to perform single, well-defined functions and have relatively simple, parameterized interfaces. So, in answer to our original question, the architecture is less than satisfactory and there would seem to be a good case for a certain amount of re-design work.

2.2 Quantitative design evaluation

Despite the advent of both design methods and evaluation criteria, the process of generating and analyzing software architectures remains a subjective and skilful process. Design methods such as structured design [40] or Jackson system development [21] may direct the software designer away from less fruitful solutions; they may provide useful insights, but they are not mechanistic; there remains a degree of choice. There is a need for a more objective basis for assessing architecture. Even the concepts of module coupling and cohesion can be quite difficult to apply in practice, especially for large systems comprising hundreds rather than a handful of modules. For these reasons software engineers have sought to use measurement as an aid to software design.

This section describes four classes of design metric. These are metrics based upon calling structure, ripple analysis, information flow and cluster analysis. This is representative of work in the field but it is by no means exhaustive. For a more comprehensive picture the reader is referred to a survey such as [16].

(i) Calling graph metrics

The earliest design metrics were based upon module calling structures, that is, module hierarchy charts without module interface information. The modules are treated as nodes and the calls as edges of a graph. A good example is the graph impurity measure of Yin and Winchester [44]. Their aim was to assess an architecture in terms of the complexity of calling hierarchy. An ideal architecture was thought to exhibit the properties of a pure tree, where every module has only a single calling parent and, therefore, there only exists a single calling path from the root, or top level module to each leaf module. Figure 2.5 shows two architectures. The left hand architecture is a pure tree, whilst the right-hand architecture has two additional module calls (from `A` to `G` and `F` to `G`), causing the structure to deviate from a tree and introducing additional calling complexity.

The formula for deriving the graph impurity measure, `C`, is:

$$C = e - n + 1 \tag{2.1}$$

where `e` is the number of edges or module calls and `n` is the number of nodes or modules. For a pure tree `C` will be zero. For the right-hand architecture in Figure 2.5 the `C` metric is $9 - 8 + 1 = 2$. In other words, two edges must be removed in order to obtain a pure tree.

Although Yin and Winchester intended the measure for other purposes, it does give a measure of the level of component re-use within a system architecture. They

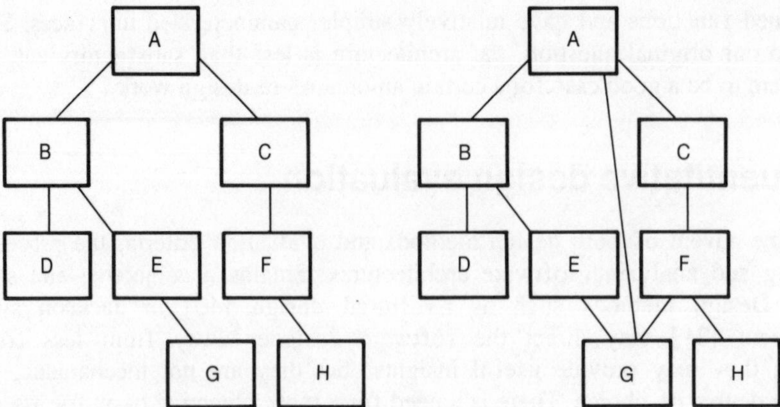

Figure 2.5 The Yin and Winchester graph impurity metric

also extended the metric definition to include data structures in the system graph. This metric is known as C′. A further suggestion was to analyze trends for the metric across levels of the calling hierarchy, the suggestion being that a sudden increase in the C or C′ values might indicate a structural weakness.

Assessment

The empirical support for the general use of these measures is not strong. They also suffer from being difficult to interpret. On the one hand, we would wish to reduce the complexity of the calling structure, and, on the other, we would wish to promote component re-use. Unfortunately, Yin and Winchester's metrics do not differentiate between these two conflicting objectives.

(ii) Ripple analysis metrics

The second class of metrics is based upon ripple analysis, such as the ripple metric of Yau *et al.* [42, 43]. In this case their primary concern was with software maintenance and the objective was to measure a design's resistance to change. In a poor design a simple maintenance change will ripple through a large number of modules, whereas good design will contain the change within a single module. A typical example would be modifying the reactor control system shown in Figure 2.4 to poll an increased number of sensors. This simple change ought to only impact one or two modules – perhaps GET-SENSOR-READING and CHECK-SENSOR-NO – but in fact the change will propagate and will also require modifications to be made to HANDLE-PROCESS.

The Yau and Collofello approach is to take a representative maintenance task and analyze how the change is propagated through the system architecture. Their choice of a representative task is to modify a single variable. This is because it is a fundamental task, common, they argue, to all more complex maintenance work.

They break down their analysis into two classes of ripple effect:

- inter-module change propagation;
- intra-module change propagation.

In order to derive the inter-module propagation, information is required concerning module interfaces and global data structures. This is readily available from a module hierarchy diagram. By contrast, intra-module propagation requires internal module details concerning local variables and control flow which is unlikely to be available prior to coding.

Figure 2.6 shows an example of how intra-module propagation can create additional inter-module ripples. In this case the assignment statement within module B has the impact of linking module C to a change in the variable x within module A.

Assessment

To calculate the worst case ripple effect, both inter-module and intra-module analysis is required. Although an attempt has been made to infer the metric from purely design information [22], the results were considered unreliable. So, it would appear that, to calculate the worst case ripple effect, code is required. This is a major drawback to an otherwise promising method of quantitative design analysis as it delays feedback into the software development process critically: discovery of potential maintenance problems is only made once coding is complete.

(iii) Information flow metrics

The third class of metrics that we wish to examine are those based upon the notion of information flow. Pioneering work is described in the doctoral thesis of Henry and subsequently in [11–14]. The basic concept is that module couplings occur via information flows. Examples of information flows are parameter passing and shared data structures. If a flow exists between modules A and B, then one module is potentially able to influence the behaviour of the other and hence they are coupled in some way. As with module coupling and the ripple metrics, such connections are minimized in an ideal system architecture. This is because they make modules more difficult to develop, understand and modify in isolation.

Henry and Kafura [11–14] defined two types of information flow: local flows based upon a parameter passing mechanism and global flows based upon data structures shared between at least two modules.[8] Once all the flows in a system

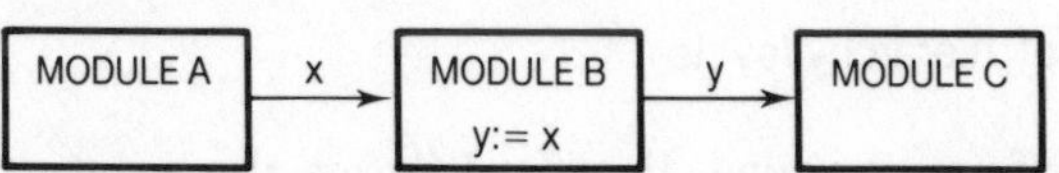

Figure 2.6 The impact of intra-module change propagation

[8] Note that Henry and Kafura use the term 'module' to mean a collection of modules, and 'procedure' to mean a single module. In order to maintain consistency with the remainder of this chapter, their terminology will not be used.

architecture have been identified the information flow complexity may be computed for each module and then summed across the system.[9] At a module level the measure can be used to isolate the potentially critical parts of an architecture, particularly the most error-prone and difficult to maintain. It can also be used to look for sharp rises in the number of information flows between levels in a module hierarchy.

Figure 2.7 shows the Henry and Kafura metric plotted on a level-by-level basis for an imaginary system. Here it is evident that there is an extremely sharp rise in the metric between levels 4 and 5 of the architecture, possibly indicative of a missing level of procedural refinement; in other words, that the designer has proceeded too rapidly from high level abstract functions to very primitive low level functions, without any intermediate functions. If this were the case, a remedy might be to introduce an additional level or levels between the present levels 4 and 5.

Assessment

Henry and Kafura attempted to validate their particular information flow measure against change data for the UNIX operating system. Other researchers have explored the relationship between such measures and the maintainability of the delivered system [22, 31, 33, 39], whilst others have focused upon reliability [23, 25] and, yet again, implementation effort [34]. Although results have been somewhat varied, particularly concerning details of definition, the overall pattern is indicative of a significant relationship between this class of system architecture measure and a range of quality factors of the resultant software system. For this reason Section 2.3 covers the topic in detail.

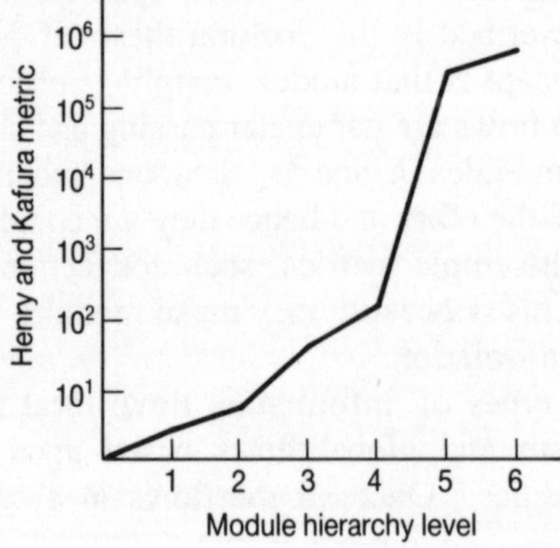

Figure 2.7 Trend analysis of hierarchy levels

[9] In addition to using counts of information flows, Henry and Kafura also recommend the inclusion of a factor to represent internal module complexity. In their empirical analysis of UNIX change data, they used module length in lines of code (LOC). However, it is not clear that this improves predictive performance [23, 31]; moreover such measures cannot be taken until well after the architectural design is complete. For these reasons LOC is excluded from their metric.

(iv) Cluster analysis

A final class of design metric consists of those based upon cluster analysis. Cluster analysis is an analytic technique for grouping similar objects. There is a variety of algorithms for determining similarity but all are based upon a similarity matrix which details each object and its strength of association with every other object. Dubes and Jain [9] provide a good introduction to the technique and choice of algorithm. For system architecture, the usual choice of object is the module and the indicator of similarity is the count of inter-module couplings, see, for example, the work of Belady and Evangelisti [2], Hutchens and Basili [15] or Ince and Shepperd [18, 19].

Consider the following example of five modules `A`–`E`. The number of couplings between modules is shown in the matrix below.

	A	B	C	D	E
A		0	5	1	1
B			0	1	1
C				4	2
D					1

This matrix indicates that there are no couplings between modules `B` and `C` but that there are five couplings between `A` and `C`. The simplest algorithm is that of nearest neighbour, so in this case the nearest neighbours are modules `A` and `C`, so these modules will be combined into a single cluster, the similarity matrix re-computed and the next nearest neighbour sought. This process continues until all the modules have been clustered. The process can be represented pictorially as a dendogram (see Figure 2.8).

It can be observed that the first two modules to group are modules `A` and `C`, followed by `A + C` with `D`, followed by `A + C + D` with `E` and finally module `B`. At this point the clustering ceases since there are no further ungrouped modules. A software tool is essential, given the need to re-compute the similarity matrix after each clustering, otherwise it is very arduous indeed to derive a dendogram by hand.

Module dendograms have a variety of applications.

First, Hutchens and Basili [15] have argued that the dendogram shape can be used to provide information about the choice of system architecture. They suggested that there are a number of general classes of architecture, including the 'planetary system' and the 'black hole'. 'Planetary systems' exhibit a number of distinct subsystems or clusters and usually a larger cluster that forms the core of the system (see Figure 2.9(a)). 'Black holes' are characterized by a single dominant cluster and can be suggestive of a lack of information hiding or critical components highly

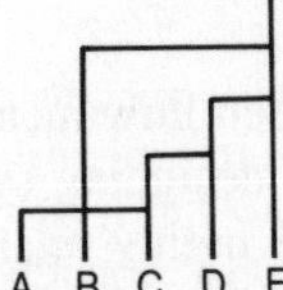

Figure 2.8 A cluster analysis dendogram

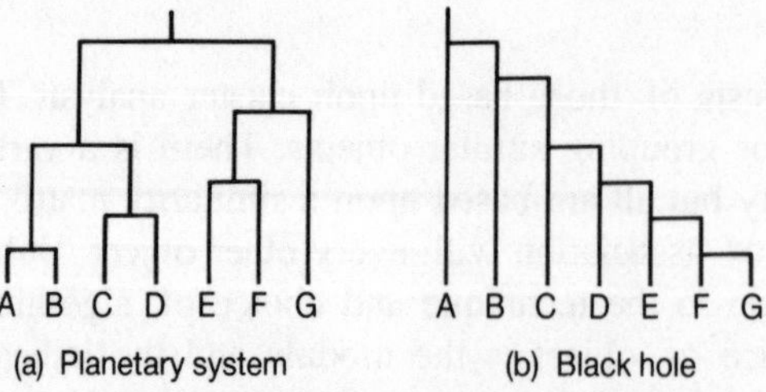

Figure 2.9 Classes of module dendogram

coupled to many parts of the system (see Figure 2.9(b)). Attractive as the notion of dendogram 'finger prints' is, it is vulnerable to the choice of clustering algorithm and so the same similarity matrix can lead to different shapes. This must be borne in mind when applying the 'finger print' approach.

Second, the dendogram can be used as a form of 'ideal' architecture with which to compare the proposed design. The more the two structures deviate, the less good the proposed solution. The reason the dendogram can be considered as an idealized design is because modules in close proximity have the most in common and couplings will be over the shortest possible distance.

Third, is the possibility of automatic generation of software designs or at least a first attempt which could then be further optimized by hand. This is still a highly speculative area with few practical contributions.

Assessment

The greatest weakness with the cluster analysis approach is its vulnerability to the choice of clustering algorithm. The same similarity matrix can yield quite different dendograms according to the choice of algorithm. Even the nearest neighbour algorithm, which would seem to be a very reasonable approach intuitively, suffers from certain weaknesses including a tendency to form bridges between quite distinct clusters on the strength of a single strong coupling between two members of the two subclusters. The approach has yet to be subjected to much empirical evaluation, and therefore remains an unproven, if intriguing, method of analyzing software structures quantitatively.

2.3 Applying information flow metrics

In this section we examine the class of metrics known as information flow measures in detail and consider how they can be applied to the problem of designing system architecture. The concept of information flow between modules is highly related to that of module coupling. The greater the number of flows between a module and its environment, the more highly coupled it will be and the less attractive the architecture. This is because the flows are channels through which changes to a module can flow out and impact other modules, much in the sense of the Yau and Collofello ripple metrics [42]. Moreover, high numbers of connections increase the number of additional modules with which a software engineer needs to deal in order to understand and manipulate a module. The adverse effect upon interface complexity will also make it difficult to replace or to re-use.

In order to measure information flows within a system architecture we need some more formal definitions. Although there exist a number of interpretations of the basic information flow concept, we will use the approach defined by the author [33, 34] and known as `IF4`, since it has the merit of being the most straightforward member of this class of metrics.[10]

`IF4` – like the Henry and Kafura measure from which it is derived – identifies two basic types of information flow: local and global. The former is based upon explicit communication between two modules as implemented by parameter passing, whereas the latter occurs by means of shared data structures.

(i) *Local information flows.* Such a flow is defined to exist whenever a module invokes another module and passes an argument, or whenever a module returns a result after elaboration. Figure 2.10(a) illustrates a local flow from module `A`, the calling module, to module `B` via the parameter `x`. This can be represented by the triple ⟨`A, x, B`⟩. Conversely, Figure 2.10(b) depicts a flow from module `B` to `A` via the result `B` which can be represented as ⟨`B, B, A`⟩.

The following code fragment is one possible implementation of the local flow given by Figure 2.10(a). Here, module `A` calls `B` and passes it a parameter `x`, hence module `A` is able to influence `B` since the value of `x` may determine the behaviour of `B`. Note that there is no flow from `B` to `A` because there is no mechanism whereby `B` is able to communicate with `A`.

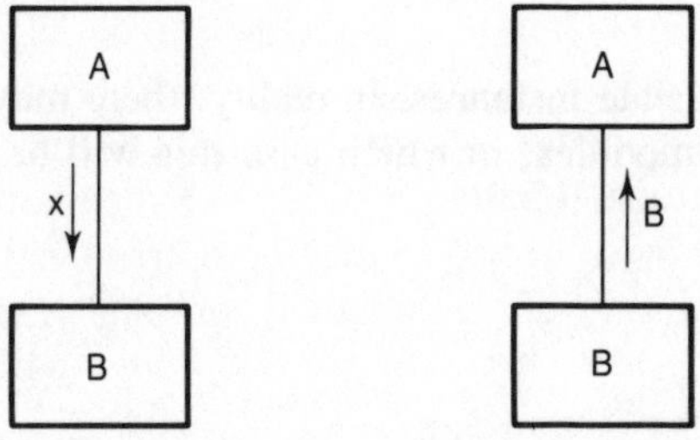

(a) Module call with argument (b) Module call with result

Figure 2.10 Local information flows

[10] For a detailed comparison of the different information flow counting approaches the reader is referred to Ince and Shepperd [17]. In brief, however, the argument is that the original Henry and Kafura model [11] is (i) inconsistent in that it defines global flows but does not utilize them, (ii) arbitrary in including indirect flows on some but not all occasions, and (iii) an overly complex synthetic as a consequence of its attempt to combine module control information with information flow.

```
procedure B (x: integer);
begin
  ...
end; {B}

begin {A}
  B(x)
end {A}.
```

The next fragment of code is a realization of the information flow shown by Figure 2.10(b). Again, module A calls module B, but instead receives, rather than passes, parameter B.[11] This design implies that because there is no flow of information from module A to B, A is unable to influence B.

```
function B: integer;
begin
  ...
end; {B}

begin {A}
  writeln(B)
end {A}.
```

Of course these are the simplest possible instances. In reality, there may exist more than one information flow between modules, in which case this will be represented as a set of triples, for example:

$$\langle A, x, B \rangle$$
$$\langle A, y, B \rangle$$
$$\langle A, z, B \rangle$$

indicates that there are three flows from module A to module B.

(ii) *Global information flows*. The other type of information flow is known as a global because it occurs whenever one module writes to a global data structure and a second module reads from the same data structure.

Figure 2.11 depicts the simplest possible example of a global information flow, where module A updates the data structure DS and module B retrieves from the same data structure. This is the second type of coupling between the two modules, since A

[11] For those unfamiliar with Pascal syntax, the result of the function call B is, in this case, an integer type named B.

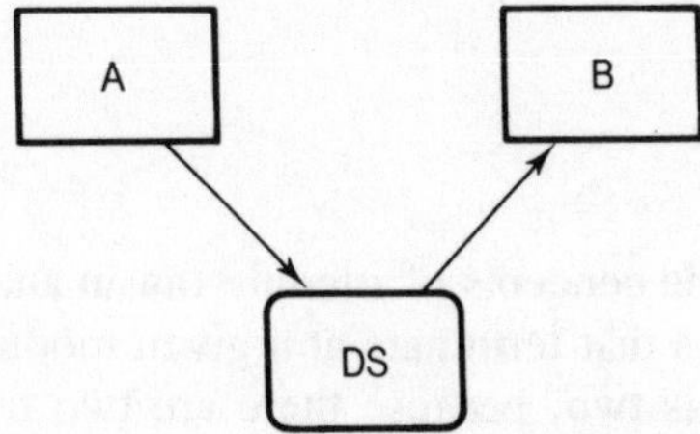

Figure 2.11 Global information flow example

can potentially modify the behaviour of `B`. The flow is represented by the triple ⟨`A, DS, B`⟩, in a manner similar to local flows, as this view of system architecture is less concerned with the precise mechanism by which the information flow occurs than with the fact that the flow exists. Note that such a flow can exist irrespective of the location of the modules in the calling hierarchy. It is not necessary, for instance, for `A` and `B` to have a common parent in the system architecture and indeed it is the 'long distance' couplings which can cause particular difficulties with the comprehension and maintenance of software.

A more complex example is presented in Figure 2.12. Here module `A` has three subordinates. Module `B` returns a value `x` which is passed via module `A` to module `C`, which in turn outputs variables `y` and `z` as parameters, of which `y` is used as an argument in the call of module `D`. Module `B` writes to the `MASTER-FILE` and modules `C` and `D` read from it. Information flow analysis yields the following triples.

Local flows:

⟨A, x, C⟩
⟨A, y, D⟩
⟨B, x, A⟩
⟨C, y, A⟩
⟨C, z, A⟩

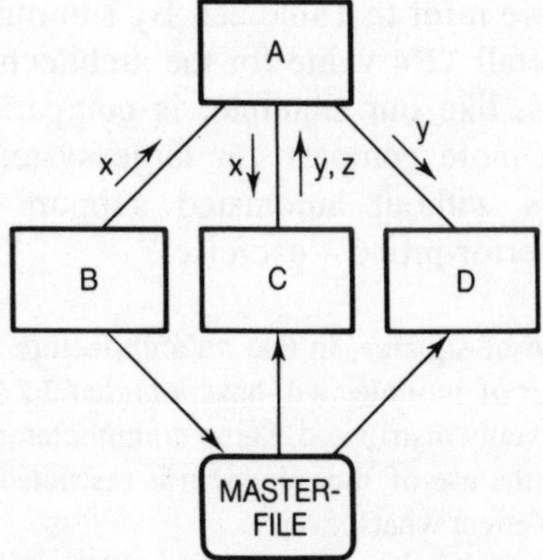

Figure 2.12 Information flow analysis

Global flows:

⟨B, MASTER-FILE, C⟩
⟨B, MASTER-FILE, D⟩

Information flow measures also make use of the concepts of module fan-in and fan-out. Fan-in is the number of information flows that terminate at a given module. In the above example, the fan-in for module `C` is two, because there are two triples, with `C` as the destination attribute (⟨`A, x, C`⟩ and ⟨`B, MASTER-FILE, C`⟩). Be aware that fan-in does not distinguish between local and global flow. Likewise, fan-out is the number of information flows that emanate from a given module. So, for the same example, the fan-out for module `B` is three (⟨`B, x, A`⟩, ⟨`B, MASTER-FILE, C`⟩ and ⟨`B, MASTER-FILE, D`⟩).

The next step when calculating the information flow measure, `IF4` is to tabulate the fan-in and fan-out for each module and then derive the fan-in–fan-out product which represents the number of information paths through the module. Returning to the above example, we can derive Table 2.1.

An interesting feature of using the product of the fan-in and fan-out is that those modules that act as sources or sinks, within the system architecture, have zero values. Typically, such modules are the initialization or close down routines which only have flows in one direction.

The final step is to compute the `IF4` measure for the entire system architecture which is given by:

$$IF4 = \sum_{i=1}^{i=n} (FI_i \, . \, FO_i)^2 \qquad (2.2)$$

where `n` is the number of modules within the architecture, and FI_i and FO_i are the fan-in and fan-out values, respectively, for the `i`th module. The quadratic form of the `IF4` definition has the effect of amplifying the contribution of modules with high fan-in fan-out products.[12] A secondary metric, $IF4_i$ is also defined as:

$$IF4_i = (FI_i . FO_i)^2 \qquad (2.3)$$

So, to complete the example in Table 2.1, we refer to Table 2.2. By summing the $IF4_i$ values from Table 2.2 we obtain an overall `IF4` value for the architecture of 52. Although the analysis for trivial systems, like our example, is comparatively straightforward, the problem becomes much more complex for large systems. In particular, identifying all the global flows without automated support is an exceedingly time consuming – not to mention error-prone – exercise.[13]

[12] The effect of the exponent is that of a least-sum-of-squares, in that an architecture with `n` information flows that cluster around a small number of modules will have a higher `IF4` value than one with the same number of flows but more evenly distributed. Some commentators have questioned the value of this approach; however, if the use of measurement is restricted to the analysis of modules based upon rank order it has no effect whatsoever.

[13] For a description of an automated tool developed by the author to compute a range of information flow related metrics, refer to [32].

Table 2.1 Example information flow analysis

Module	Fan-in (FI)	Fan-out (FO)	FI.FO
A	3	2	6
B	0	3	0
C	2	2	4
D	2	0	0

Table 2.2 The computation of information flow metrics

Module	Fan-in (FI)	Fan-out (FO)	FI.FO	$IF4_i$
A	3	2	6	36
B	0	3	0	0
C	2	2	4	16
D	2	0	0	0

Interpretation

However, it is all very well to provide a software designer with measurements, but we must also consider what they mean and how they might be employed. Given that the choice of architecture has a major bearing upon a whole range of quality factors, and that module coupling is a significant criterion with which to evaluate architecture, it is useful to provide a designer with numerical feedback at design time.

The first type of application of information flow measures is to highlight modules that exhibit unusually high degrees of connection or coupling with their environment. This type of analysis relies principally upon weak ordering[14] and the identification of outliers or abnormal components. In the example given by Table 2.2, we can derive an ordering: (`D = B < C < A`). This highlights module A as the most tightly coupled module, that is, the module with the greatest number of information flow connections. Alternatively, even a simple visual inspection identifies module `A` as an outlier.[15] Both approaches flag module `A` as a design component that merits particular attention. The designers need to ask themselves whether this number of module connections is necessary? Whether an alternative can be found with a lower level of coupling as captured by the information flow metric.

[14] That is, measurement based on an ordinal scale (see Chapter 1).

[15] There exists a more formal approach, known as outlier analysis. This is concerned with the identification of abnormal values, and uses a range of techniques such as boxplots, the construction of confidence intervals, residual analysis or simply ranking values and using the upper and/or lower quartile or deciles. Chapter 7 provides more details of some of these analytic techniques.

The second application of the information flow measure is to assess whole system architectures. Here the metric can be used to compare two or more candidate architectures. The strength of this use of design metric is that the analysis and decision making can be carried out early on in a software project, before the bulk of the project resources are committed. However, once the choice of architecture has been frozen by implementing it as code, any changes will be very costly, and in most organizations – very improbable.

A worked example

We now seek to apply our ideas on information flow metrics to the reactor control system first introduced in Figure 2.4. To help the reader the information flow triples are listed (module names are abbreviated to their acronyms).

There are thirteen local information flows, namely:

⟨GMT, max-temp, HP⟩
⟨GSR, sensor-no, HP⟩
⟨GSR, temp, HP⟩
⟨GSR, err-f, HP⟩
⟨HP, sensor-no, CSN⟩
⟨HP, last-sensor-no, CSN⟩
⟨CSN, err-f, HP⟩
⟨HP, temp, CT⟩
⟨HP, sensor-no, CT⟩
⟨CT, err-f, HP⟩
⟨CT, op-shutdown-f, HP⟩
⟨S, err-f, HP⟩
⟨CFOI, op-shutdown-f, CT⟩

and fifteen global flows:

⟨I, first-time, HP⟩
⟨I, reactor-status, CFOI⟩
⟨I, reactor-status, S⟩
⟨I, reactor-status, HP⟩
⟨HP, reactor-status, CFOI⟩
⟨HP, reactor-status, S⟩
⟨HP, max-temp, CT⟩
⟨CSN, reactor-status, CFOI⟩
⟨CSN, reactor-status, S⟩
⟨CSN, reactor-status, HP⟩
⟨CT, reactor-status, CFOI⟩
⟨CT, reactor-status, S⟩
⟨CT, reactor-status, HP⟩
⟨CFOI, reactor-status, S⟩
⟨CFOI, reactor-status, HP⟩

Parenthetically, it is interesting to note how visual appearances can be deceptive; more information flows stem from the three data structures than from the six parameterized interfaces.

By summing the $IF4_i$ values from Table 2.3 the system wide metric IF4 can be computed as 8914. However, as a starting point we consider the individual module values. Inspection of Table 2.3 reveals that module HANDLE-PROCESS represents almost 90% of the total IF4 score. That this is an outlier value is made even clearer from the frequency histogram given in Figure 2.13. The median $IF4_i$ value is 25, whilst HANDLE-PROCESS has a score of 8281, which suggests that this module would repay closer study. Note that the informal discussion upon coupling and cohesion based upon the ideas of Stevens *et al.* (Section 2.1.3) arrives at a similar conclusion. Examination of the system architecture in Figure 2.4 reveals that this module has five subordinate components, that is, the largest span of control within the structure. In addition to the couplings that this implies, it is also coupled to other modules via all three global data structures and, as has already been noted, these are responsible for more information flows between modules than all the parameterized interfaces combined. In particular, the data structure reactor-status is responsible for no less than fourteen of these information flows.

Table 2.3 The computation of information flow metrics

Module	Fan-in (FI)	Fan-out (FO)	FI.FO	$IF4_i$
REACTOR SYSTEM	0	0	0	0
INITIALIZE	0	4	0	0
HANDLE-PROCESS	13	7	91	8281
GET-MAX-TEMP	0	1	0	0
GET-SENSOR-READING	0	3	0	0
CHECK-SENSOR-NO	2	4	8	64
CHECK-TEMP	4	5	20	400
SHUTDOWN	5	1	5	25
CHECK-FOR-OPERATOR-INPUT	4	3	12	144

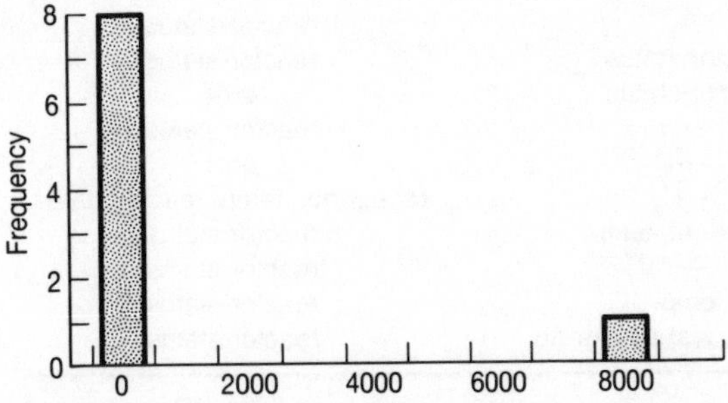

Figure 2.13 Frequency histogram of $IF4_i$ values

From the information flow analysis, we conclude that the HANDLE-PROCESS should be re-designed and that the designer also ought to re-consider the role of the data structure reactor-status. Whilst considering the re-design it is useful to re-visit the design evaluation criteria of module coupling and cohesion. The metric is highlighting the component HANDLE-PROCESS as being the most strongly coupled in the system. The high coupling is also suggestive of a lack of module cohesion. In this architecture, it would seem that HANDLE-PROCESS performs a wide range of functions, rather as one might expect from its somewhat nebulous title. For example, the task of obtaining the maximum safe temperature for a process (GET-MAX-TEMP) appears to be unrelated to the main objective of monitoring and checking the sensors whilst the reactor is active.

Figure 2.14 presents a modified architecture. The major changes concern the role of the module HANDLE-PROCESS, which is now restricted to the more cohesive

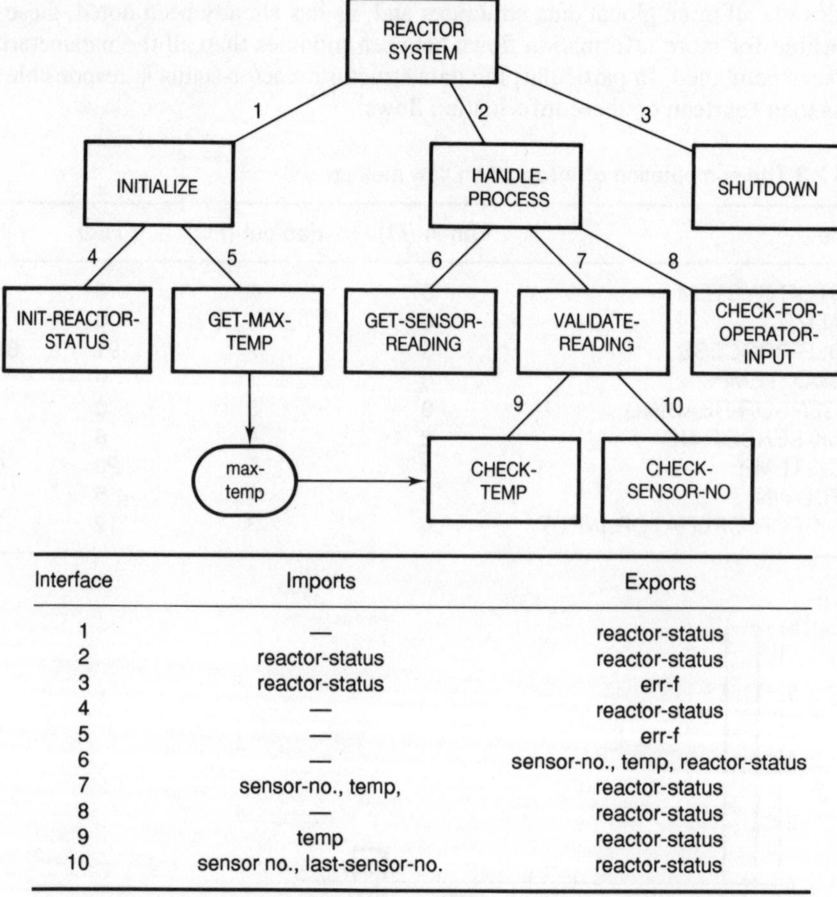

Interface	Imports	Exports
1	—	reactor-status
2	reactor-status	reactor-status
3	reactor-status	err-f
4	—	reactor-status
5	—	err-f
6	—	sensor-no., temp, reactor-status
7	sensor-no., temp,	reactor-status
8	—	reactor-status
9	temp	reactor-status
10	sensor no., last-sensor-no.	reactor-status

Figure 2.14 A modified architecture for a reactor control system

function of monitoring the reactor vessel whilst the process is active. As a result the function `GET-MAX-TEMP`, which is only required prior to commencing the process, is moved to be part of the initialization function. `SHUTDOWN` is also moved from the scope of `HANDLE-PROCESS` since it does not contribute to the function of monitoring the process. An additional level of abstraction is introduced for the validation of sensor inputs in the form of the `VALIDATE-READING` module. Last, the global data structure reactor-status is eliminated and instead this information is communicated via the module calling interfaces, thereby reducing the number of module couplings.

Although, the above changes to the system architecture might seem intuitively reasonable, we have little objective data upon which to decide between the first and second structures. For this reason the information flow measures are re-computed in Table 2.4. Again, we commence with the information flow triples.

There are nineteen local information flows, namely:

⟨I, reactor-status, RS⟩
⟨RS, reactor-status, HP⟩
⟨HP, reactor-status, RS⟩
⟨RS, reactor-status, S⟩
⟨S, err-f, RS⟩
⟨IRS, reactor-status, RS⟩
⟨GMT, err-f, RS⟩
⟨GSR, sensor-no, HP⟩
⟨GSR, temp, HP⟩
⟨GSR, reactor-status, HP⟩
⟨HP, sensor-no, VR⟩
⟨HP, temp, VR⟩
⟨VR, reactor-status, HP⟩
⟨CFOI, reactor-status, HP⟩
⟨VR, temp, CT⟩
⟨CT, reactor-status, VR⟩
⟨VR, sensor-no, CSN⟩
⟨VR, last-sensor-no, CSN⟩
⟨CSN, reactor-status, VR⟩

but only one global flow:

⟨GMT, max-temp, CT⟩

The systemwide value for the `IF4` metric is 689 compared with 8914 for the first architecture: a substantial reduction[16] despite the introduction of two new modules.

[16] One should beware of making inappropriate inferences. It is not clear that this measurement is based upon the ratio scale; hence, assertions such as the second architecture is 11.3 times better than the first architecture are invalid. For the time being we will restrict ourselves to weak ordering (i.e. ordinal scale) and so merely propose that the second architecture has less information flow complexity under our model than the first architecture.

Table 2.4 The computation of information flow metrics

Module	Fan-in (FI)	Fan-out (FO)	FI.FO	$IF4_i$
REACTOR SYSTEM	5	2	10	100
INITIALIZE	0	1	0	0
HANDLE-PROCESS	6	3	18	324
SHUTDOWN	1	1	1	1
INIT-REACTOR-STATUS	0	1	0	0
GET-MAX-TEMP	0	1	0	0
GET-SENSOR-READING	0	3	0	0
VALIDATE-READING	4	4	16	256
CHECK-FOR-OPERATOR-INPUT	0	1	0	0
CHECK-TEMP	2	1	2	4
CHECK-SENSOR-NO	2	1	2	4

At the individual module level the most noticeable change is the decrease in the $IF4_i$ value for the module HANDLE-PROCESS. Referring to the graphical output of Figure 2.15, it is clear that no individual component stands out as an outlier quite to the same extent as in the first architecture (Figure 2.13).

Thus, we can conclude that the use of information flow based measurement supports the choice of the second rather than the first architecture for the reactor control system. The author describes a more detailed example based upon the original Henry and Kafura measure in his tutorial paper [36].

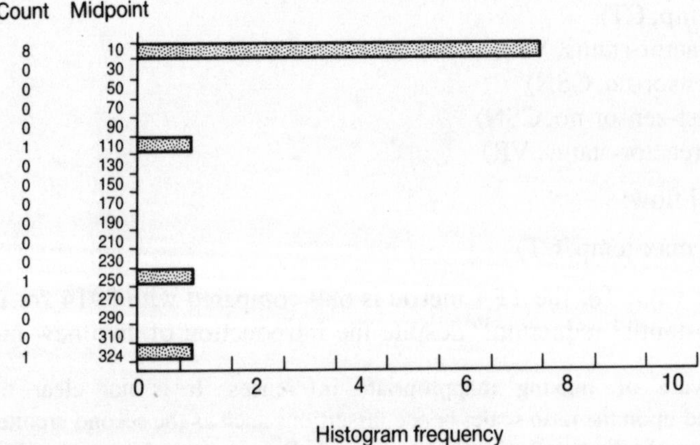

Figure 2.15 Frequency histogram of $IF4_i$ values for the re-designed architecture

Discussion

How useful are these quantitative approaches to system architecture evaluation? To some extent they overcome the disadvantages associated with the subjectivity of module coupling and cohesion. The objective nature of the analysis lends itself to automation, a useful feature when dealing with large architectures. We have seen how they can support a software engineer carrying out high level design tasks, either by comparing candidate architectures or by pinpointing possible problem areas. Such measures can also be useful for projects during maintenance phases, for example by offering the means to prevent or limit the degradation in structure typically associated with the ageing of software [24]. Where severe degradation has already occurred, information flow metrics can help to identify those parts of the system that would most benefit from re-engineering.

However, the information flow measures make a number of assumptions which may not always be warranted. First, the approach treats information flows – be they booleans or complex structured types – as if they were all the same size, mainly because the additional information to discriminate between flows is not generally available at the high level design stage.[17] Should detailed data definitions or a data dictionary be available, then it would seem wise to count primitive data elements.

Second, there is an assumption of equivalence in module size. This approach only counts flows that cross module boundaries so a large module can mask many couplings by subsuming them into a single module. Taken to its extreme, a designer could produce an architecture with zero coupling by using a single, monolithic module: hardly good practice!

Despite the limitations that these assumptions impose, the information flow metrics can provide useful information regarding module coupling. Module cohesion is, however, a more difficult issue since it is more a matter of the purpose of each module which requires semantic understanding of the module descriptions than a matter of structure. The result is that design measures, at best, highlight consequences of low module cohesion.

2.4 Multidimensional models

From the preceding section, we have seen that measuring information flows of a software system architecture can offer more objective information over and above that provided from an analysis based solely upon the subjective design evaluation

[17] There is a case for eliminating duplicate information flows between modules in situations of incomplete knowledge concerning data size, the reason for this being that summing flows of such varying size may generate more 'noise' than useful information and in such circumstances a simple measure based upon the number of module connections, rather than 'band width', may be more effective. Empirical studies have shown this to be the case, at least on some occasions [34].

criteria. However, there are limitations to the information flow approach. Although empirical studies have shown a strong overall relationship between information measures and implementation and maintenance difficulty, a number of data points deviated significantly from this relationship [34, 37]. Closer examination suggests that in most cases these 'abnormalities' can be explained by the presence of unusually large modules. The inference is that system architecture is too complex to capture easily with a single metric or dimension. We must explore the possibility of constructing more complex models that are able to integrate more than one dimension, such as module coupling and module size. But before embarking upon multidimensional modelling we briefly consider the concept of module size.

2.4.1 How small is too large?

Ever since the beginning of the 1970s, when the concept of modular software first became popular, there has been much debate concerning upper limits for module size. In general, most interest has centred upon finding a quantitative figure, for example 100 lines of code (LOC), which could then be applied as a quality check on a simple accept/reject basis. Many organizations and software standards have incorporated such limits. Typical values have been 50, 100 or 200 LOC but, as Bowen points out [4], with little rationale or validation.

One of the difficulties with using LOC on this accept/reject basis is that on its own it represents an extremely naïve model of modularity. Modules that have a high LOC value may be lacking functional cohesion. It may be that they could be usefully decomposed into more primitive functions. For example, the module `DO-COMPANY-ACCOUNTS` may well exhibit functional cohesion, yet its monolithic nature and the fact that it will almost inevitably contain many useful subfunctions strongly suggest decomposition. On the other hand, it is equally possible that there is no particular problem, merely that the module's task requires more programming language statements to implement than some other tasks. Probably the wisest approach is to use module size as an indicator of potential problems and use a length threshold to trigger a special review process.

More serious, from our perspective of providing quantitative support for the software designer, is the matter of timeliness. The big disadvantage with LOC as a measure of module size is that it is unavailable whilst high level design decisions are being made. For this reason we now consider some alternatives to LOC for measuring module size.

Card and Agresti [5] have attempted to tackle the problem by defining a metric for internal module complexity. Although it is unclear from an operational viewpoint exactly what is intended by complexity, it would seem at the very least to be strongly associated with module size. Their measure counts the number of module inputs and outputs as an indicator of the size of the module task. A high count indicates a large or complex task, whereas a count of, say, zero or one suggests a trivial function. The number of subordinate modules is then used to assess the extent to which work is distributed amongst modules, the idea being that if a module has many subordinate modules, then much of its task can be delegated to other modules and it will be correspondingly smaller and simpler. This gives a size measure, S of:

$$S = v/(f + 1) \quad (2.4)$$

where v is the sum of the module inputs and outputs, and f is the number of subordinate modules.

Unfortunately, the metric is still vulnerable to the use of very large modules. Since the size of a module task is defined in terms of movement of data across module boundaries, it will fail to include any work that is completely internal to a module. The metric also assumes – like the information flow metrics – that data objects are of uniform size. A report could constitute a single module output but actually require a considerable amount of processing to generate it, compared with, for instance, a simple count of records. A third concern is that the metric performed poorly when empirically validated by a data set of sixty-one modules [35]. The measure failed to identify the two largest modules and produced no meaningful correlation with module size in terms of LOC, decision counts or the number of variables used (see Table 2.5).

The reason for the poor performance shown by the low correlation coefficients is that increasing the number of subordinates often increases the size, and arguably the complexity, of a module as additional work is involved in scheduling the module calls. Moreover, a module often has a large number of subordinates, precisely because it performs a large task or set of tasks.

Another possible measure of module size that could be derived from a system architecture is DeMarco's bang metric [8]. This metric requires data flow diagrams (DFD) and entity-relationship diagrams (ERD). An interesting aspect of his work is that he distinguishes between two classes of system: those that are 'function-strong' and those that are 'data-strong'. 'Function-strong' systems are characterized as those that are dominated by functional or operational complexity. Good examples are control systems, such as the reactor system we examined previously, and

Table 2.5 Correlations with the Card and Agresti intra-modular complexity metric

Factor	Spearman correlation coefficient (r)[18]
Decision count	0.018
Module variable count	0.205
LOC	0.067

[18] Correlation coefficients, of which the Spearman coefficient is an example, are indicators of statistical association between two variables. As the value tends towards 1 (or −1) so the relationship becomes stronger. Zero implies no discernible relationship. The relationships in Table 2.5 are weak and not statistically significant. But more of this in Chapter 7.

telecommunication systems. At the other end of the spectrum are 'data-strong' systems, which are characterized by highly complex data and relationships between individual data elements. Management information systems and computerized library databases are examples of 'data-strong' systems. Obviously, many systems will be hybrid in that they possess elements of 'function-strong' and 'data-strong'. In such circumstances it may be possible to break the overall system into subsystems and conduct the analysis at this level.

Given that classifying projects can be a rather subjective process, DeMarco provides a method of distinguishing between function- and data-strong systems. This is based upon the ratio of the count of entity relationships (RE) taken from the ERD, and the number of primitive functions (FP) taken from the DFD. In both cases we are only concerned with that portion of the system that is to be automated. DeMarco suggests the following boundary values for classification purposes:

$RE/FP < 0.7$	'function-strong' system
$RE/FP \leq 1.5$	hybrid system
$RE/FP > 1.5$	'data-strong' system

However, it is likely that these values will require adjustment to suit different measurement environments.

For 'function-strong' systems, the bang metric can be calculated for each primitive function – those data transformations that are not further decomposed – as follows:

$$CFP_i = fw_i \cdot TC_i \cdot \log_2(TC_i) \qquad (2.5)$$

where CFP_i is the corrected bang metric for the ith primitive function, fw_i is a function complexity weight (see Table 2.6) and TC_i is the sum of data inputs and outputs of this ith primitive function. From this, a systemwide measure can be derived, assuming n primitive functions:

$$\text{Function bang} = \sum_{i=1}^{i=n} CFP_i \qquad (2.6)$$

Table 2.6 Bang metric function complexity weights

Function type	Weight (fw)	Function type	Weight (fw)
data direction	0.3	text manipulation	1.0
simple update	0.5	output generation	1.0
separation	0.6	tabular analysis	1.0
amalgamation	0.6	initiation	1.0
arithmetic	0.7	synchronization	1.5
edit	0.8	display	1.8
storage management	1.0	computation	2.0
verification	1.0	device management	2.5

For 'data-strong' systems, the bang metric is derived, for a system of n data objects or entities, as follows:

$$COBI_i = RE_i \cdot dw_i \tag{2.7}$$

$$\text{Data bang} = \sum_{i=1}^{i=n} COBI_i \tag{2.8}$$

where RE_i is the count of relationships of the ith data object, dw_i is a data weighting factor obtained from a table supplied by DeMarco (see Table 2.7) and $COBI_i$ is the corrected object increment, effectively the contribution of the ith data object to the overall bang measure for the system data model.

Assuming that primitive functions can be equated with modules, it would seem possible to use CFP_i as a crude size indicator. It is less obvious how the bang metric for data-strong systems can be applied to measuring module size, other than to determine which modules access which data objects and then to use the appropriate $COBI_i$ value. Furthermore, there is limited empirical support other than DeMarco's original data and it is clear that there is a need for extensive tailoring. Finally, it is not obvious precisely what is being measured. DeMarco suggests that the metric is a 'quantitative indicator of net usable function from the user's point of view'. This is not strictly so. It might be better viewed as a weighted composite of design size and structure measures that can be used as an input to a prediction system for net usable function. The verdict, as for so many other metrics, is inconclusive; more evidence is required.

A third approach is the module work metric [35, 37] based upon the traceability of functional requirements onto a module hierarchy. Functional requirements are behavioural features that are required of a software system, for example to print a report, validate an account number or send a signal to a hardware device. Non-functional requirements are constraints, for example that the maximum response

Table 2.7 Bang metric function complexity weights

Relationship count (RE)	Weight (dw)[19]	Corrected object increment (COBI)
1	1.00	1.0
2	1.15	2.3
3	1.33	4.0
4	1.45	5.8
5	1.56	7.8
6	1.63	9.8

[19] The derivation of these weights is slightly obscure, especially if one considers the inter-weight differences, which are 15, 18, 12, 11, 7 respectively. This highlights the discontinuity between the RE values of 2 and 3.

time for a query must not exceed five seconds under certain circumstances, or that the system must be easy to use. The functional requirements can be constructed into a hierarchy – this is frequently implicit from the structuring of the specification document, for example from the paragraph numbering. Consider the requirement to add a new customer account. This comprises a number of more primitive requirements such as obtain customer details, generate an account number, set the initial account balance and so forth. From a hierarchical viewpoint we have:

add a new account
  obtain customer details
  generate an account number
  set initial account balance

Once the three primitive requirements are satisfied, then the higher level or more abstract requirement 'add a new account' can also be considered to be satisfied. In terms of a module hierarchy, the higher level modules inherit the requirement satisfaction up the structure.

The metric uses the number of primitive functional requirements that are to be implemented by each module, combined with the number of subordinate modules needing coordination. This gives an advantage in that it will be independent of module boundaries. In order to derive the work metric for each module the following steps are required.

1. Construct, from the system specification, the functional requirements hierarchy.
2. Using the design documentation, derive the module calling hierarchy.
3. For each module, determine which primitive requirements are implemented, either in full or in part, thereby establishing P_i (the set of primitive requirements satisfied by the `i`th module).
4. For each module calculate $Rmax_i$, that is, P_i plus any inherited requirements from subordinate modules.
5. For each module calculate $Rmin_i$, that is, $Rmax_i$ with all more primitive requirement groupings replaced by higher level or more abstract requirements wherever possible. For example, if a module inherits the functional requirements `{a, b, c}` and a higher level requirement `D` has been defined as `{b, c}`, then $Rmin_i$ will be `{a, D}` and $Rmax_i$ will be `{a, b, c}`.
6. Calculate the scheduling work of each module such that:

$$s_i = \#(Rmax_i) + \#(Rmin_i)$$

   where # denotes set cardinality.
7. Estimate empirically a value for the coefficient α which weights the contribution of scheduling work relative to implementing primitive functional requirements. This is most easily accomplished by analyzing code from existing software systems to determine the proportion of

statements associated with control compared with those implementing actual functions.[20] Note the inequality $\alpha > 0$ which requires that scheduling – where present – must make a non-zero contribution to a module's workload.

8. Calculate $\mathtt{work}_i$ for each module as:

$$\text{work}_i = r_i + \alpha \cdot s_i \qquad (2.6)$$

What support exists for such a module size measure? Using the same data as were used to assess the Card and Agresti intra-modular complexity empirically, Table 2.8 shows the strength of association between the work metric and various module size indicators. All correlations have less than one chance in a thousand of being chance as opposed to statistically significant relationships. This is strongly suggestive of a relationship between the work metric and module size, at least for these data.

Probably the biggest single disadvantage with the work metric is establishing the requirements traceability, particularly for industrial scale software systems. Certainly, the use of both structured specification techniques and tool support are essential. This, at least for the time being, is likely to severely restrict its use.

2.4.2 Putting it all together

The preceding section examined a number of ways of measuring the size of modules at design time. We now move on to consider techniques for integrating more than one measure into a single model, in this case of system architecture. There is general recognition of the fact that software engineering processes and products are frequently too complex to be easily represented by a single measure. Unfortunately, there is rather less agreement as to how this is best accomplished. Broadly speaking, researchers have adopted one of three approaches: the use of n-ary relations where n is the number of measures, the use of compound measures and the use of n-dimensional classification.

The first technique, that of n-ary relations, is the most common for dealing with multiple measures. For example, if it was desired to describe the code for a module

Table 2.8 Correlations with the work metric

Factor	Spearman correlation coefficient (r)
Decision count	0.895
Module variable count	0.694
LOC	0.927

[20] Results from a small study by the author suggested a value of $\alpha = 0.33$; however, it is likely that this will vary from environment to environment.

using lines of code (LOC), the number of subordinate modules (`m`) and the number of local variables (`v`), it would be necessary to use a ternary relation of the form ⟨`LOC, m, v`⟩. Although this is quite straightforward, there are problems. Suppose there are two modules `A` and `B` which have the following measurement values:

$$A = \langle 50, 2, 5 \rangle$$
$$B = \langle 30, 5, 5 \rangle$$

These modules are extremely difficult to compare. We cannot easily determine which module is worse or more complex, since $\mathtt{LOC}_A > \mathtt{LOC}_B$, $\mathtt{m}_A < \mathtt{m}_B$ and $\mathtt{v}_A = \mathtt{v}_B$. It might be that `LOC` is considered to be more significant than `v`, though this is not made explicit with this approach. Even if it were, we do not know how much more significant `LOC` is than the number of modules. Relations at least provide some information but place the onus of interpretation upon the user.

The second approach to integrating measurements is to devise a compound measure from the individual measures by means of weights. Using the same example, a module complexity measure might be proposed as:

$$a_1 \cdot LOC + a_2 \cdot m + a_3 \cdot v$$

where a_1, a_2 and a_3 are coefficients that determine the relative weights or contribution of each individual measure to the compound measure. This would seem attractive and to solve many of the difficulties inherent with the first approach; unfortunately there are deep theoretical problems unless the measures are all derived from the same dimension. In the situation where we have executable lines of code (`ELOC`), comment lines (`CLOC`) and blank lines (`BLOC`) it is perfectly legitimate to construct an overall length measure as:

$$LOC = ELOC + CLOC + BLOC$$

Here the individual measures are unweighted. Frequently, measures drawn from the same dimension will only differ in terms of unit, for example length, in which case the choice of weight will be such as to convert the measures into the same unit. If object code is either measured in bytes (`b`) or words (`w`) we could construct the following:

$$\text{length} = a_1 \cdot w + a_2 \cdot b$$

To measure in bytes, and assuming words are four bytes in length, then $\mathtt{a}_1 = 4$ and $\mathtt{a}_2 = \mathtt{1}$. By contrast, it would not be acceptable to sum separate measures drawn from different dimensions and treat the sum as a single measure. Apart from possible problems of differing scales, the resulting composite will not have any empirical meaning. Returning to the module example of LOC, number of subordinates and local variables, there is no basis for determining the value of the weights. How many LOC is a subordinate worth? How many subordinates are equivalent to a local variable? What is the composite of these three module measures?[21] Such questions are meaningless and illustrate the problems inherent in this strategy. This is not to say that one might not seek to construct a prediction system – for instance to predict the number of defects within a module – along such lines but this is quite distinct from claiming to combine unrelated primitive measures as some valid composite.

A third approach to integrating more than one measure is to classify using n-dimensional scatterplots. Each dimension is partitioned into classes of interest, typically two. An information flow measure could be divided into normal values and high values, perhaps using the upper quartile as the break point. The classification scheme can then be constructed using the product of all dimensions, thereby yielding m^n classes, where m is the number of partitions for each dimension and n the number of dimensions.

The three module measures from our example can be combined into a simple system of eight classes as follows:

low LOC, low m, low v
low LOC, low m, high v
low LOC, high m, low v
low LOC, high m, high v
high LOC, low m, low v
high LOC, low m, high v
high LOC, high m, low v
high LOC, high m, high v

Obviously, a system with too many classes will be rather intractable to analyze. Used judiciously, however, this approach enables the user to assess each measure in the context of the other two measures without having to construct meaningless composite measures. It is also simpler to analyze than n-ary relations since the number of cases is vastly reduced, so the interpretation of each case can be more easily defined.

2.4.3 Information flow and module size

This section applies the n-dimensional classification technique to the system architecture measures of information flow and module size. Previously, we have considered the limitations of measuring inter-module information flow without also assessing module size quantitatively. This is because there exists the possibility of masking information flows by moving module boundaries; a very large module could contain many flows, but only those that connect to other modules will be counted.

[21] In an attempt to find an answer to the question of the meaning of composite measures of the form $X = a_1 \cdot m_1 + a_2 \cdot m_2 ... + a_n m_n$, many measurement workers have used such non-operational terms for X as complexity or quality. In practice, this normally means that a prediction system has been constructed where X is some measurable attribute of the module that is not known at the time of measuring $m_1, m_2, ..., m_n$. This is discussed in more detail in Chapter 1.

Conversely, if only module size is used to analyze software architecture, then small but highly coupled modules will not be detected.

The information flow measure used is $\mathtt{IF4}_i$ and the measure of module size is the work metric, though, clearly, the principles remain the same even if other indicators of coupling and size are adopted. For this example, we will use the data set of sixty-one modules from the empirical study described in [37]. Due to the skewed nature of the data, rankings rather than absolute values are used so that the scatter plot is easier to inspect visually. The $\mathtt{IF4}_i$ and work metric rankings are plotted for each module in Figure 2.16, where a value of 1 indicates the lowest measurement value and a value of 61 the highest value. Ties are ranked at the mid-point position. Each measure is partitioned into two categories, low values (or, rather, ranks) and high values of potential concern. The break point used is the upper quartile, so in this case ranks 47 and above fall into the high value category. With two dimensions and two categories we obtain a four-class classification scheme, as illustrated by the different shaded areas in Figure 2.16. The modules fall into the following classes:

low $\mathtt{IF4}_i$, low $\mathtt{work}_i$ (43 modules)
low $\mathtt{IF4}_i$, high $\mathtt{work}_i$ (4 modules)
high $\mathtt{IF4}_i$, low $\mathtt{work}_i$ (5 modules)
high $\mathtt{IF4}_i$, high $\mathtt{work}_i$ (10 modules)

The low $\mathtt{IF4}_i$, low $\mathtt{work}_i$ modules are not a cause for concern to the software designer. The 43 modules from our empirical analysis in this class had an average error rate of 0.07 known defects per module. This contrasts with an average defect rate of 0.58 for modules drawn from the other three categories.

The second class of modules consists of those with low $\mathtt{IF4}_i$ and high $\mathtt{work}_i$ values. These are modules that, whilst not having a particularly complex interface with their environment, are abnormally large in terms of either the number of

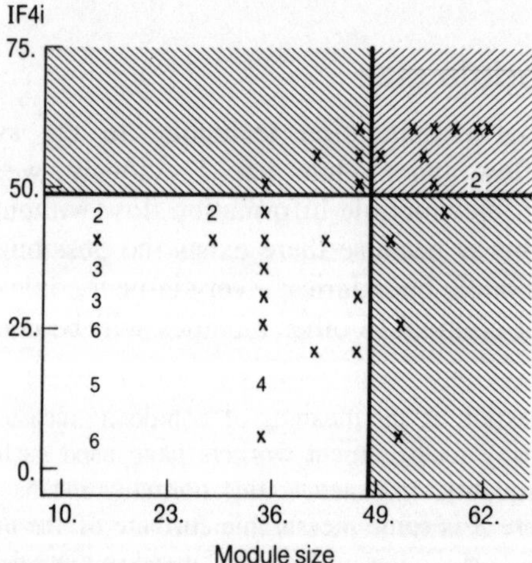

Figure 2.16 Two dimensional analysis of system architecture

functions or the amount of scheduling work, they perform. Often, the problem with such modules is a lack of cohesion due to multiple functions, though the functions may well be closely related – perhaps communicational or temporal strength cohesion – since the module does not exhibit high levels of inter-module coupling. The usual remedy, therefore, will be to divide the module into smaller components, one for each individual function.

The third class of modules consist of those possessing high $\mathtt{IF4}_i$ but low $\mathtt{work}_i$ metric values. This is indicative of modules with large interfaces with their environments. Nor can it be concluded that the lack of size implies high cohesion. High coupling suggests that there is a problem with the functionality of the module. Most common in these circumstances are misplaced modules. Failing to locate a module as a subordinate to whatever procedural abstraction it supports can greatly increase the amount of 'traffic' in an architecture and the level of coupling of the modules involved. An example is contained in the original reactor control system in Figure 2.4 and is reproduced in part in Figure 2.17. Here the module `CHECK-FOR-OPERATOR-INPUT (CFOI)` is placed as a subordinate of `CHECK-TEMP (CT)` rather than `HANDLE-PROCESS (HP)`, the procedural abstraction that it actually supports. As a consequence, `CT` has additional couplings in order to channel information from `CFOI` to `HP`. If `CFOI` were moved to be a direct subordinate of `HP`, this would reduce the level of coupling for `CT` and would have no impact upon `HP` (refer to Figure 2.18).

Another possible cause of modules with normal size but high coupling is missing levels of procedural abstraction. Figure 2.19(a) illustrates an example. Here, the module `OPEN-NEW-ACC` performs a range of subfunctions including obtaining the necessary data, validating it and setting up the appropriate entries in an accounts database. However, in this particular architecture the designer has failed to identify the procedural abstraction of validation. The consequence is that `OPEN-NEW-ACC` has to have detailed knowledge of how the validation is performed. This increases its span of control considerably, makes the module more difficult to understand since

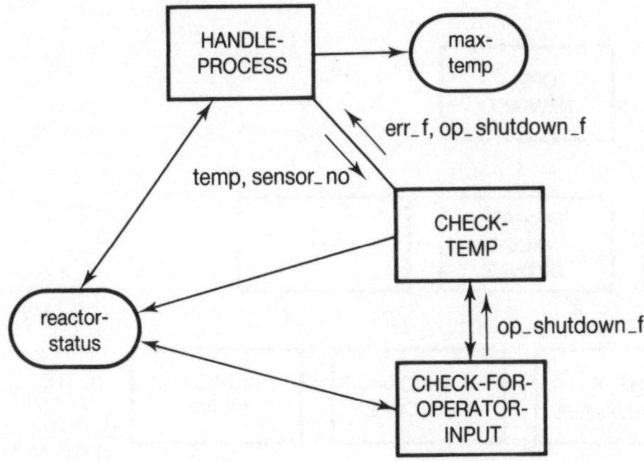

Figure 2.17 A misplaced module example

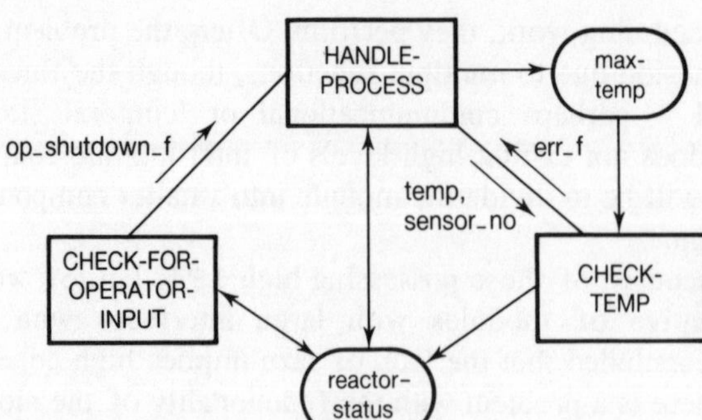

Figure 2.18 Repositioning a misplaced module

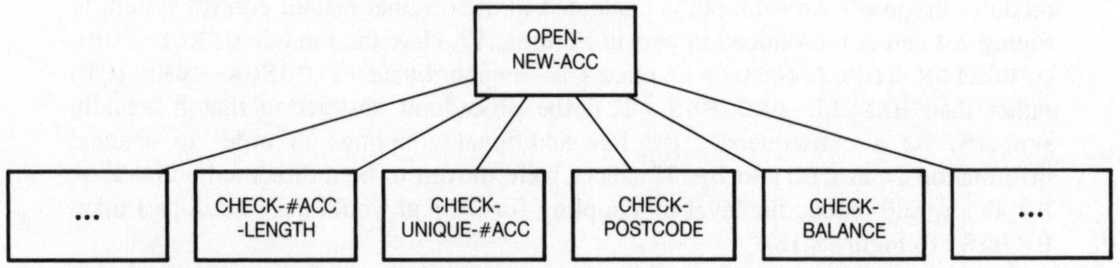

Figure 2.19(a) Missing procedural abstraction

the software engineer will have to infer the abstraction and inhibits re-use because four rather than one module calls will be required. Even if the correct four modules are identified, there remains the distinct possibility of calling them in different sequences, with ensuing potential for unexpected and unpleasant side effects. These problems occur despite the fact that each module exhibits high levels of cohesion.

The remedy, as revealed by Figure 2.19(b), is to introduce a new module to

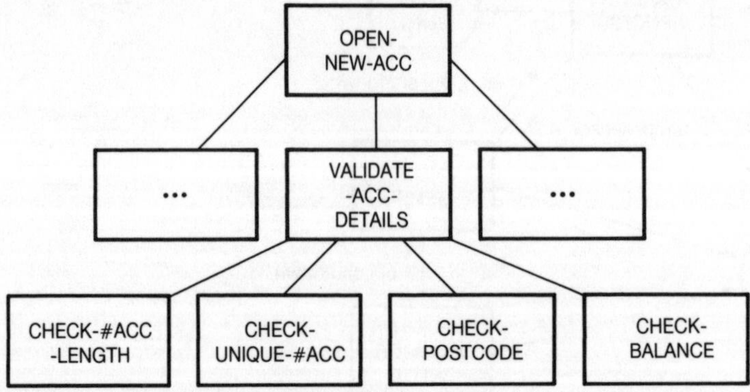

Figure 2.19(b) An additional level of procedural abstraction

represent this missing procedural abstraction; hence, the new module VALIDATE-ACC-DETAILS. This immediately reduces the span of control and the level of coupling for the module OPEN-NEW-ACC by shielding it from details of how validation is performed.

Yet another reason for high levels of coupling in modules is the absence of data hiding. Applying the Parnas principle of information hiding [30] to data structures suggests that the actual structure should be visible to as few modules as possible. Violation of this principle leads to system architectures with high numbers of global flows associated with a small number of global data structures. The reactor-status data structure contained within the original reactor control system (see Figure 2.4) is a good example, where a single read access by the CHECK-TEMP module results in couplings to no less than five other modules. The solution – other than assessing whether the access is necessary in the first place – is to provide a small number of service modules through which all global data structure access takes place. Figure 2.20(a) and (b) shows a stylized architecture without and with data hiding.

Note that the introduction of the two service modules PUT-DS and FETCH-DS hide the data structure DS from modules A, B, C and D. This brings many of the benefits that a database management system provides in separating the application systems from the physical data.

The final class of modules from the multi-dimensional analysis consists of those that have both high $IF4_i$ and high $work_i$ metric values. Clearly, these are the greatest cause for concern since they have complex interfaces and are abnormally

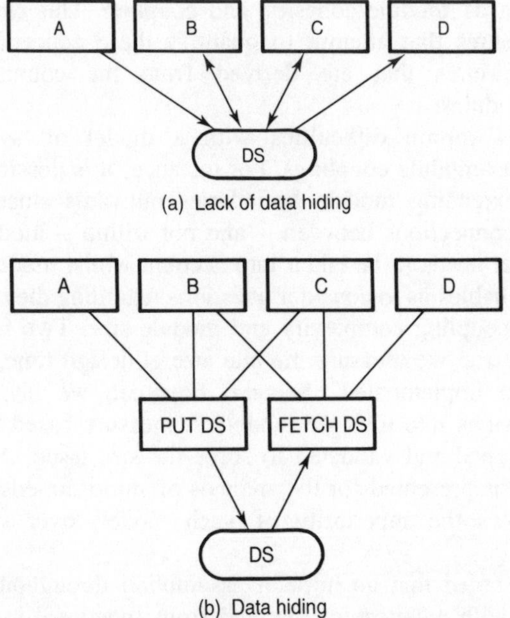

Figure 2.20 The impact of data hiding upon module coupling

large; in other words there are problems of module coupling and cohesion. Possible causes include one or more from: multiple functions, misplaced modules, missing procedural abstractions and insufficient data hiding. Empirical analysis of thirteen separate system architectures [38] suggests that missing levels of procedural abstraction is the most widespread type of design fault.

It is important to emphasize that a single metric would only have identified two out of the three classes of problem module. For our data set this means that four or five problem modules – approximately 6–8% of the total module population, or 21–26% of the problem modules – would, potentially, have gone unnoticed. This provides empirical support for the notion that more sophisticated models of software architecture, that is, those based upon more than one dimension, *can* have enhanced explanatory power. Such power is at the cost of increased development and validation costs.

2.5 Summary

Software design is the process of making choices about system architecture given a particular set of requirements. Such choices can have a profound impact upon the resultant software, including the ease of coding and testing, the potential for re-use and maintainability. The problem then becomes: upon what basis should designers make these decisions? Independent empirical studies, such as the Troy and Zweben [41] investigation, lend credence to the belief that software designers should pay attention to the evaluation criteria of module cohesion and coupling. This chapter has reviewed a number of measures that attempt to quantify these concepts, in particular information flow measures that are derived from the counts of information couplings between modules.

More careful scrutiny reveals certain difficulties with a model of system architecture based solely upon inter-module couplings. For instance, it is possible to disguise information flows by extending module boundaries outwards since the coupling measures only address connections between – and not within – modules. Consequently, a second factor that needs to be taken into account whilst modelling architecture is module size. This enables us to consider questions regarding the trade-off between module interface or coupling complexity and module size. Two issues make this problematic. First, how can we measure module size at design time, that is, before the module has been implemented? Second, how can we integrate measures of two separate dimensions into a single model? A measure based upon requirements traceability is developed and validated to solve the size issue. An n-dimensional classification scheme is presented for the analysis of multi-dimensional models. Empirical evidence shows the superiority of such models over single measure based approaches.

Rather belatedly, it should be noted that an implicit assumption throughout the chapter has been that of dealing with architectures derived from functional models and therefore best suited for what DeMarco termed 'function-strong' systems [8]. The components of these architectures are modules, that is, functional units, their interfaces, shared data structures and data structure accesses. This vocabulary can be rich enough for modelling functional aspects of system architectures but it is quite restrictive in other circumstances. Database designers [29], for example, have a quite different vocabulary in order to model the architecture of their systems, using entities, attributes and relationships (entity–relationship diagramming) or the mathematical structure of relations. Presently, there are few measures for this class of architectural model, excepting some preliminary work described by Gray *et al.* [10].

Another area of modelling outside the scope of the functional view described in this chapter, is object-oriented (OO) architecture [3, 27]. Here our view of a module as a functional unit is inadequate. The object-oriented view is to encapsulate both function and data into a single structure, the class. Moreover, interface connections are more subtle than the parameter (local) and shared data structure (global) connections of a functional architecture. Possible connections are between subclasses and parents (via inheritance and specialization mechanisms): the subclass `CLERK` might inherit services, usually termed 'methods', from its parent class `EMPLOYEE`. In addition there is the binding of generic services to different classes and services that link more than one object, for instance returning a book will alter the state of both the borrower and the book.

The complexity of different types of interaction within an OO architecture demands a greater level of sophistication in our measurement approaches. Moreover, many of the interactions cannot be resolved by the traditional type of static analysis described within this chapter. Consequently, developing useful quantitative models of OO architectures is still very much an open research topic. Chidamber and Kemerer [6] have suggested a suite of six candidate metrics which have been widely adopted, although certain definitional problems have been noted [7].

Although this chapter has focused upon software architecture measures there are a number of more general principles, as follows:

- The collection and possible use of measures without some clearly articulated and coherent model on which to base their meaning is futile.
- Models should be validated; a powerful technique for accomplishing this is empirical validation.
- The use of measurement can greatly facilitate objective assessment of candidate solutions and also highlight unusual or anomalous components within an individual solution.
- Models based upon more than one measurable dimension typically have additional explanatory power, but at the cost of further complexity and validation difficulties.

2.6 Exercises and further reading

1. 'In fact, the goal of the design process is never a "best" design. Instead, it is an "adequate" design that satisfies the requirements and design goals and has a reasonably good structure.' (Barbara Liskov and Jon Guttag [26].) To what extent do you agree with this quotation? Does the use of measurement make any difference?

2. Using the `IF4` information flow measure, 'analyze the following system architecture. Identify any weak points and suggest improvements. Does the measure support your modifications?

Interface table for the project scheduler system

Interface no.	Imports	Exports
1		cmnd
2	cmnd	err_f, sched_list
3	sched_list	
4	err_f	response
5	cmnd	err_f
6		err_f
7		err_f
8		err_f
9		err_f
10		err_f, sched_list

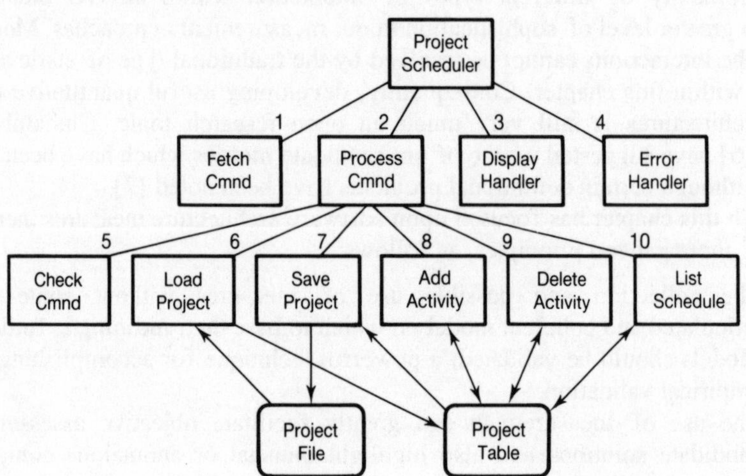

3. Review any system architecture that you have access to. List and classify any design defects. How do your findings compare with those reported by the author in [38]?

Booch, G., 'Object-oriented design', *IEEE Transactions on Software Engineering*, **12**(2), 211–21, 1986.

The majority of design metrics implicitly assume some form of module decomposition, as typified by Stevens *et al.* [40]. This paper offers a concise description of a contrasting approach to software development. A helpful case study is included.

Error type	Frequency	% of systems affected
Missing level of abstraction	13 (22%)	92
Multiple functionality	7 (12%)	38
Split functionality	5 (8%)	38
Misplaced functionality	6 (10%)	31
Duplicated functionality	5 (8%)	31
Lack of data object isolation	20 (34%)	54
Duplicate data objects	0 (0%)	0
Over-loaded data objects	3 (6%)	15
Total errors	59	

Meyer, B., *Object-oriented Software Construction*, Prentice-Hall, Hemel Hempstead, 1988.

A comprehensive text on object-oriented development, with many examples on design. The book also introduces the programming language Eiffel as a suitable vehicle for realizing the various object-oriented design constructs such as inheritance and polymorphism.

Parnas, D.L., 'On the criteria to be used in decomposing systems into modules', *CACM*, **15**(2), 1053–8, 1972.

Despite its brevity and vintage, arguably one of the most important articles to be written on system architecture. Parnas introduces his principle of 'information hiding', that is, modules hiding design decisions from the rest of the system, as a criterion for dividing systems into modules. Essential reading for all software designers!

Stevens, W.P., G.J. Myers, and L.L. Constantine, 'Structured design', *IBM Sys. J.*, **13**(2), 115–39, 1974.

This paper provides a most useful summary of the design evaluation criteria of module coupling and cohesion. In addition there are a number of other heuristics to guide a software designer in producing a system architecture. Recommended.

Troy, D.A. and S.H. Zweben, 'Measuring the quality of structured designs', *J. of Syst. and Softw.*, **2**(2), 113–20, 1981.

A major empirical analysis of many of the quantitative aspects of software system architecture. The authors conclude that there is considerable support for the design evaluation criteria of module coupling and cohesion.

References

[1] Alexander, C., *Notes on the Synthesis of Form.* Harvard University Press: Cambridge MA, 1964.

[2] Belady, L.A. and C.J. Evangelisti, 'System partitioning and its measure', *J. of Syst. and Softw.*, **2**, 23–9, 1981.

[3] Booch, G., *Object Oriented Design with Applications.* Addison-Wesley: 1990.

[4] Bowen, J.B., 'Module size: a standard or heuristic?', *J. of Syst. and Softw.*, **4**, 327–32, 1984.

[5] Card, D.N. and W.W. Agresti, 'Measuring software design complexity', *J. of Syst. and Softw.*, **8**, 185–97, 1988.

[6] Chidamber, S.R. and C.F. Kemerer, 'A metrics suite for object oriented design', *IEEE Trans. on Softw. Eng.*, **20**(6), 476–93, 1994.

[7] Churcher, N. and M.J. Shepperd, 'Comment on "A metrics suite for object oriented design"', *IEEE Trans. on Softw. Eng.*, 1995.

[8] DeMarco, T., *Controlling Softw. Projects. Management, measurement and estimation.* Yourdon Press: NY, 1982.

[9] Dubes, R. and A.K. Jain, 'Clustering methodologies in exploratory data analysis', in *Advances in Computing*, Vol. 19, M.C. Yovits, ed., Academic Press: 1980.

[10] Gray, R.H.M. *et al.*, 'Design metrics for database systems', *BT Technol. J.*, **9**(4), 69–79, 1991.

[11] Henry, S. and D. Kafura, 'Software quality metrics based on inter-connectivity', *J. of Syst. and Softw.*, **2**(2), 121–31, 1981.

[12] Henry, S. and D. Kafura, 'Software structure metrics based on information flow', *IEEE Trans. on Softw. Eng.*, **7**(5), 510–17, 1981.

[13] Henry, S. and D. Kafura, 'The evaluation of software systems' structure using quantitative software metrics', *Softw. Pract. and Experience*, **14**(6), 561–73, 1984.

[14] Henry, S., D. Kafura and K. Harris, 'On the relationship among three software metrics', *ACM SIGMETRICS Performance Evaluation Review*, **10**(Spring), 81–8, 1981.

[15] Hutchens, D.H. and V.R. Basili, 'System structure analysis: clusterings with data bindings', *IEEE Trans. on Softw. Eng.*, **11**(8), 749–57, 1985.

[16] Ince, D.C. and M.J. Shepperd, 'System design metrics: a review and perspective', in *Proc. Software Engineering '88*, ed. Pyle, I.C. Liverpool University: IEE, 1988.

[17] Ince, D.C. and M.J. Shepperd, 'An empirical and theoretical analysis of an information flow-based system design metric', in *Proc. 2nd European Softw. Eng. Conf.*, eds. Ghezzi, C. and McDermid, J.A., Springer-Verlag: Warwick, UK, 1989.

[18] Ince, D.C. and M.J. Shepperd, 'Quality control of software designs using cluster analysis', in *Proc. 1st European Software Quality Conf.*, Vienna: EOQ, 1989.

[19] Ince, D.C. and M.J. Shepperd, 'The use of cluster techniques and system design metrics in software maintenance', in *Proc. UK IT'90 Conf.*, Southampton, UK: IEE/DTI, 1990.

[20] Jackson, M.A., *Principles of Program Design.* Academic Press: London, 1975.

[21] Jackson, M.A., *System Development.* Prentice-Hall: Hemel Hempstead, UK, 1982.

[22] Kafura, D. and G.R. Reddy, 'The use of software complexity metrics in software maintenance', *IEEE Trans. on Softw. Eng.*, **13**(3), 335–43, 1987.

[23] Kitchenham, B.A., 'An evaluation of software structure metrics', in *Proc. COMPSAC '88*, Chicago, IL.: IEEE, 1988.

[24] Lehman, M.M. and L.A. Belady, 'A model of large system development', *IBM Syst. J.*, **15**(3), 225–52, 1976.

[25] Linkman, S.G., 'Quantitative monitoring of software development by time-based and intercheckpoint monitoring', *Softw. Eng. J.*, **5**(1), 43–9, 1990.

[26] Liskov, B. and J. Guttag, *Abstraction and Specification in Program Development.* MIT Press: Cambridge, MA, 1986.

[27] Meyer, B., *Object-oriented Software Construction.* Prentice-Hall: Hemel Hempstead, UK, 1988.

[28] Myers, G.J., *Reliable Software through Composite Design*, Petrocelli/Charter, New York, 1975.

[29] Navathe, S.B., 'Evolution of data modeling for databases', *CACM*, **35**(9), 112–23, 1992.

[30] Parnas, D.L., 'On the criteria to be used in decomposing systems into modules', *CACM*, **15**(2), 1053–8, 1972.

[31] Rombach, H.D., 'A controlled experiment on the impact of software structure on maintainability', *IEEE Trans. on Softw. Eng.*, **13**(3), 344–54, 1987.

[32] Shepperd, M.J., 'A metrics based tool for software design', in *Proc. 2nd Intl. Conf. on Softw. Eng. for Real Time Systems*, ed. Wilson, D.R. The Royal Agriculture College, Cirencester, UK: IEE, 1989.

[33] Shepperd, M.J., 'Early life cycle metrics and software quality models', *Information and Softw. Technol.*, **32**(4), 311–6, 1990.

[34] Shepperd, M.J., 'An empirical study of design measurement', *Softw. Eng. J.*, **5**(1), 3–10, 1990.

[35] Shepperd, M.J., 'Measuring the structure and size of software design', *Information and Softw. Technol.*, **34**(11), 756–62, 1992.

[36] Shepperd, M.J. and D.C. Ince, 'Metrics, outlier analysis and the software design process', *Information and Softw. Technol.*, **31**(2), 91–8, 1989.

[37] Shepperd, M.J. and D.C. Ince, 'The multi-dimensional modelling and measurement of software designs', in *Proc. Annu. ACM Comp. Sci. Conf.*, ed. Rine, D.C. Washington DC: ACM Press, 1990.

[38] Shepperd, M.J. and D.C. Ince, 'The use of metrics for the early detection of software design errors', in *Proc. BCS/IEE Software Engineering '90*, ed. Hall, P.A.V. Brighton, UK: IEE, 1990.

[39] Shepperd, M.J. and D.C. Ince, 'Design metrics and software maintainability: An experimental investigation', *J. of Softw. Maint.*, **3**(4), 215–32, 1991.

[40] Stevens, W.P., G.J. Myers and L.L. Constantine, 'Structured design', *IBM Syst. J.*, **13**(2), 115–39, 1974.

[41] Troy, D.A. and S.H. Zweben, 'Measuring the quality of structured designs', *J. of Syst. and Softw.*, **2**(2), 113–20, 1981.

[42] Yau, S.S. and J.S. Collofello, 'Some stability measures for software maintenance', *IEEE Trans. on Softw. Eng.*, **6**(6), 545–52, 1980.

[43] Yau, S.S., J.S. Collofello and T. MacGregor, 'Ripple effect analysis of software maintenance', in *Proc. COMPSAC '78*, IEEE, 1978.

[44] Yin, B.H. and J.W. Winchester, 'The establishment and use of measures to evaluate the quality of software designs', in *Proc. ACM Softw. Qual. Ass. Workshop*, 1978.

Chapter 3

Quality

Not measuring quality has a disastrous effect on morale. Of all the gripes I hear at my seminars, the most frequent is, 'Nobody in my organisation cares about quality, only about quick delivery of even the shoddiest product.' (Tom DeMarco [5].)

Synopsis

In which we consider the meaning of software quality and how it might be assessed quantitatively. The relationship between quality standards, quality plans and quality metrics is investigated and a framework is advocated. Two types of application for quality metrics are proposed: they can be used either in a diagnostic or a discrepancy indication capacity. Examples of the former include setting an upper limit for module size and examples of the latter include statistical process control.

3.1 Quality under control

Product quality is obviously another key management concern. Increasingly, society is dependent upon computer based systems, and as these systems become more and more endemic, so their quality acquires a greater and greater significance. Quality is, however, a multi-faceted characteristic. It encompasses a whole range of different factors ranging from operational ease through to reliability. Quality is also dependent upon whose perspective is being considered, because quality, like beauty, is in the eye of the beholder. For example, customers will see quality quite differently from the maintenance team, who, in turn, will have quite a different view from the IT director. Furthermore, when considering quality it must be recognized that code is only one of the many products produced by a software project. Managers must also address the quality of the various intermediate project products: specifications, designs, user documentation and test plans, to name but a few.

There is no shortage of agreement that quality is a good thing. The difficulties lie first in defining the quality levels that are required and second in obtaining these desired quality levels. Measurement enables the project manager to transform fuzzy quality aspirations into operational definitions, without which it is difficult to establish the presence, or otherwise, of quality in any product. As an illustration contrast the quality requirement that a system be robust with the operational definition that it fail no more than once per 1000 hours under given operating conditions. The latter approach provides feedback to drive processes that build the quality product, since it can be determined whether the product requires further testing, modification and so forth.

If we wish to be able to control or manage quality, then we need to be able to measure it. And being able to measure quality makes it possible to define quality targets unambiguously. Otherwise, it is difficult to state with any degree of confidence whether a product has met a particular quality requirement, and quality control degenerates to an exercise in supposition and wishful thinking.

3.2 Defining quality

First, what do we mean by quality, and, in particular, what do we mean by software quality? The standard definition, taken from (ISO 8402), is:

> *the totality of features and characteristics of a product, process or service that bear on its ability to satisfy stated or implied needs.*

Clearly, such a definition is fairly all embracing, so it is important to be able to provide more specific and objective quality definitions. This is the key to being able to measure quality. As Tom Gilb [10] recommends, avoid fuzzy statements! He gives an example of a quality requirement for the 'consistent commonality of data (common data)' which is so meaningless as to make it impossible to assess whether an information system actually possesses this characteristic, let alone to what degree. Transforming such a vague notion of quality into something measurable is an iterative process of refinement. The first step might be to establish the following:

- the quality attribute;
- the object of interest;
- the perspective.

So, in this case, the quality attribute is consistency, the object is the information system and the perspective is presumably that of the customer. It is essential, however, to check as it can modify our understanding of the quality attribute considerably. The next step is to consider what is meant by consistency – here it is defined as the absence of contradictory information in the database at any one point in time. Then there is the problem of how to measure the presence or absence of contradictory information. One solution might be to develop a special purpose testing tool that makes n thousand random database accesses and tests these for consistency. Finally, it is useful to express quality expectations in terms of quantitative levels: target, minimum acceptable and present situation. Where measurements are only estimates, this must be made explicit so as to prevent a spurious sense of precision. We are all familiar with wild guesses dressed up as 83.619%!

To try to circumvent some of these problems, the headings (adapted from [10]) in Figure 3.1 can be used as a framework for describing quality characteristics in a precise and measurable way. None the less difficulties remain. For instance, how reliable is the consistency testing tool? Is it truly random, or is there a bias which might distort our measurements? Can it check for all types of inconsistency? Also, what about the inconsistency detection rate? It is arguable that there are two separate, but related, quality factors, namely, the detected and undetected inconsistency rates. Indeed, it may well be the latter that really concern the information system customer. Despite these potential difficulties, this structured approach to quality measurement represents a real step forward. The definition of consistency might be contentious but at least it is explicit. The consistency measurement might be naïve but at least it is objective and repeatable. It offers the manager some basis for understanding where the project is in quality terms, coupled with a view of where the customer wants the project to be.

None the less, there remains a danger that the above approach to the quality metrics can lead to an excessively simplistic view. Normally, a project manager has to deal with multiple quality factors. Many quality factors are not independent, for example minimizing mean response time for an interactive system could be achieved

Consistency definition:

QUALITY ATTRIBUTE = consistency
OBJECT = information system
PERSPECTIVE = customer
SCALE = probability of a data element being consistent with all other elements in the system
TEST = 1000 random record sample checked by the database consistency testing program
NOW = 85–90% (estimated)
MINIMUM = 90%
TARGET (11:94) = 99.9%

Figure 3.1 A quality definition framework

Table 3.1 Quality factor trade-off matrix

Quality factor	Priority	Timeliness	Security	Usability
Timeliness	Essential			
Security	Essential	–ve		
Usability	Desirable	–ve	0	
Maintainability	V. desirable	–ve	0	0

by sacrificing maximum response times. On the other hand, other quality factors are linked such that improving one factor will lead to improvements in other factors. A good example is that improving code readability will have a positive impact upon reliability and maintainability. Similarly, resource constraints on the project have the effect of linking different quality factors. Extra effort devoted to improving product maintainability is at the cost of, say, the clarity of the user documentation.

A simple, but effective method for at least highlighting interactions between quality factors is to use a matrix.[1]

Table 3.1 shows a highly simplified set of quality factors, and their interrelationships. A '0' indicates no direct relationship, '+ve' indicates that, by pursuing one quality factor, the other will be increased as a side effect, and '–ve' indicates a conflict. In this case there is a conflict between timeliness and all the other three factors. The conflict could be resolved by examining the relative priorities, so in this case usability and maintainability might have to be sacrificed, at least in part for timeliness. The conflict between timeliness and security will be less easy to resolve and would require further management attention. Obviously, this matrix is a gross simplification of reality, but it at least offers a method for reviewing the situation in a structured and explicit fashion.

3.3 Quality standards

It has been suggested that there exist two types of manager. Type I is bright and enthusiastic and knows that standards are a waste of time. Type II is battered, more experienced, doesn't enjoy standards but knows they are essential [23]. The aim of this section is to increase the proportion of type II readers!

Standards may not enjoy much of a reputation at present, but there is increasing recognition of their important role. Unfortunately, as in many technical areas, there seems to have been a proliferation of terminology. The following glossary is offered as a small redress.

[1] The use of a matrix to track software quality factors is extended considerably by the QFD method [2]. See Chapter 5 for a fuller account of this method as applied to software systems.

Glossary of quality terms

BS5750 Part 1: British standard equivalent to ISO 9001.
EN 29001: European standard equivalent to ISO 9001.
ISO 8402: Definition of quality vocabulary.
ISO 9001: International quality management and quality assurance standard for manufacturing processes.
ISO 9000-3: the interpretation of ISO 9001 with regard to the software industry.
Quality assurance (QA): defining, reviewing and improving the Quality Management System (QMS), coupled with maintaining confidence that the QMS is being properly adhered to.
Quality control: the set of operational techniques and activities necessary to satisfy the quality requirements for a product or service.
Quality management system (QMS): a statement by the software developer of the strategy and tactics for obtaining the desired quality levels as economically as possible.
Quality plan: the tailoring or interpretation of the QMS to a particular project.
Quality policy: the 'overall quality intentions and objectives of an organization formally expressed by senior management' (ISO 8402).
TickIT: an initiative commissioned by the Department of Trade and Industry, based upon ISO 9001, for the certification of quality management systems (QMS) and the accreditation of QMS assessors [7].

In an effort to tackle the widespread problems relating to quality, a series of standards has been developed by the various standards bodies, most notably the International Standards Organisation (ISO). The approach embodied by the ISO 9000 [15, 16] series of standards has been to focus upon the engineering process, the argument being that a high quality process will result in the manufacture of high quality products. The ISO 9001 Standard describes twenty requirements of a quality management system (QMS) which are then used as a yardstick for judging quality, that is, the extent to which processes conform to the documented QMS. The excerpt

4. Design Control: procedures are required for the control of the design function including: a design/development programme with assigned responsibility and adequate resources allocated; the identification and control of organisational and technical interfaces; preparation and maintenance of drawings; consideration of regulatory requirements and the establishment of design review procedures.

The design stages need to cover: design and development planning; design input, output, verification and changes.

20. Statistical Techniques: where it is appropriate, procedures are required for identifying adequate statistical techniques for verifying the acceptability of process capability and product characteristics. (ISO 9001 – 1987.)

on p.72 from [16], of paragraphs 4 and 20, provides an indication of the nature of these requirements.

As the more astute reader might have noticed, this approach is fairly general to any manufacturing process! For instance, the standard does little more than highlight the importance of statistics and the need for their disciplined and appropriate application. Effectively, the standard provides a framework and a set of yardsticks by which to assess a production process. It does not spell out in minute detail exactly what must be done at each and every stage of the process. The ISO 9000-3 standard, however, attempts to make the ideas behind ISO 9001 more relevant to software engineering. Again, to provide a flavour of ISO 9000-3, an excerpt from paragraph 6.4 on measurement is given.

6.4 Measurement

6.4.1 Product measurement

Metrics should be reported and used to manage the development and delivery process and should be relevant to the particular software product.

There are currently no universally accepted measures of software quality. However, at a minimum some metrics should be used which report field failures and/or defects from customer's viewpoint. Selected metrics should be described such that results are comparable. ...

6.4.2 Process measurement

... Here, as for product metrics, the important thing is that levels are known and used for process control and improvement and not what specific metrics are used. The choice of metrics should fit the process being used. ... (ISO 9000-3 – 1991:)

The standard reiterates the point made earlier in this chapter: that there are no simple universal quality metrics. Moreover, it is appropriate to consider both the nature of the product being developed and the process by which it is being developed. The customer's perspective on quality must be regarded as paramount, and if measurement is to be used for comparison, then sufficient contextual or environmental information must be recorded in order to prevent invalid inferences. The fact that Project A appears to be 250% more productive than Project B may be less significant than it first appears, if Project A is working on a small commercial system using tried and tested technology, whilst Project B is developing a 10 million LOC, time critical, embedded aerospace system.

A key feature of the ISO approach is the central role of the QMS, which is, in the words of the TickIT Guide [7]:

> the enabling mechanism within an organisation which coordinates and controls the functions necessary to achieve the required quality of product or service as economically as possible.

Typically, the QMS will be documented in a quality manual or handbook. Since the QMS will necessarily be very complex, it is often structured in a hierarchical fashion reflecting the organizational structure. Such a structure is given in Figure 3.2.

At the highest level, within the QMS, there will be some general statement of quality policy which will essentially be an indication of the scope of the organization's commitment to quality. This general statement is refined into more detail as a set of quality procedures documented in the organization quality manual. The manual can then be instantiated into quality plans targeted at specific projects. Each project might have a highly standardized plan, or the plan could be significantly adapted to local factors and specific project requirements. To some extent the degree of flexibility in quality plans is in part dependent upon diversity within the organization, but also upon the organizational culture. Each quality plan will comprise various quality control procedures for a project. Part of an example software quality plan is given on p. 75.

Equally important is the concept of quality assurance (QA), that is, that 'aspect of the overall management function that determines and implements the quality policy' (ISO 8402), and it divides into two areas of responsibility [20]:

- determination and improvement of the QMS;
- checking that pre-determined quality control techniques and activities are properly undertaken.

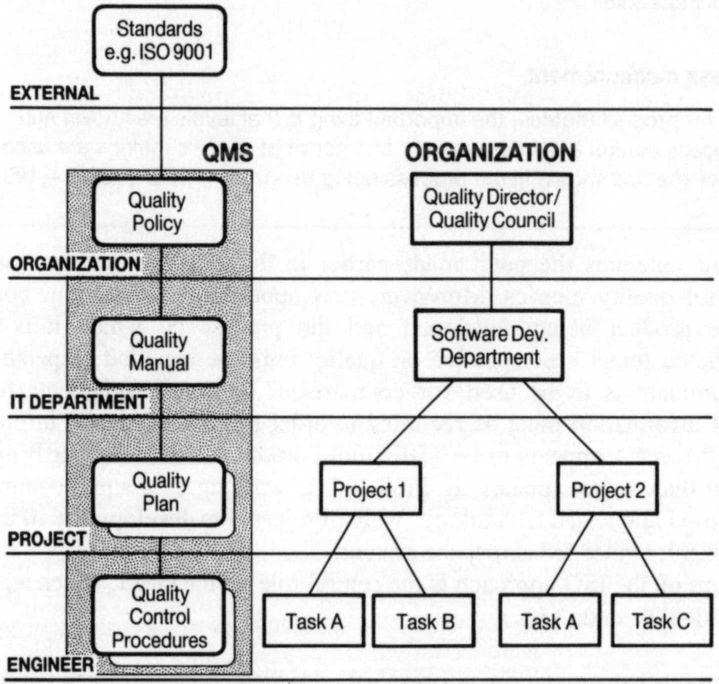

Figure 3.2 Hierarchy in a quality management system

SOFTWARE QUALITY PLAN – PROJECT BUFFPOOL

Reference: Buffpool/QP/1.00 **Date:** 30.11.94

PURPOSE

1. This Plan details the procedures to be followed in order to maintain the quality of all products forming part of Project Buffpool.
2. Project Buffpool is a small computer system designed to reconstruct a piece of text from a number of disk files.
3. Project deliverables are as follows:
   - Management and standards documentation and plans
   - Design documentation
   - Source code documentation
   - Test/output documentation

REFERENCE DOCUMENTS

4. Documents used in this plan are:
   - XYZ quality manual (Version 1.01)
   - Project plan
   - Terms of reference – project manager
     - QA manager
     - configuration manager
     - programmers
   - ADA Programming Codes of Practice (Version 3.01)
   - ISO 9000-3
   - Object Oriented Design Codes of Practice (Version 1.00)

MANAGEMENT

Organization

5. The project team structure is:

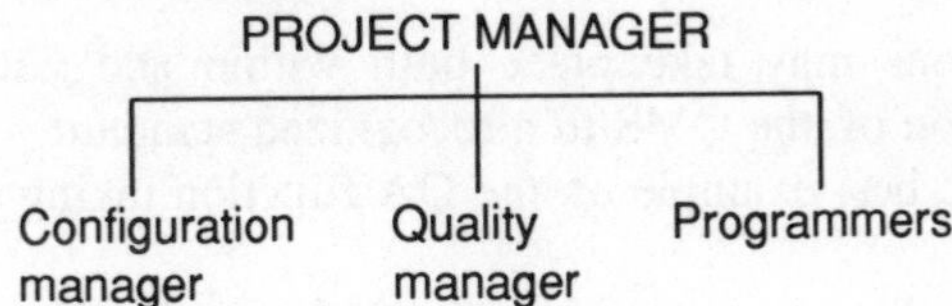

Scope

6. This plan covers all aspects of the project development lifecycle from detailed design (previous stages have been supplied by the customer) to delivery.

continued

continued

Responsibilities

7. All members of the project will be involved in detailed design, coding and testing. ...

Documentation

8. Each document produced during the project will be checked by the QA manager and, when accepted, will come under configuration control. ...
9. As a minimum the following documentation is required: ...

STANDARDS, PRACTICES AND CONVENTIONS

10. OOD will be utilized as the design medium for the project following practices described in the Object Oriented Design Codes of Practice, excepting that JSD style notation will be employed. ...

REVIEWS AND AUDITS

11. Preliminary design review – to validate the technical feasibility of the initial software design.
12. Critical design review – to verify the compliance of the detailed designs to the high level design and software requirements. ...

CONFIGURATION MANAGEMENT

...

PROBLEM REPORTING AND CONTROL

...

Both these functions may take place both within and without the organization. External certification of the QMS to a recognized standard – for instance ISO 9001 or BS5750 – is the best example of the QA function taking place from without the organization.

The other widely known approach is the Software Engineering Institute's process maturity model, originally developed to establish the competence of software developers tendering for the US Department of Defense (DoD) [13, 14]. On occasions, however, quality audits are carried out internally either for the purpose of improving the QMS or to check that a project is conforming to its quality plan. Such internal audits may carry less objectivity than those carried out by external staff and there can be difficulties in exposing non-conformances, especially if a more senior member of staff is the culprit!

We have already suggested that a quality management system may not be greeted with unalloyed joy. Frewin [9] identifies a number of reasons for such resistance, as follows:

- quality management is seen as an 'add-on' to product development and maintenance;
- staff do not like having their work monitored;
- QMSs are thought to be too restrictive, stifling the flair and creativity of engineers.

In addition, many of the quality issues imply long rather than short term costs and when under pressure it is the long term issues that are sacrificed. Typically, maintainability – which is often perceived by the development team as somebody else's problem[2] – will be traded for timeliness or meeting a delivery date. Related, is the problem noted by Tom DeMarco [5], that of costs migrating to the least well monitored area, typically the rather intangible area of quality. The result can be software engineers treating quality as an expensive luxury. A more objective, quantitative view of quality can help to raise the perceived importance of quality. Work done in this area can more easily be recognized, and is thus no longer regarded as an 'add-on'. The measurement of quality makes the monitoring of staff's work more impartial and gives a fairer picture since quality as well as productivity is being assessed. Lastly, the prospect of measurement should support software engineers in making more reasoned judgments, as opposed to stifling their creativity.

3.4 Quality metrics

There have been many and varied attempts to identify a measure of quality over the past twenty years. In the main, these attempts have focused upon the product of code. Unfortunately, most work has been severely handicapped by the extremely fuzzy notion of quality, verging on the almost metaphysical in many instances, with the result that quality has been interpreted as meaning almost any product attribute under almost any circumstance. This was frequently expressed in terms of minimizing complexity. Code that was complex would be less reliable, more difficult to maintain, more costly to develop and so forth. Thus, *if* complexity could be captured as a simple measurement, then the exercise of maximizing quality would merely be one of minimizing the complexity metric. The trouble is, our notions of complexity are almost as metaphysical as those of quality. A key point is that both quality and complexity are best viewed not as intrinsic properties of software engineering artefacts but as properties of the interaction between the users, the task and the artefact. For example, my view of software complexity will depend upon

[2] Unfortunately, in many software engineering organizations, maintenance is often literally somebody else's problem, as it is still regarded in many quarters as an unprestigious activity fit only for newcomers and those who have transgressed!

(i) myself, (ii) what I am trying to accomplish with the software and (iii) the software itself. Focusing solely upon the software could lead to a very confused picture. The end user may consider the software to be simple to use for a particular purpose, whilst maintainers might see the same software as their worst nightmare come true when trying to adapt it in a certain way!

Despite these complications, considerable energy has been devoted to finding complexity metrics, typically derivable from code. The best-known is the family of measures collectively known as software science[3] [11] and the cyclomatic number[4] of a program's flow graph [19]. The problem with such approaches is that the search for *the* complexity metric is akin to the search for the elixir of life! It is highly doubtful that such a metric exists. We have already considered how complex modern software systems can be, and the suggestion that all aspects of such systems may be usefully captured by a single measure strikes one as rather fanciful. Effort is better focused upon more tractable measurement problems. Indeed, subsequent work has indicated considerable difficulties with the use of these code metrics as such simplistic indicators of quality.[5] It has also revealed that, almost invariably, these metrics are most strongly associated with the simple size measure LOC.

Notwithstanding these difficulties, quality metrics have an important role to play in the management and development of software projects. Card [4] suggests that such metrics can be usefully employed in two distinct ways:

(i) diagnostic metrics;
(ii) discrepancy metrics,

where diagnostic metrics are concerned with identifying sources of potential problems, whilst discrepancy metrics are indicators of actual problems.

(i) Diagnostic quality metrics

A major application of metrics is to identify quality problems before they occur so that appropriate action can be taken. Clearly, the earlier the measurements can be

[3] Software science metrics are based on four simple code properties, the number of unique operators n_1 (assignment, mathematical functions, etc.), the number of unique operands n_2 (variables, constants, etc.), the total number of operators N_1 and the total number of operands N_2. These basic counts are then combined into a number of equations which, it was claimed, are related to program difficulty, D given as $(n_1/2)*(N_2/n_2)$ and implementation effort, E given as $D*N*\log_2 n$, where $N = N_1 + N_2$ and $n = n_1 + n_2$.

[4] The cyclomatic number, v is a graph theoretic measure equivalent to the number of linearly independent circuits in a strongly connected graph G and is $e - n + 1$, where e is the number of edges and n the number of nodes. This is of interest to a software engineer when the control flow of a piece of procedural code is represented as a graph so that statements are nodes and the transfers of control are edges. The cyclomatic number will be the number of basic paths through the code, from which all paths can be generated. More simply, it is the program decision count plus one!

[5] See, for example, [12, 18] on software science and [21] on cyclomatic complexity.

obtained the greater the scope for problem avoidance. For this reason the system architecture metrics described in Chapter 2 offer considerable advantages over the more traditional code based quality metrics.

Table 3.2 illustrates some sample quality metrics that can be employed in a diagnostic capacity as part of a review process. It is important to warn against the naïve use of metrics. Software developers are well able to maximize one or two simple quantitative indicators of quality, particularly if it is believed that they are also being used to assess performance. For example, if module length is used as a quality metric, it is easy to partition modules into smaller components without necessarily contributing anything to the modularity of the system. Consequently, there is a danger that quality metrics can cause unintentional side effects and contribute little to software quality. These issues are explored in considerably more depth in Chapter 5; for the time being we just sound a note of caution.

(ii) Discrepancy quality metrics

Metrics of quality discrepancy tend to be straightforward counts of incidents that

Table 3.2 Sample diagnostic quality metrics

Metric	Typical usage	reference
Cyclomatic complexity (v(G))	Set a threshold such that modules will not *usually* exceed V(G) = 10, which equates to nine decisions	McCabe [19].
Module LOC	A high value for module length can indicate inadequate modularization and problems of a monolithic structure. Some organizations have set fixed upper limits (e.g. 50 or 100 LOC), although the evidence to justify this view is limited [1]	Chapter 2, Bowen [1]
Module fan-out	An unusually high value (outlier) for the number of subordinate modules can be indicative of a missing level of abstraction and/or high functionality	Kitchenham [17]
Yin and Winchester's C_i	The C metric can be computed by level within a module hierarchy and a sharp increase can warn of a missing level of abstraction	Chapter 2, also Yin and Winchester [24]
IF4	A high value indicates a component which is excessively coupled to its environment which can lead to problems with re-use, comprehension and maintenance	Chapter 2, also Shepperd [22]

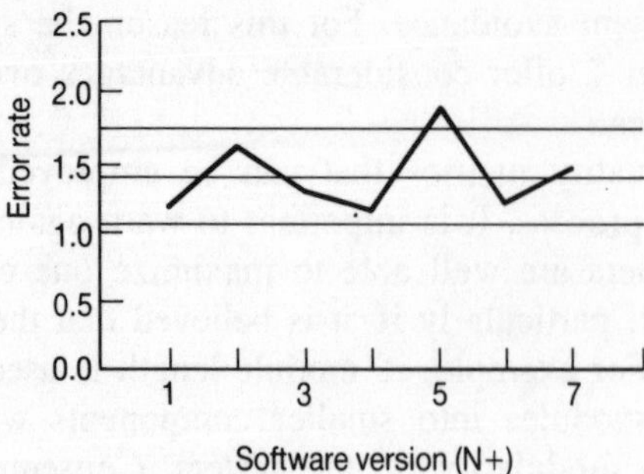

Figure 3.3 Statistical process control

have occurred, for example the design errors found by inspection, the number of known system errors and the count of QMS non-conformances. It is usually helpful to collect additional information such as the type of error (e.g. logical, requirements, etc.), when it was committed and when it was detected. Such data can then be analyzed for the purpose of process improvement. If a large number of errors of a particular type are made during one part of the software development process, then steps can be taken to reduce the likelihood of making such errors or to trap them earlier.

Another increasing popular application of discrepancy type metrics is to support statistical process control (SPC). Briefly, this technology – widely used in other production processes – is based upon the premise that high quality processes exhibit stable quality levels and that these trends should be made visible using a control chart [3, 4].

Figure 3.3 illustrates a typical control chart which reveals how current performance compares with expectations based upon past experience. The wavy lines represent upper and lower control limits and the unbroken line the norm or expected error rate. Wide deviations are a cause for concern and exceeding control limits should trigger project management action to search for problems with the process and institute remedial action. So, for example, the error rate for release N + 5 can be seen to exceed the upper control limit[6] and is indicative of problems which are brought back under control by subsequent releases. Obviously, where the process is unstable (corresponding to a level one in the SEI process maturity model [13]), this technique will not be valuable since it is difficult to determine norms and there will be no reason to expect consistent quality levels. For further details refer to [6].

[6] Upper and lower control limits are determined by reference to past performance. Typically, they are set two standard deviations above and below the mean performance, although this assumes something corresponding to a normal distribution of variations from the mean. For a more detailed discussion of the statistical niceties refer to Chapter 7.

3.5 Summary

To summarize, controlling quality is a major part of a project manager's work. Developing and maintaining low quality products is expensive, both in terms of reworking costs and in loss of markets. In order to be in a position to control quality, managers must first be able to measure: this requires objective and measurable definitions.

Measurement forms an essential part of any quality management system and is obligatory under the ISO 9001 quality standard. Given the demands and diversity of quality measurement, no single metric, or indeed pre-defined set of metrics, will suffice. Instead, we have argued that quality measurement requires a framework that is simple, flexible yet makes explicit the purpose of the metric and how it is to be used.

There still remain many problems associated with the application of quality metrics. In particular, single metrics are not sensitive to problems of quality factor trade-offs and the need for the project manager to satisfy – if not maximize – a number of objectives simultaneously. Despite these reservations, a more quantitative approach to quality is essential if software engineers are ever to make progress in controlling the quality of software and related artefacts.

3.6 Exercises and further reading

1. Using the following failure data construct a statistical control chart to identify which, if any, releases might cause a project manager concern. Assume that the

Release	errs/KLOC
1	2.3
2	2.0
3	1.9
4	2.9
5	2.4
6	2.2
7	2.3
8	2.6
9	2.0
10	2.2
11	1.7
12	2.5
13	2.1
14	2.7
15	2.3

development process is stable and that the control limits should be set at ±2 standard deviations (σ) from the mean.

2. Peter Mellor in Chapter 6 of [8] describes the conceptual schema of a software reliability database. Design and implement a software metrics database suitable for a small software development organization that is thinking of collecting quality metrics from their design inspection process.

Card, D.N., 'Software product assurance: measurement and control', in *The Software Life Cycle*, D.C. Ince and D. Andrews, eds., Butterworth–Heinemann: Oxford, 1990.

A good overall account of quality control and quality metrics including an introduction to statistical process control and the equations that lie behind quality charts.

Cobb, R.H. and H.D. Mills, 'Engineering software under statistical quality control', *IEEE Softw.*, **7**(6), 44–54, 1990.

An interesting article on the application of statistical process control to software production as part of the 'Cleanroom' model.

Deming, W.E., *Out of the Crisis*. MIT Press: Cambridge Mass., 1986.

The classic work on quality. A must for anyone interested in pursuing this topic further.

Kan, S.H., V.R. Basili and L.N. Shapiro, 'Software quality: an overview from the perspective of total quality management', *IBM Syst. J.*, **33**(1), 4–19, 1994.

This paper gives a good introduction to the TQM view of software quality.

References

[1] Bowen, J.B., 'Module size: a standard or heuristic?', *J. of Syst. and Software*, **4**, 327–32, 1984.

[2] Brown, P.G., 'QFD: echoing the voice of the customer', *AT & T Tech. J.*, **70**(2), 18–32, 1991.

[3] Card, D.N., 'Statistical process control for software?', *IEEE Softw.*, **11**(3), 95–7, 1994.

[4] Card, D.N., 'Software product assurance: measurement and control', in *The Software Life Cycle*, D.C. Ince and D. Andrews, eds., Butterworth-Heinemann: Oxford, 1990.

[5] DeMarco, T., *Controlling Software Projects. Management, Measurement and Estimation*. Yourdon Press: NY, 1982.

[6] Deming, W.E., *Out of the Crisis*. MIT Press: Cambridge Mass., 1986.

[7] DTI, TickIT Guide to Software Quality Management System and Certification using EN29001. Issue 2.0, Department of Trade and Industry, 1992.

[8] Fenton, N.E., *Software Metrics: A rigorous approach*. Chapman Hall: London, 1991.

[9] Frewin, G.D., 'Software quality management', in *Software Reliability Handbook*, P. Rook, ed., Elsevier Applied Science: 1990.

[10] Gilb, T., *Principles of Software Engineering Management*. Addison-Wesley: 1988.

[11] Halstead, M.H., 'Advances in software science', in *Advances in Computers*, M. Yovits, ed., Academic Press: NY, 1979.

[12] Hamer, P.G. and G.D. Frewin, 'M.H. Halstead's software science – a critical examination', in *Proc. 6th Intl. Conf on Softw. Eng.* Tokyo: IEEE, 1982.

[13] Humphrey, W.S., 'Characterising the software process: a maturity framework', *IEEE Softw.*, **5**(2), 73–9, 1988.

[14] Humphrey, W.S., *Managing the Software Process*. Addison-Wesley: 1989.

[15] ISO 9000-3, Quality management and quality assurance standards – Part 3: Guidelines for the application of ISO 9001 to the development, supply and maintenance of software. Standard No. 9000-3: 1991(E), International Organization for Standardization, 1991.

[16] ISO 9001, Quality systems – Assurance model for design/development, production installation and servicing capability. Standard No. 9001 (Part 1), International Organization for Standardization, 1987.

[17] Kitchenham, B.A., L.M. Pickard and S.J. Linkman, 'An evaluation of some design metrics', *Softw. Eng. J.*, **5**(1), 1990.

[18] Lassez, J.L. *et al.*, 'A critical examination of software science', *J. of Syst. and Softw.*, **2**, 105–12, 1981.

[19] McCabe, T.J., 'A complexity measure', *IEEE Trans. on Softw. Eng.*, **2**(4), 308–20, 1976.

[20] Ould, M.A., 'Quality control and assurance', in *Software Engineer's Reference Book*, J.A. McDermid, ed., Butterworth–Heinemann: Oxford, UK, 1991.

[21] Shepperd, M.J., 'A critique of cyclomatic complexity as a software metric', *Softw. Eng. J.*, **3**(2), 1–8, 1988.

[22] Shepperd, M.J., 'An empirical study of design measurement', *Softw. Eng. J.*, **5**(1), 3–10, 1990.

[23] Stevens, R., 'Creating software the right way', in *Byte*. August 1991.

[24] Yin, B.H. and J.W. Winchester, 'The establishment and use of measures to evaluate the quality of software designs', in *Proc. ACM Softw. Qual. Ass. Workshop*. ACM 1978.

Chapter 4

Management and measurement

You can't control what you can't measure. (Tom DeMarco [22].)

Synopsis

In which we explore the relationship between software project management and measurement. The chief task of management is control; yet control without measurement is a very feeble affair. Having studied the measurement of software quality in the preceding chapter, we go on to focus upon two additional management applications: productivity and effort prediction. It is shown how measurement can be applied to each area. Here the problem is to obtain an appropriate measure of output. The classic approach of lines of code and the more recent function based measures are covered. Predicting software project effort, and hence cost and duration, is another management concern. We review various prediction models – including COCOMO and function points – together with some model calibration techniques to enable models to be fitted to specific environments. In conclusion, we note that simple models are not only more tractable but often yield more accurate results.

4.1 The role of the project manager

Software projects are amongst some of the most complex of human endeavours. A typical example is the three million lines of code in the GPT digital telephone switchboard System X. They can also span many years and involve hundreds, even thousands, of staff – as in the case of the IBM OS/360 project. Yet, surprisingly, coding is seldom the major activity. Analysis of project costs at the European Space Agency revealed that, on average, coding consumes no more than 10–15% of total project resources [50]. In any case, it comes too late on in a project to enable strategic decisions to be made or for the correction of major mistakes. Projects also embrace requirements capture: what does the customer or user actually want? Specifying, designing, testing, training and documenting are also extremely important stages of a project. Furthermore, the project seldom comes to an end with the delivery of the completed software. Typically, the maintenance of an existing system consumes even more resources than does its initial development. This might range from the removal of defects detected after the software has been installed, to major enhancements and extensions to cater for changing business needs and user requirements. Ensuring that the correct version of each system component is in operation is a further headache, especially if the system comprises hundreds of modules, with complex inter-dependencies and where there may exist tens, if not hundreds, of versions of many of the components. Tackling this type of problem is a subdiscipline in its own right, generally known as configuration management.

It is not difficult, therefore, to appreciate that software projects demand very careful planning and control if they are to be successful. More than ten years ago, Barry Boehm suggested that 'poor management can increase costs more rapidly than any other factor' [14]. A more recent empirical study of the design stages of a software system concluded that the influence of managerial and communication factors far outweighed the impact of more technical issues [19].

> Poor software design and project control have put a £619m project for improving the UK's air defence network five years behind and still unable to meet the contract specification.
>
> (*Computing*, November 1990.)

Thus, there can be little doubt of the central importance of project management if we are to be successful software engineers.

But what does project management involve? First and foremost management is about control. Given the levels of complexity demanded of modern software systems we can hardly allow the project to run itself: coordination, planning and monitoring are essential. Obviously the concerns of a project manager are many and varied, just as projects and organizational environments themselves will be varied. Nevertheless, the following important areas of management can be identified:

- visibility;
- productivity;
- quality;
- prediction;
- improvement.

It is worth briefly examining each of these five areas in turn.

Visibility. This is the need for the project manager to be aware of, and to monitor, the current state of a project. The aim is to avoid surprises, especially unpleasant ones! It is also to provide feedback, so that the manager is able to judge the effect of a particular decision. Measurement can make a key contribution as it enables subjective opinions such as 'I think module `A14` is nearly completed' to be transformed into rather more objective statements such as 'Module `A14` is already 25% larger, in terms of lines of code (LOC) than predicted, and has consumed 90% of its allocated time resource.' But, beware of the famous 90:90 syndrome where a task is 90% complete for 90% of its duration. Software developers are renowned optimists and the 90% complete might not be a measure; it could merely be an aspiration. It is also interesting to note – though not always appreciated – that too much information can be as unhelpful as too little. This can be a particular problem for managers of very large projects. Which are the key indicators, the warning signs, the areas requiring immediate attention amongst a morass of weekly returns, fault reports and the suchlike? The problem is not merely one of collecting measurements. They must also be analyzed!

Productivity. This is another extremely important concern for any manager. There are clear links with measurement since subjective opinion is somewhat vulnerable to bias, particularly in such a charged area as productivity. Naturally, I believe myself to be highly productive! Obviously, my CASE tool contributes more to productivity than that of a rival vendor!

There are two distinct aspects to productivity. The first aspect is the area of individual or group performance. Many commentators strongly advise against measuring individuals; rather they advise working at the level of teams or projects. Certainly, this would seem to be less invidious than the prospect of applying doubtful measures which fail to encompass any notion of quality for individual appraisal. However, a team level productivity measurement can yield valuable information by indicating good or poor organization and straightforward or complex application areas. It is also a vital input for cost estimation, a subject that we will return to later in this chapter. The second aspect of productivity is the impact of different methods and tools upon output. Neglect of this aspect leaves the manager exposed to the claims and counterclaims of sales people and zealots.[1] Despite the difficulties associated with productivity measurement, it forms an essential basis for cost and resource prediction. Consequently, we will return to it in the section on resource prediction, p. 99.

Quality. Product quality is obviously another key management concern. Increasingly, society is dependent upon computer based systems, and as these systems become more and more endemic, so their quality acquires a greater and greater significance. However, as has been demonstrated in Chapter 3, without measurement quality is difficult to control as there are no objective means of determining what level of quality is required and whether that level has been attained or not.

Prediction. The ability to manage a project is greatly enhanced by the ability to predict, and as a result, take the appropriate anticipatory action. Moreover, the earlier on in a project that the prediction can be made, the greater the benefit, since this offers the manager maximum scope for strategic decision making. Important areas for prediction are those related to project resourcing, such as cost, staff requirements and delivery date. Also of great significance is the ability to predict potential quality problems, for instance using metrics extracted from a software design to anticipate subsequent maintenance difficulties. The ability to obtain advanced warning enables the project manager to take the necessary action and minimize the amount of re-work. By contrast, realization that a unit is unusually defect prone during acceptance testing can be extremely expensive to rectify, particularly if the root cause is specification or design inadequacies. Indeed, it has been suggested that, for a large project, the repair costs are typically a hundred times greater for errors found once the software has been installed compared with errors detected during the requirements specification phase [14].[2] This obviously excludes any costs that derive from the fault such as loss of business goodwill.

Improvement. Here, the concern is to improve either the process or the product. In recent years there has been a growing appreciation of the relationship between process and product – a 'good' process is one that produces high quality products.[3]

[1] Despite the importance of objective measurement, it is remarkable how little quantitative work has been conducted on the impact of various methods, tools and languages upon the software engineering process; instead, the value of formal methods, GOTO-less coding and so on is accepted almost without question. Consider the following two examples. A careful review of the empirical evidence, by Vessey and Weber, found little or no support for the benefits, in particular, of structured programming [51]. Likewise, the Basili and Perricone study of error-prone software [10] challenges the orthodoxy of the desirability of small modules since they found that, within certain limits, the larger modules had lower defect densities. The moral is clear: a degree of agnosticism is a healthy trait for the software engineer.

[2] Fagan [25] quotes a range of 10–100 from studies of large projects at IBM.

[3] Clearly, there is a danger of circularity when one defines a good process as one which produces good products; none the less, it is important to focus upon how to build high quality software in the first place, as opposed to attempting to impose quality after it has been developed.

For example, there has been a great deal of interest in the process maturity and improvement work carried out by the Software Engineering Institute at Carnegie Mellon [26], based upon a five level model of process maturity. The levels range from level one, where processes are *ad hoc* and therefore not repeatable, through successive levels to level five, where processes are being optimized.

One would expect the search for improvement to be unequivocally founded upon measurement; that, at a minimum, software engineers would measure before and after the putative improvement in order to establish its efficacy. Unfortunately, as with productivity, most evidence remains at a speculative and anecdotal level. In terms of the maturity model, most software development organizations remain at the lower levels of process capability, where little use is made of measurement. This ought to be a major area of concern for software project managers.

Software engineering project management is diverse and often complex. Yet, ironically given its central importance, relatively few projects exhibit much evidence of effective management. An indicator of the scale of the problem is the study of US defence projects, which found that almost half of all projects fail to deliver at all (see Table 4.1). This might seem slightly extreme, and it must be noted that the study was conducted more than ten years ago. None the less, 100–200% cost and schedule overruns are still quite typical. Likewise, with reliability rates of eight defects per thousand delivered LOC, considered to be the UK industry norm (*Computer Weekly*, December 1989), or in the range of 5–30 defects per 1000 LOC in the USA [42], there are few grounds for complacency.

The central theme of this book is the need to make greater use of measurement within software engineering. Nowhere is this need more compelling than in project management. Current usage of metrics by managers is – by and large – extremely limited; yet, as DeMarco observes, without measurement there can be little meaningful control. This lack of control is the principal contributor to the problems described above. In the next section we will examine some specific techniques for measuring quality leading to quality control. The subsequent section deals with resource prediction and the final section briefly addresses some of the managerial issues relating to the introduction and usage of metrics.

Table 4.1 Software project outcomes

47%	Paid for but not delivered
29%	Delivered but not used
19%	Abandoned or re-worked
3%	Used after changes
2%	Used as delivered

Source: US Government Accounting Office 1979.

4.2 Productivity

4.2.1 Why measure productivity?

Whilst discussing the scope of the project manager's role, we have already identified productivity to be a major area of concern and an obvious application for measurement. Clearly, productivity is important in its own right: for cost containment; for the assessment of competing methods, techniques and tools; for monitoring performance. But it also forms an essential basis for effort estimation and project scheduling.

The standard definition of productivity is:

Rate of output per unit input

Unfortunately, in the case of software development, despite the fact that the various inputs can be readily identified – principally software engineering effort – the outputs are rather more elusive. What is a suitable unit of software output? For more conventional manufacturing, the answer would be relatively straightforward: the number of artefacts produced, be it biros or socks. This would suggest a productivity measure of biros produced per person per unit time, perhaps an hour. Software differs somewhat from biro or sock manufacture in that almost all effort is devoted to producing the first system, and subsequent systems may be copied almost without cost.

Other problems associated with software development productivity include the issue of quality. Am I being productive if I produce large amounts of software that contain abnormally high defect levels and an impenetrable user interface? We also need to consider the question of productivity over what time scale. Short term productivity, say until delivery of the software, may be easier to collect but could be vulnerable to costs being deferred until maintenance. It would be possible to appear to be highly productive by omitting to test the software at all, allowing all the defect removal work to be treated as maintenance, thereby excluding the testing, debugging and repair costs and consequently enhancing productivity. Obviously, this is rather an extreme case, but it does illustrate the dangers of basing our view of productivity upon only part of a project. At the other end of the spectrum is the long term perspective of productivity, based upon the entire life time of the system. Although this might seem to offer a solution to the problems associated with shorter term definitions, in practice it is difficult to apply since a project can last for more than twenty years – an unacceptably long period of time to wait for productivity feedback! Moreover, interpretation of the results will be difficult due to the multiplicity of productivity factors, many of which can be time dependent, for example improvement in development technology over the years. Probably the most important lesson to draw is the need to avoid a simplistic interpretation of productivity measures. Productivity in the absence of quality is worthless.

4.2.2 Productivity measures

To return to the problem of productivity measurement, there are two general approaches to the problem of software output. Typically, lines of code are used as an indicator of output size. The chief alternative is an attempt to capture the level of functionality, or the size of the system requirements to be implemented, known as function points. We will review each in turn.

(i) Lines of code

The most common measure productivity, then, is:

LOC/person month

But how do we count lines of code? Some of the problems are best indicated by a simple example. Given below is a fragment of a program, laid out in two different ways. In the first case we might decide that there are six LOC, whilst in the second, only two LOC. And this is despite the fact that both fragments will compile into identical object code and will exhibit identical behaviours.

```
IF a=b THEN
  a := 3
ELSE
  a := 4;

b := a * b;
```

```
IF a=b THEN a:=3 ELSE a:=4;
b:=a * b;
```

Jones [30] reports at least twelve definitions for LOC including the following:

- counting delimiters (semicolons for Pascal and full stops for COBOL);
- executable LOC (excludes the declaration part of code);
- non-commentary source LOC.

He also notes variations of 5:1 between the extremes, which suggests that it is important to define a counting convention carefully [4] and then rigorously adhere to it. This is best achieved using a special purpose counting tool. None the less, there remain significant difficulties with LOC as a measure of software productivity. It can be easily manipulated – usually upwards! It will penalize well-designed but shorter programs. The measure will be language dependent so that comparisons between languages, or indeed mixed language implementations, will present difficulties. The

[4] Probably the most authoritative treatment of LOC counting conventions is [49].

classic example is assembler versus a fourth generation language (4GL), where the assembler programmer may appear to be more productive since an assembler program with similar functionality to the 4GL program will be many times longer. Other areas of difficulty include the re-use of existing code, the fact that many important project activities, such as specification, design and documentation, are completely ignored. The treatment of maintenance productivity is also less amenable to the LOC style of approach.

Despite these, and many other, objections, LOC based definitions of productivity are in widespread use and, when used wisely, can yield valuable information. Furthermore, many of the problems relating to language and layout can be overcome by the simple expedient of counting the size of the object code in bytes.

(ii) Function points

An alternative software output measure for establishing productivity is function points (FP). This yields a productivity measure of:

FP/person month

Function points were developed by Allan Albrecht, working in the late-1970s at IBM [3]. The basic principle was to focus upon the size of the requirements specification, or the system functionality, as opposed to the size of the code to implement the specification, the reason being that this enables us to have a more user centred view of productivity – after all the user cares more about what functionality the system has than how it is coded. Function points also enable our view of productivity to be more development technology independent. A problem with LOC definitions is that changing the development technology, say from a 3GL to a 4GL with a database management system, can render productivity comparisons very difficult. It is highly probable that the 4GL will be more compact than the 3GL, with the result that there could well be a spurious decline in productivity. Function points measures circumvent such problems. They may also be collected much earlier in a project than LOC since all that is necessary is the availability of a detailed requirements specification, rather than the finished code. For these reasons there has been a rapid growth of interest in FP techniques, both for productivity assessment and also as an effort estimation technique.

Although there have been a number of modifications to, and extensions from, the original FP method, Albrecht's work has been the most influential so we will consider it in some detail. The method that we will describe is that originally given by Albrecht and subsequently codified by IFPUG [27] into a highly detailed set of rules.

The starting point for FP counting is to analyze the requirements specification in order to isolate the basic function types. Albrecht identified the following five classes of function:

- external input types (e.g. file names);
- external output types (e.g. reports, messages);

- enquiries (interactive inputs needing a response);
- external files (i.e. files shared with other software systems);
- internal files (i.e. invisible outside system).

The process of trying to identify the various functions requires some skill and judgement, and is not easily automated without modifying the counting rules and using a machine readable requirements notation. A consequence is that an element of subjectivity enters into the measurement process, though commentators vary in their opinion of its significance. One experiment reported significant variations between analysts measuring the same specification [40]. A more recent survey by Kemerer [34] indicates that within organizations variation due to counting differences might be nearer to 10%.

Once the various function types have been isolated they must be classified according to their complexity in order to derive a weighted count known as the unadjusted function count (UFC). So, for example, a system comprising three simple and one complex external input together with two average external outputs would score $(3+3+3+6+5+5=25)$ function points (see Table 4.2).

An immediate question is how do we decide upon the complexity level of each function? In an attempt to make this an objective process, the levels are defined by reference to two out of three of the following counts: file accesses, record type accesses and data elements. Tables 4.3 and 4.4 provide the exact levels. For example,

Table 4.2 Basic weights for function types

Function type	Simple	Average	Complex
External input	3	4	6
External output	4	5	7
Logical internal file	7	10	15
External interface	5	7	10
External enquiry	3	4	6

Table 4.3 Determination of function type complexity levels

Function type	Determinants								
	#files			#rec. types			#data elems.		
	1	2	3	1	2	3	1	2	3
Ext. input	0–1	2	≥3				1–4	5–15	≥16
Ext. output	0–1	2–3	4				1–5	6–19	≥20
Logical int. file				1	2–5	≥6	1–19	20–50	≥51
Ext. interface file				1	2–5	≥6	1–19	20–50	≥51
Ext. enquiry	Use the greater of the input and output components								

Table 4.4 Function type complexity scores

Score	Complexity
2–3	simple
4	average
5–6	complex

an External Input that references four files and nine data types would score five (3 + 2), resulting in a function type complexity classification of 'complex' from Table 4.4. In the past, flexibility to adjust the classification by one was permitted due to additional complexity factors; however the general consensus now is that this leads to an unacceptable level of subjectivity, which, especially in the area of productivity, could lead to undesirable complications.

However, in addition to the raw information processing implied by a specification upon a system, Albrecht considered that there might be other factors that could influence the 'size' of the functional requirements for a system. These are encapsulated into fourteen general system characteristics (GSCs) that contribute to an overall value adjustment factor (VAF) for a system.[5] These are listed in Table 4.5. Each factor is rated in terms of its degree of influence (DI) on a scale of 0 (not applicable) to 5 (essential). The DIs for all fourteen factors are summed in order to derive a Total Degree of Influence (TDI).

$$VAF = 0.65 + (0.01 * TDI)$$

Thus the VAF may range from 0.65 to 1.35. This is then used to modify the unadjusted function count as below:

$$FP = UFC.VAF$$

So, a relatively straightforward system on a single processor, without performance constraints will tend to have a low VAF, perhaps in the range of 0.65 to 0.85, which will have the effect of reducing the raw or unadjusted function count. On the other hand a distributed, interactive system, with complex processing and highly time critical, will tend to have a TDI of well above unity, perhaps in the range of 1.15 to 1.35. Clearly, this will inflate the UFC. For an 'average' system, that is, one where the VAF has a value of one, and therefore makes no adjustment, the average value of each GSC will be 2.5, slightly less than 3, which is defined as being of average influence. (The moral is to be careful when applying the concept of average to an ordinal scale, that is, one in which the size of the intervals are unknown. For a fuller discussion of the issues of scale and measurement refer back to Chapter 1.)

[5] In the earlier literature the general system characteristics are referred to as information processing complexity characteristics and the sum of these characteristics as the technical complexity factor (TCF). They are, however, unchanged in other respects excepting minor details of definition for the individual GSCs.

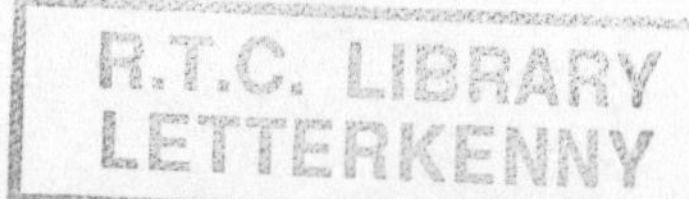

Table 4.5 General system characteristics

1. Data communications	8. On-line update
2. Distributed data processing	9. Complex processing
3. Performance	10. Re-usability
4. Heavily used configuration	11. Installation ease
5. Transaction rate	12. Operation ease
6. On line data entry	13. Multiple sites
7. End user efficiency	14. Facilitate change

A function point example

A simple information system is required for a bank. It will enable new customers to be added, and deleted, from a customer file. The system must also support paying in and withdrawal transactions, and will display a warning message if the borrower has an excessive overdraft. Customers can query their account balance via a terminal. A report of overdrawn customers can be requested.

The first step is to identify the various function types from the specification.

In Figure 4.1 we highlight the various function types to illustrate the process of analyzing a textual specification. Remember that FP analysis is – with the exception of internal files – concerned with functions that cross system boundaries, either with another software system, as in the case of external interfaces, or with the users, as in the case of external inputs, outputs or queries. A top level or context data flow diagram can be extremely helpful in identifying functions. So, we have as external inputs:

add new customer
delete customer
paying in transaction
withdrawal transaction
request a report of overdrawn customers[6]

as external outputs:

warning message of an excessive overdraft
report of overdrawn customers

as an external enquiry:

account balance query

and as an internal file:

customer file.

[6] This request is viewed as an external input and output as opposed to an enquiry, due to the fact that there can be a significant time delay between the request for the report and its production.

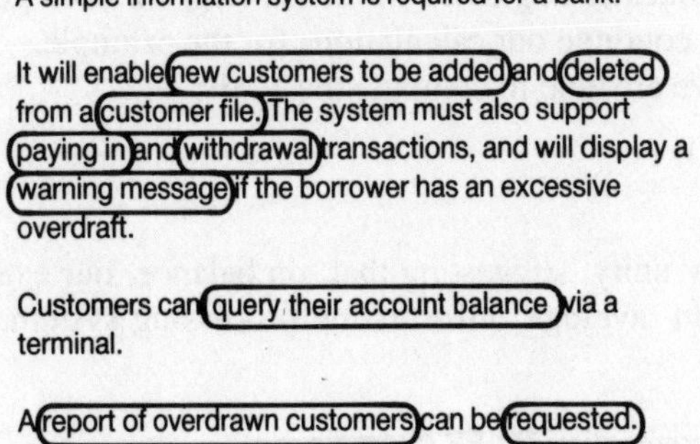

Figure 4.1 Requirements specification for the function point example

Note that in this instance there are no external interfaces as the system appears to be self-contained and does not communicate with other software systems. In practice this is an unlikely state of affairs as the above example, would form a subsystem of a larger banking system with interfaces to statistical analysis, direct debit and many other subsystems.

The next step is to count file accesses and numbers of record types and data elements. Hypothetical values are given in Table 4.6.

Note that all the functions are classified as simple when applying the IFPUG guidelines to this example. This suggests a certain lack of sensitivity for comparatively small systems such as this example, where a single internal file is accessed by all transactions.

Table 4.6 Determination of function complexities

Function	#files	#rec. types	#data elems.	Complexity	Score
add new customer	1	–	10	S	3
delete customer	1	–	2	S	3
paying in transaction	1	–	2	S	3
withdrawal transaction	1	–	2	S	3
request a report of overdrawn customers	1	–	0	S	3
warning msg of an excessive overdraft	1	–	4	S	4
report of overdrawn customers	1	–	8	S	4
account balance query (output more complex)	1	–	3	S	3
customer file	–	1	12	S	7
Total					33

Table 4.7 shows some possible values or degree of influence (DI) for each general system characteristic to enable us to continue our calculations for the example.

Using the total TDI value of 30 we are able to compute the VAF:

$$\begin{aligned} VAF &= 0.65 + (0.01 * 30) \\ &= 0.95 \end{aligned}$$

The value for VAF is slightly below unity, suggesting that, on balance, our example will be slightly less complex than an 'average' information processing system. This

Table 4.7 Total degree of influence calculation for FP example

General system characteristic	DI	Notes
1. Data communications	3	On line data collection for a batch process and query system
2. Distributed data processing	3	Distributed processing and transfer of data are on line, but in one direction only
3. Performance	3	On line response time is critical during business hours, though the reports are only required by the next business day
4. Heavily used configuration	2	Assuming the system will run on an existing computer system, there will be some security and timing constraints
5. Transaction rate	4	The high transaction rates demanded by the specification warrant performance analysis in the design phase
6. On line data entry	5	More than 30% of all transactions are on line data entry (mainly payments and withdrawals)
7. End user efficiency	4	The high level of efficiency needs special design considerations, to minimize key strokes and mistakes
8. On line update	4	On line update of a major internal file, the CUSTOMER FILE with recovery against the loss of data
9. Complex processing	1	Generally simple, other than the need to provide extensive audit facilities for security reasons
10. Re-usability	0	No special requirement to re-use code
11. Installation ease	0	No special requirements
12. Operation ease	1	Effective startup, backup and recovery procedures are required for the operations staff
13. Multiple sites	0	Only installation
14. Facilitate change	0	No special requirement for flexible queries or user driven control tables
TDI	30	

seems plausible as the example is a much trivialized banking system, although it is both highly transaction driven and interactive. The VAF is then used to adjust the UFC to arrive at the final FP score, so we have:

$$\begin{aligned} FP &= VAF * UFC \\ &= 0.95 * 33 \\ &= 31.35 \text{ function points} \end{aligned}$$

How can this information be used? Recall, that we are attempting to gauge output in order to assess productivity, hence we return to formulation of productivity as:

FP/person month

This has some notable advantages over the more conventional LOC view. First, it gives us programming language independence. Consider the situation where two programmers are both implementing the above banking system. In the one case the programmer uses COBOL, whereas in the other case a 4GL is employed. The first program is 3323 LOC in length and takes six months, whereas the 4GL program is 1254 LOC in length and takes three months. If we simply apply LOC as a measure of output, then the COBOL programmer would appear to be significantly more productive, since we have:

$$3323/6 = 553.83 \text{ LOC month}^{-1}$$

compared with

$$1254/3 = 418 \text{ LOC month}^{-1}$$

This is a counterintuitive result since the 4GL programmer has developed the same system in half the time of the COBOL programmer. An FP view of output overcomes this difficulty since we focus upon the delivered functionality of the system, not a by-product of how it happens to be implemented. So, we obtain:

$$31.35/6 = 5.23 \text{ FP month}^{-1}$$

compared with

$$31.35/3 = 10.45 \text{ month}^{-1}$$

We now see that the 4GL programmer is in fact twice as productive as the COBOL programmer. However, we still need to be cautious about making value judgements since there are at least two unknowns: personal ability and the impact of using a more advanced technology. It is not evident whether the second programmer is more capable, or is merely provided with more productive tools, or a combination of both.

A second benefit from the FP approach to productivity is that the output measure can be derived as soon as the requirements specification is available. This helps to assess the productivity of activities such as design. With LOC, however, output size will be nothing more than an estimate until after the coding has been completed.

Despite these undoubted advantages, there remain a considerable number of difficulties with function points as they are presently defined. A major concern is the derivation of the weights for the function types. Albrecht stated that these were determined by 'debate and trial' ([5], p. 639) using data collected from various IBM projects during the late-1970s. In addition, Albrecht justified the weights in terms of their 'relative value of the function to the customer/user' ([5], p. 639). These two factors are independent and may frequently conflict. The desirability of a function to a customer does not influence the cost to implement. Indeed, the desirability of a function may vary over time and between different customers.

Returning to measurement basics, another concern with function points is the problem of exactly what is being measured? The unadjusted FP count is a complex, synthetic and dimensionless measure derived from the following:

- the primitive counts of file access, record type access and data elements referenced per function type;
- counts of five classes of function type.

The adjusted FP count is also a complex, synthetic and dimensionless measure derived from the following:

- the unadjusted FP count;
- fourteen general system characteristics, each on a six point ordinal scale.

Synthetic measures are difficult to validate and also result in a loss of information, making them difficult to interpret. We are also in danger of confusing the measure with the prediction system. The main application for function points is to predict software project effort and, as consequence, the definition of FPs is modified to take into account various factors that are likely to impact project effort, such as complexity and so forth. This is all well and good but it leads to a blurring of the measure and the prediction system. As Dijkstra wisely remarked many years ago, we must have a 'separation of concerns'.

A measure should be an attribute of, in this case, a requirements specification document. Unfortunately, given the complex and synthetic nature of FPs it is unclear exactly what the attribute is. It would seem to be the size of the requirements specification plus something, and this is unfortunate. If it were size alone then it could be more easily used as one, of several, inputs to a prediction system, as illustrated by Figure 4.2. This additional complexity leads to calibration difficulties when we attempt to use FP based effort prediction models (see Sections 4.4.3 and 4.4.4).

A third area of difficulty lies in the subjectivity of the counting process, despite the highly detailed counting rules produced by such organizations as the International Function Point Users Group (IFPUG). Low and Jeffery report 30% variation between different analysts as being typical, once rogue data from inexperienced

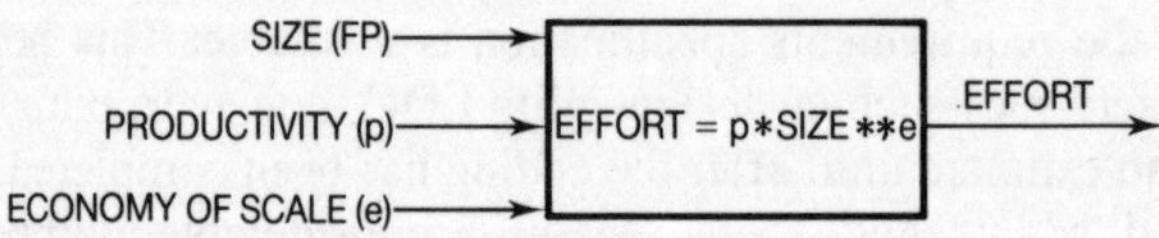

Figure 4.2 Function points and an effort prediction system

analysts have been removed. As a result it can be difficult to automate. It is also difficult to apply to maintenance, as opposed to new development work. Furthermore, it is not based upon organizational needs, for example is it productive to produce functions irrelevant to the user?

Last, function points are strongly oriented to traditional data processing type applications based upon information systems. The concepts of queries and files do not fit comfortably with modern real-time and embedded software systems. A number of extensions have been proposed to overcome these shortcomings, although none have been validated externally.

To re-cap, once counting irregularities can be overcome, function points contain several distinct advantages over LOC for productivity measurement for information systems. They have yet to be proved for real-time and embedded systems. The reader is left with some health warnings to aid in their effective use.

Some function point health warnings

'We found a disciplined process was an essential ingredient to meaningful productivity measurement.' [3]

'... important to ensure that differences in estimated function points and SLOC could not arise from imprecise specifications.' [40]

'comparisons between organizations must be handled carefully unless they are using the same definitions.' [3]

'Sort projects into related groups. Analyze related groups separately.' [4]

Productivity summary

A quantitative view of productivity is an important aspect of a project manager's role. It helps cost containment as it forms a basis for comparing different software development methods and technologies. We have emphasized the need to approach individual performance with considerable caution. None the less, productivity measurement can help to identify variation in productivity levels, which can be quite considerable. There does not exist any one good measure of software productivity, so, often, the best strategy is to use several measures including quality indicators. For, after all, do we really want our software engineers to be churning out, at high speed, large volumes of poor quality, unreliable and difficult to maintain software?

4.3 Effort prediction

4.3.1 A simple effort prediction model

We now turn to effort prediction. Strictly speaking, effort and cost prediction models are not the same. A project will incur costs other than staffing; however, for most software projects staff represent the major, and least certain, cost component. None the less, we need to be aware of the fact that there certainly will be other costs including equipment, training, secretarial support and so forth. A major concern for any software project manager is cost and delivery date estimation. How much will a given software system cost to produce? When will it be ready? How many staff will be required? Furthermore, we would like answers very early on in the project, when information is least available. Despite the importance of accurate prediction, the software engineering industry has had a poor track record [28, 38].

In the preceding section we considered productivity measurement in its own right. It is, however, an essential base for software cost estimation. If we do not know at what rate software engineers are able to output software – however it might be measured – it is not possible to make predictions concerning project effort.

The simplest effort prediction models take the following form:

$$\text{effort} = p * S$$

where p is a productivity coefficient (1/productivity rate) and S is the size of the software system to be developed. Obviously, both must have similar units, for example, function points. Once values for p and S are known, for instance if the productivity rate is 6.5 FP per month, making $p = 0.1538$, and the size is 430 FPs, then we have:

$$\begin{aligned}\text{effort} &= 0.1538 * 430\\ &= 66.134 \text{ person months}\end{aligned}$$

Such an approach to effort estimation makes the simplifying assumption that the relationship between effort and size is a linear one. However, most models allow for non-linearity by introducing an economies, or dis-economies, of scale exponent. Hence we now have:

$$\text{effort} = p * S^e$$

where $0 < e$.

An early predictive model of this form was published by Walston and Felix [52], who carried out an empirical study of sixty projects at the IBM Federal Systems Division during the mid-1970s. They concluded that effort could be approximately modelled as:

$$\text{effort} = 5.2 * \text{KLOC}^{0.91}$$

where the units for effort are person months (PM). This gives a productivity of about 250–350 LOC per person month.[7] Note the choice of lines of code as the

[7] There is evidence that productivity has increased since the Walston and Felix study, which used data from the early- to mid-1970s. David [20] reports an average productivity level for 1985 of 650 LOC per person month, whilst Duncan [23] describes average productivity levels at DEC in excess of 2000 LOC per person month. Although one needs to be a little cautious in generalizing from such figures, they would seem to suggest a significant improvement over the past twenty years. For this reason alone, re-calibration, from time to time, of the effort prediction models is essential as the coefficients are unlikely to remain constant (see Section 4.3.4).

measure of output; also that with an exponent of less than unity the model suggests economies of scale. In other words, there is scope for greater productivity when building large software systems as opposed to small systems. Possible justifications are that larger teams can afford more specialization, that some overheads are of a relatively fixed size, for instance progress meetings, and also that the impact of fixed costs, such as acceptance testing, are minimized.

Table 4.8 illustrates the impact of project size upon productivity. A 1000 KLOC project would have a 50% higher productivity level than a 10 KLOC project. Moreover, a 20 000 KLOC project would be even more cost effective. Such an outcome would not accord with the generally held view that software projects of this scale are approaching the limits of what is presently feasible, *vide* the Strategic Defense Initiative. This highlights some of the limitations of this fairly simplistic approach to cost estimation.

An interesting feature of the Walston and Felix work is their identification of a list of productivity factors that can modify the basic relationship. A total of twenty-nine factors was collected, including interface complexity, user participation in requirements specification and personnel experience. One difficulty arising from having so many factors is that – as Walston and Felix admit – there can exist many complex inter-dependencies, which hinder detailed analysis of the impact of each individual factor and also introduce calibration difficulties (see Section 4.3.4).

Although one might expect the Walston and Felix approach to be relatively straightforward, in practice there are many problems. Different investigators have identified quite different values for the economy of scale coefficient e, as revealed by Table 4.9.

The variation would suggest that, at the very least, there do not exist any universal cost estimation models and that values for the coefficients must be individually estimated for each software development environment. Banker and Kemerer go further and argue that the relationship between size and productivity is a more complex one than that indicated by the above models. If fixed project costs are significant, then they will have a considerable impact upon productivity; however, as a project increases in size this will start to be outweighed by the communication overheads described by Brooks [16], hence productivity will peak at a certain level,

Table 4.8 Productivity and project size using the Walson and Felix model

Effort (PM)	Size (KLOC)	KLOC/PM
42.27	10	0.24
79.42	20	0.25
182.84	50	0.27
343.56	100	0.29
2792.57	1000	0.36

Table 4.9 Summary of effort prediction models

Data set	n	Mean SLOC	Mean FP	e
Yourdon [21]	17	34K	na	0.72
Kemerer [33]	17	220K	1013	0.79
Walston [52]	60	20K	na	0.91
Behrens [12]	22	na	146	0.94
Bailey [6]	19	29K	na	0.95
Belady [13]	33	92K	na	1.06
Wingfield [53]	15	180K	na	1.06
COCOMO [14]	63	67K	na	1.11
Albrecht [5]	24	66K	648	1.49

Source: Banker and Kemerer [9].

referred to as the most productive scale size (MPSS), and then decline. How close a project is to the organization's MPSS will therefore have a major impact on effort estimation. Unfortunately, identifying the MPSS requires a lot of project cost data and will tend to be clouded by the many other factors that can influence productivity. Furthermore, it may not even be stable over time.[8] Clearly, even simple effort prediction models are not all that simple!

4.3.2 COCOMO

Now we turn to what is probably the best-known example of a cost model, that proposed by Boehm in 1981. It was derived from his analysis of data from sixty-three projects at TRW Inc. and is called the constructive cost model or COCOMO for short. The COCOMO model comes in three flavours: basic, intermediate and detailed. In this chapter we will focus upon the intermediate model;[9] however, for a thorough coverage of the detailed model the reader is referred to [14], a monumental work and recommended reading for anyone who is a serious student of cost estimation.

The models come in two parts and assume relationships between the following:

- size measured in thousands of delivered source instructions (KDSI) and effort;
- effort and elapsed time.

[8] There is some debate between Kitchenham and Banker *et al.* as to the most appropriate form of prediction system. The interested reader should refer to [35] and [7].

[9] Note that the detailed model is essentially the same as the intermediate version other than that the effort is estimated separately for the four phases of development, namely, product design, detailed design, coding and unit test and, last, integration and test. Also the software product is analyzed in terms of a three level hierarchy: module, subsystem and system. However, in principle the approach remains the same.

This leads to two equations, the first of which is of the general form of the effort prediction models described above to determine person months (PM):

$$PM = a(KDSI)^{e}$$

where a and e are model coefficients. The second equation predicts total, or elapsed, development time (TDEV) as a function of the total effort:

$$TDEV = c(PM)^{d}$$

with c and d as coefficients.

It is useful for a project manager to be able to predict how long a project will take, as well as much it will cost. From his experience as project manager of the IBM OS/360 project, Brooks realized that staff and time are not necessarily interchangeable [16]; very often, adding additional staff to a late project can render it even later. The reason for this is not difficult to determine: new staff have a learning overhead and impose an additional within-project communication burden upon the existing staff.[10]

A major feature of Boehm's approach is that the model coefficients are dependent upon the type of project. In essence, software projects are classified into the following three distinct classes or modes:

- organic – small teams, familiar application;
- semi-detached – intermediate mode between organic and embedded;
- embedded – complex organization, tightly coupled software and/or hardware with many interactions, limited experience.

Developing a pay-roll or a student grade information system would normally be considered to be organic mode projects; certainly, this would be the case if the project members had had prior experience of this type of application. At the other end of the spectrum, developing aerospace or nuclear reactor control systems would be examples of embedded mode projects. An interactive banking system might be somewhere in the middle. The distinctions between the types of project mode are not absolute and require a fair degree of judgement.

Table 4.10 Coefficient values for development modes

Development mode	a	e	c	d
Organic	3.2	1.05	2.5	0.38
Semi-detached	3.0	1.12	2.5	0.35
Embedded	2.8	1.20	2.5	0.32

[10] Assuming that each project member must communicate with all other project members the number of communication links will be $n(n-1)/2$, where n is the number of project members. For a large project, adding even one additional member can have a significant impact.

Boehm provides separate values for the model coefficients dependent upon project mode (see Table 4.10). The impact of the different coefficient values upon development mode productivity is best shown graphically. Figure 4.3 shows that organic mode development will have the highest level of productivity in terms of KDSI output per person month, leading to the lowest effort estimates for a project of a given size. Note that O represents organic mode, I intermediate mode and E embedded mode.

In addition, Boehm identifies fifteen productivity factors – often referred to as cost drivers – which are used to adjust the nominal effort estimate obtained from the model. These fall into four categories, and are listed in detail in Table 4.11. Each factor has between four and six ratings with a mid-point, or nominal, value of one. For further details regarding rules for assigning ratings the reader is referred to [15] or, for the last word, to [14]. The factors are then multiplied to arrive at an effort adjustment factor which is used to modify the basic effort estimate. Thus, if all factors have nominal ratings the product will be unity, which will have no effect upon the nominal effort estimate. In many ways the productivity factors are analogous to the general system characteristics for FP counting, though there exists more flexibility in that different factors have varying impacts. Furthermore, the range of adjustment is considerably more wideranging, from a maximum of 72.38 for the worst case to a minimum of 0.089 for the best case. Once the total predicted effort has been determined, COCOMO then allows project duration to be estimated using the TDEV equation.

In summary, there are five steps for using the intermediate COCOMO model to derive project effort estimates:

1. Identify the project development mode.
2. Estimate the project size in KDSI and derive a nominal effort prediction.

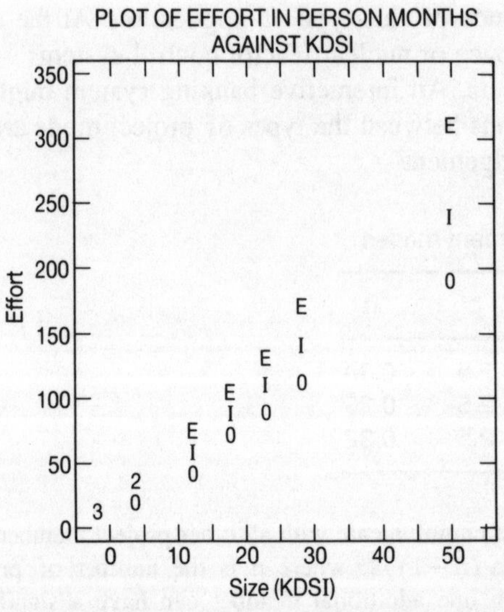

Figure 4.3 Development mode and productivity

Table 4.11 COCOMO productivity factors

Productivity factor	Ratings					
	V. low	Low	Nominal	High	V. high	Extra high
PRODUCT ATTRIBUTES						
RELY Required softw. reliability	0.75	0.88	1.00	1.15	1.40	
DATA Database size		0.94	1.00	1.08	1.16	
CPLX Product complexity	0.70	0.85	1.00	1.15	1.30	1.65
COMPUTER ATTRIBUTES						
TIME Execution time constraint			1.00	1.11	1.30	1.66
STOR Main storage constraint			1.00	1.06	1.21	1.56
VIRT Virtual machine volatility		0.87	1.00	1.15	1.30	
TURN Computer turn-round time		0.87	1.00	1.07	1.15	
PERSONNEL ATTRIBUTES						
ACAP Analyst capability	1.46	1.19	1.00	0.86	0.71	
AEXP Application experience	1.29	1.13	1.00	0.91	0.82	
PCAP Programmer capability	1.42	1.17	1.00	0.86	0.70	
VEXP Virtual machine experience	1.21	1.10	1.00	0.90		
LEXP Prog. language experience	1.14	1.07	1.00	0.95		
PROJECT ATTRIBUTES						
MODP Use of modern programming practices	1.24	1.10	1.00	0.91	0.82	
TOOL Use of tools	1.24	1.10	1.00	0.91	0.83	
SCED Development schedule[11]	1.23	1.08	1.00	1.04	1.10	

Source: Boehm [4]

3. Using the cost drivers compute the effort adjustment factor.
4. Calculate the predicted project effort using the nominal effort and the effort adjustment factor.
5. Compute the project duration.

A COCOMO example

We will use the same banking system as the FP counting example referred to in Figure 4.2. The first question is that of development mode. Given the small size of the application and the fact that a similar system has already been developed, the

[11] The SCED productivity driver concerns schedule compression. Productivity will be lowered if an extremely tight delivery date is required due to the fact that larger projects have a greater internal communications overhead. More surprising is the loss of productivity for extended project schedules, suggesting that if a project falls below an optimum size there can be a resultant loss of productivity arising either from lack of specialization and for the need for staff to become 'Jacks of all trades', or from high staff turnover if specialists are employed.

building society system, organic mode would seem to be the most suitable choice. Possibly if the system were larger and the interactive and distributed aspects more significant, one might consider it to be semi-detached; however, there are no hard and fast rules.

The next task is to estimate the size of the system in terms of KDSI. This immediately highlights a drawback with the COCOMO approach, as this information is unavailable early on in the project when we most wish to obtain our effort prediction. The choice of programming language will also have a bearing upon the estimate.

Setting aside inspired guesswork, there are a number of estimation techniques[12] that we could employ, including the following:

- bottom–up [14];
- analogy [18, 43];
- Delphic approach [14].

The bottom–up method relies on the fact that it is often easier to estimate for the various subcomponents and then sum the parts, than to estimate for the system as a whole. For the banking system one might identify the following subsystems:

- customer file management;
- interactive query handler;
- daily report generation.

An estimate can then be produced of length for each subcomponent, which can then be added to arrive at the total length estimation. One problem with this method is that it very often misses out the 'glue' to build the parts together. For instance, initiation, close down and interrupt routines will almost certainly be required for our system, yet there is a danger that they will not be accounted for in any of the subcomponent estimates. A common remedy is to increase the total estimate by a fixed amount – perhaps 20%, though the exact level is more a matter of intuition than science – to try to compensate for such omissions.

As the name suggests, estimating by analogy involves searching for one or more completed projects in similar domains and then modifying the size as appropriate. Analogies may be sought at either the total project or the subsystem level. Cowderoy and Jenkins suggest the following steps:

1. Select analogies and rank in order of applicability.
2. Assess similarities and differences.
3. Assess quality of analogy itself, for example how reliable was record keeping?
4. Consider known special cases, for example ignore team X as they don't use the SSADM development method.
5. Modify the analogy to reflect the current situation.

[12] Note that these are general estimation techniques and could equally well be applied to direct estimation of project effort as software size.

Figure 4.4 shows how size data from an analogous system can be used to generate estimates for the new banking system. Note that, in this case, the three COCOMO product cost drivers, plus programming language information, are used to help to assess the validity of the analogy. In this case the analogy is not exact; our estimator believes that the new system will be 20–40% larger and 50% will be developed using a 4GL rather than COBOL. Assuming that a conversion factor is known between the two programming languages, then we are in a position to produce upper and lower bounds for our estimate of 4.256 and 3.648 KDSI.

Despite the simplicity of the concept, there are significant problems, including how to find an analogy in the first place, especially within a large organization, and how to gauge the representiveness of the analogy once found.

The third technique for estimation is one described by Boehm in [14], known as the Delphi method. It relies upon expert judgement but attempts to overcome the problems of individual bias. Briefly, the steps are as follows:

1. The experts receive the specification and estimation form.
2. There follows discussion of the product and estimation issues.
3. The experts produce individual estimates.
4. The estimates are tabulated and returned to the experts.
5. Only the experts' personal estimates are identified (see Figure 4.5).
6. The experts meet to discuss results.
7. The estimates are revised.
8. The cycle continues until an acceptable degree of convergence is obtained.

Figure 4.5 shows a typical form that might have been returned after the first round of estimates. Note that at this stage there is still a considerable scatter of estimates. Note also that the median rather than the average estimate is highlighted. This is to

OLD PROJECT (Building Society System)

CMPLX = nominal
DATA = nominal
RELY = high
LANGUAGE = 50% COBOL, 50% C

LENGTH = 4 KSDI

NEW PROJECT (Banking System)

CMPLX = nominal
DATA = nominal
RELY = high
LANGUAGE = 50% 4GL, 50% C
size = 20–40% larger

LOW LENGTH = 4 * 1.2 * (0.38 * 100/50)
HIGH LENGTH = 4 * 1.4 * (0.38 * 100/50)

Figure 4.4 Estimation by analogy

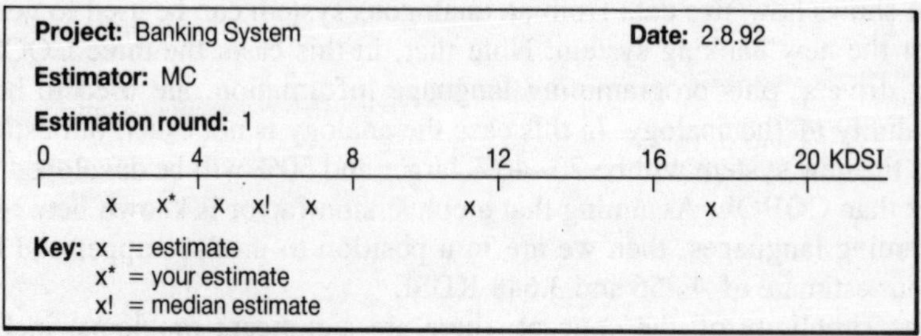
Project: Banking System **Date:** 2.8.92

Estimator: MC

Estimation round: 1

Figure 4.5 Delphi estimation form

prevent one or two rogue estimates having a disproportionate impact upon the estimation process. Chapter 7 provides a fuller discussion of the limitations of means.

Returning to our example, by whatever estimation method or, better still, methods, we need to generate an estimate of software size in KDSI as the primary input into the COCOMO effort model. For the purposes of this example we will assume a size of 4.5 KDSI.[13]

We are now in a position to calculate the nominal development effort as:

$$\begin{aligned}\text{effort (PM)} &= 3.2 * 4.5^{1.05} \\ &= 15.52 \text{ person months}\end{aligned}$$

The third step is computing an effort adjustment factor via the fifteen productivity or cost drivers. Values are tabulated in Table 4.12. By taking the product of the individual productivity factor scores from Table 4.12 we arrive at an effort adjustment factor of 0.76 $(1.15 * 1.16 * 1.0 * 1.11 * 1.0 * 0.87 * 0.87 * 1.0 * 1.0 * 1.0 * 1.0 * 1.0 * 0.82 * 0.83 * 1.0)$. It is interesting to recall that the FP value adjustment factor had a similar effect in reducing the raw FP count (see Table 4.7).

The effort adjustment can now be used for the fourth step to modify the nominal effort prediction. Since this system is not particularly complex and modern tools and programming practices – at least as compared with the 1970s – are being used, it is not surprising that the factor is less than one. This will have the effect of reducing predicted effort.

$$\begin{aligned}\text{adjusted effort} &= \text{effort adjustment factor} * \text{nominal effort} \\ &= 0.76 * 15.52 \\ \text{predicted effort} &= 11.80 \text{ person months}\end{aligned}$$

The fifth and final step is to compute project duration using the predicted effort.

$$\begin{aligned}\text{duration} &= 2.5 * 11.8^{0.38} \\ &= 7.09 \text{ months}\end{aligned}$$

[13] Strictly speaking, the COCOMO model should not be used for systems under 5 KDSI as it will tend to underestimate the fixed project overheads.

Table 4.12 COCOMO effort adjustment factor computation

Productivity factor	Rating	Score	Comments
RELY Required softw. reliability	High	1.15	High financial loss
DATA Database size	V. High	1.16	Assume 100 000 records of 500 bytes = 50M bytes. Database size/KDSI = 12 500 12 500≥1000
CPLX Product complexity	Nominal	1.00	Control operations – nominal Computational operations – low Device-dependent operations – v. high Data management operations – nominal
TIME Execution time constraint	High	1.11	50–70% usage of available execution time
STOR Main storage constraint	Nominal	1.00	≤50% usage of storage
VIRT Virtual machine volatility	Low	0.87	Major changes less than one pa
TURN Computer turn-round time	Low	0.87	Interactive
ACAP Analyst capability	Nominal	1.00	Average ability
AEXP Application experience	Nominal	1.00	3 years' experience
PCAP Programmer capability	Nominal	1.00	Average ability
VEXP Virtual machine experience	Nominal	1.00	1 year
LEXP Prog. language experience	Nominal	1.00	1 year
MODP Use of modern programming practices	V. high	0.82	Routine use, including design and code inspections and structured code
TOOL Use of tools	V. high	0.83	Full support for all stages of software development
SCED Development schedule	Nominal	1.00	As per COCOMO development time prediction
Effort adjustment factor		0.76	

In passing, we must consider what exactly is meant by a person month. Different organizations have different definitions – Boehm uses a value of 152 hours, whilst the MoD uses 125 hours – and this can be one source of prediction error.

COCOMO assessment

That, then, is the background on COCOMO, which leaves us with the question 'how useful is it in practice?' There are a number of difficulties, many of which stem from the vintage of the data upon which COCOMO is founded. First and foremost is the problem of estimating software size in KDSI accurately early on in the project. This is the major input into the model and any inaccuracies will tend to be amplified. Also, given the number of productivity drivers, they are difficult to validate empirically, and a number would seem to be inappropriate for the 1990s, especially virtual machine volatility (VIRT) and database size (DATA). Likewise, some of

Boehm's detailed guidelines on how to rate systems for each driver would benefit from revision. Present day norms on tool support (TOOL) and modern programming practices (MODP) have progressed somewhat since the late-1970s. Another area for concern is that it is vulnerable to mis-classification of development mode. For large systems a small difference in the exponent term `e` will have a major impact upon predicted effort.

Notwithstanding these very real problems, COCOMO is an extremely influential, non-proprietary software project effort estimation model. Furthermore, it is a very comprehensive model, with extensions to deal with maintenance activities and software re-use. It helps managers to understand the impact of different factors upon project costs via the fifteen productivity drivers, and supports sensitivity or 'what-if' type analysis. This helps managers to explore the possible impact upon predicted effort of investing in advanced tools or employing more experienced software engineers, always assuming of course that the model is a good reflection of the organization's development environment, a point we will return to in Section 4.3.4.

4.3.3 Function point based prediction

An alternative to the COCOMO method of effort estimation, with its reliance upon LOC as a software size input, is to use function points (FP), as previously covered in our discussion of productivity. Such an approach is gaining in popularity, if only because FP measures are easier to obtain early on in a project than LOC.

In its simplest form, if we know the productivity for the software engineers for our particular environment as `x` FPs per month, and `p` is the productivity coefficient `(1/x)`, then we can predict effort as:

$$effort = p * FP$$

Such a view presupposes a linear relationship between size and productivity, that is, that `e = 1`. If there is reason to believe that this is not the case, the model can simply be extended along the lines of the previous effort prediction models to give:

$$effort = p * FP^{e}$$

where `e (0 < e)` is the economies of scale coefficient. As with the other models this is most likely to be effective where there is a relatively homogeneous software development environment.

The other use for FPs is to convert them into an equivalent LOC value. This can then be used as input for the more traditional effort estimation models.[14] Behrens [12], amongst others, has published a table of conversion rates, part of which is

[14] A danger to beware of is overadjustment for local factors. Suppose FPs are calculated; they will take account of many of these local factors such as processing complexity, via the general system characteristics. If the FPs are then converted into an equivalent KDSI for the COCOMO model, this factor will then be double counted via the productivity driver CPLX. One solution is to use unadjusted function points as a COCOMO input.

given in Table 4.13. Obviously, such values may have to be modified to suit each individual organization by collecting historical data of size in LOC and FPs.

Several investigations [5, 33], have found empirical support of a good relationship between FPs and LOC, at least in the sense that variation in FPs can 'explain' the majority of variation in LOC. Where there exists a fairly stable ratio between LOC of a given programming language and FPs, the conversion approach has some distinct advantages. As has already been stated, the necessary data are available early on in a project when predictions are most useful. It is based upon a more systematic measurement procedure than is LOC estimation. On the other hand, FPs are principally geared towards commercial and information system type applications, and so may not represent a real alternative for other application areas such as real-time control and scientific systems.

4.3.4 Validation and calibration

Although the various models described in this section on effort prediction may appear plausible, we must answer some difficult questions. How do we know that the effort prediction model is correct? If the model works for Developer A will it work for Developer B? How do we calibrate or tailor a model for optimal performance?

In order to have confidence in effort prediction models we need to obtain external confirmation of their efficacy, in other words to see how they perform for different investigators in environments other than the ones in which they were developed. Given that the predicted effort from a model is extremely unlikely to match actual effort exactly, what error levels should be tolerated and how can error best be measured? It might seem rather negative to focus upon errors but – as DeMarco [22] points out – by not measuring we miss out on our only opportunity to improve.

The obvious approach to error measurement is to use the difference between predicted effort (E_{pred}) and actual effort (E_{act}). The main problem with this method is that it fails to take into account the size of the project. A six person month (PM) error is serious if the project is only predicted to take three PMs of effort. On the other hand, a six PM error for a 3000 PM project would be regarded as a triumph of estimation skill.

Table 4.13 Function point to LOC conversion rates

Language	LOC per FP
Assembler	320
C	150
COBOL	106
Modula-2	71
4GL	40
Query languages	16
Spreadsheet	6

The limitations with absolute error size can be overcome using a percentage error approach, giving:

$$100\,\frac{E_{pred} - E_{act}}{E_{act}}$$

or, for more than one estimate, the mean percentage error:

$$100/n \sum_{i=1}^{i=n} \left(\frac{E_{pred} - E_{act}}{E_{act}} \right)$$

where n is the number of estimates.

The above can be quite useful for revealing any systematic bias to a predictive model, for example if the model always overestimates then the percentage error will be positive and, conversely, if it underestimates it will be negative. One weakness with mean percentage error is that it will mask compensating errors: an underestimate of 50% will counteract an overestimate of the same amount. A prediction model could perform extremely badly, but if there are as many under- as overestimates the mean percentage error could be close to zero. This can be overcome using absolute error values, as in the mean magnitude of relative error (MMRE) statistic proposed by Conte, Dunsmore and Shen [17].

$$100/n \sum_{i=1}^{i=n} \left(\frac{(|E_{pred} - E_{act}|)}{E_{act}} \right)$$

Note that n is the total number of predictions and $|E_{pred} - E_{act}|/E_{act}$ is the magnitude of relative error (MRE) for an individual prediction.

A final means of assessing predictive accuracy is by determining the percentage of estimates that fall within a certain percentage of the actual value. This is known as `PRED(n)`, where n is typically 25%. If for a certain prediction system half the estimates were within 25% of the actual value this would be recorded as `PRED(25) = 50%`. The main disadvantage of this measure is that does not say anything about the estimates that fall outside the target value.

We will now illustrate these techniques using some project data provided by [36] as part of an empirical validation exercise of the intermediate COCOMO model based upon nine projects at ICL.

From Table 4.14 and visual inspection of Figure 4.6, it is apparent that for this data set the intermediate COCOMO model tends to overestimate, that is, the predicted effort exceeds actual project effort in the majority of cases. This is reflected by the large positive value for the mean percentage error for the data set. Note that the MMRE is even greater than the percentage error showing that there is some compensation by underestimates for the overestimates, thus the actual utility of the model as a predictor of project effort, indicated by the MMRE, is even worse than that suggested by mean percentage error. Conte *et al.* [17] suggest ≤25% as an

Table 4.14 Prediction error data

Actual	Predict	Error	% error	MRE
16.70	16.20	−0.50	−2.99	2.99
22.60	21.60	−1.00	−4.42	4.42
32.20	17.50	−14.70	−45.65	45.65
3.90	17.40	13.50	346.15	346.15
17.30	10.30	−7.00	−40.46	40.46
17.70	160.80	143.10	808.47	808.47
10.10	102.70	92.60	916.83	916.83
19.30	34.00	14.70	76.17	76.17
10.60	16.90	6.30	59.43	59.43
Means			234.70	255.61

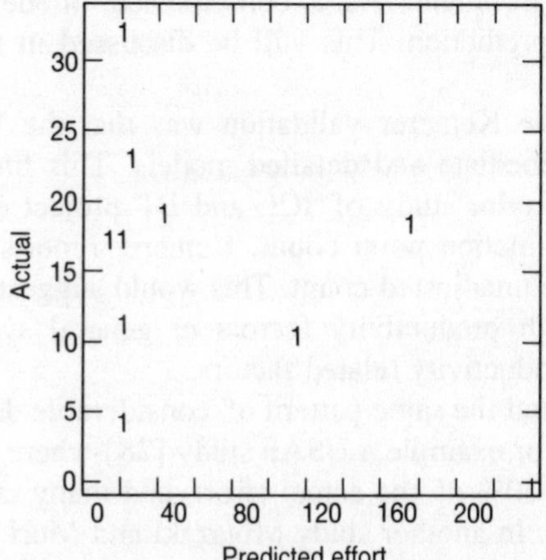

Figure 4.6 Plot of actual against predicted effort

indicator of an acceptable prediction model, so the value of 255% reveals very poor performance indeed.

We now turn to the validation of effort prediction models. There have been a number of such attempts, one of the better known having been conducted by Kemerer [33] to evaluate COCOMO, function points and two proprietary models SLIM [44, 46] and ESTIMACS [48]. The most important result was that without re-calibration all the models performed very poorly, with MMRE values of up to 772%. The results are summarized in Table 4.15. From these results, apart from concluding that none of the models is of much value, it would be tempting to suggest that ESTIMACS is the 'best' effort predictor. However, it is important to remember where the model was originally calibrated, that is, from where the values for the various coefficients have been derived. In the case of ESTIMACS and

Table 4.15 Empirical validation of cost models [33]

Model	MMRE (%)
Basic COCOMO	601
FP	103
SLIM	772
ESTIMACS	85

function points, the models have been developed in similar environments to Kemerer's validation environment: a commercial software developer. By contrast, COCOMO and SLIM were originally set up for real-time, rather than commercial, applications, so the conclusion would seem to be that the the effort models perform extremely badly outside their own environment. As a consequence, model recalibration is an essential part of effort prediction. This will be discussed in more detail in the next section.

Another disconcerting finding from the Kemerer validation was that the basic COCOMO model outperfomed the intermediate and detailed models. This finding was replicated by the Kitchenham and Taylor study of ICL and BT project effort data [36]. Likewise, with the adjusted function point count, Kemerer reports that they failed to predict effort better than the unadjusted count. This would suggest that neither of the sophisticated models, with productivity factors or general system characteristics, is effective at capturing productivity related factors.

Other empirical investigations have found the same pattern of considerable deviation between predicted and actual effort, for example a USAF study [28] where only two predictions fell within plus or minus 30% of the actual effort, and many others were in the range of plus or minus 200%. In another study Miyazaki and Mori [41] found an MMRE for COCOMO of 166% and a marked tendency to underestimate.

And if this does not seem bad enough, the reality is probably worse, as the validations are based upon *post hoc* data using actual rather than estimated KDSI or function points. It is likely that KDSI estimated early on in a project will be incorrect, leading to less accurate predictions. Early on in a project the size may well be underestimated since there will be aspects of the proposed system that will be poorly understood. As the project progresses, the size estimate will tend to improve until after the event, when the estimate will be exact, but at the same time the value of the estimate will decrease. Managers would prefer to know the cost of a project before, rather than after, its completion. In the same way, function points are more difficult to derive using high level, and often incomplete, specifications. The conclusion is that the validations of the effort prediction models will tend to be rather too favourable towards the model.

Why should the effort estimation models perform so badly, and is there any hope of improvement? Perhaps the major answer relates to calibration. The conclusion would seem to be that it is difficult to port the models to different development environments without extensive re-calibration. In the Kemerer study each model had been built in different, and in the case of COCOMO and SLIM, very different, environments to that in which they were validated. It is not surprising that productivity rates are different when building real-time, embedded, safety critical systems in C or assembler from those for developing commercial information systems using, say, a 4GL. This means that the model must be re-calibrated for each software development organization.

The second conclusion is that the models are too complex. The evidence from Kemerer and Kitchenham is that the more sophisticated versions of the models contribute nothing, and possibly detract from performance. It would seem that there is usually a significant relationship between size, however measured, and effort. Furthermore, the models need to be carefully tailored or calibrated and this process is hampered by superfluous complexity, as will be shown in the next section on the calibration process.

The third conclusion is that the effort prediction models tend to be too general. First, they would be better tailored to specific software engineering organizations, environments, methods and notations. Instead, we have increased data collection problems from a resulting proliferation of parameter and productivity drivers. Second, the highly generalized nature of the models causes counting problems due to the difficulty of providing both flexible and precise rules to cover the high level of environmental variation that a general model must necessarily address. And third, there is a failure to exploit the structure and semantics of locally used notations, methods and documentation standards, such as JSD, entity–relationship models, and data flow diagrams. Within organizations effort prediction is quite difficult enough, without endeavouring to solve the problems for the entire industry!

Calibration

By this stage it should be clear to the reader that the calibration of an effort prediction model is an extremely important step. But what do we mean by calibration? It is the process of tuning a model to fit present, local circumstances. This is accomplished by selecting values for the model coefficients and constants based upon local data, so, for the case of the simple LOC based prediction model used in Section 4.3.1:

$$\text{effort} = p * \text{SIZE}$$

we would need to find a suitable value for productivity coefficient p. Calibration is necessary because there is no universal rate of productivity. Different software developers will have varying productivity levels due to the different products being developed, the software engineering methods employed and variations in staffing policy, to mention just a few factors. Calibration is also necessary as productivity within an organization will alter over time, perhaps as a result of investment in training, use of new techniques, changes in staff recruitment and so forth.

A simple calibration example

Suppose we wish to use the above model to predict project effort, assuming that the software size is known, or can be accurately estimated. Analysis of five projects at organization A suggests that, on average, 2 KLOC of software can be produced per person month, yielding a value for the productivity coefficient of p = 1/2 = 0.5. However, if we attempt to apply this model to organization B we find that we consistently underestimate development effort: in fact organization B would appear to be only 50% as productive as organization A, so, consequently, we need to adjust the coefficient *p* to reflect this fact. A value of p = 1.0 gives the best fit for organization B (see Figure 4.7).

There are many reasons why there might be large variations in productivity between organizations, or even within different areas of the same organization, other than differences in programmer ability. Differing counting conventions, particularly in the area of recording effort,[15] is a possible explanation. Thus, calibration is necessary even when two organizations seem superficially to be comparable simply to compensate for differing counting conventions.

Stages of calibration

There are four stages to the calibration process.

1. Check that local data definitions are consistent with the model, for example the LOC counting rules and also that the productivity driver definitions can be meaningfully applied.
2. Collect effort data for a historical database.
3. Adjust the model coefficients and constants.
4. On-going re-calibration (back to step 2).

First, agree and then document the data definitions. There is little point in collecting data if it is inconsistent. This step usually turns out to be something of a

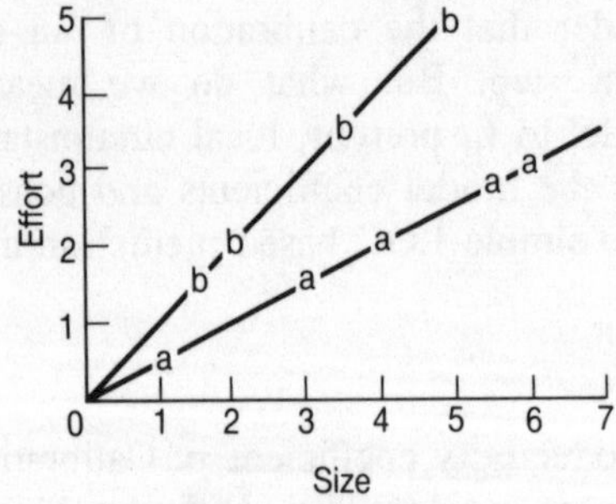

Figure 4.7 Example data to calibrate a resource prediction model

[15] Recording effort ought to, but may not, include management overheads, plus all associated requirements capture, design, documentation and quality assurance activities. However, each organization will have its own conventions.

compromise between the demands of the effort prediction model, consistency with data that has been collected in the past and expediency concerning what can be collected cheaply, accurately and with a minimum of disruption to projects. Data collection is a neglected but fundamental part of software measurement which is covered in some depth in Chapter 5.

Second, populate the database with data from past software projects. Such a historical database, whether it is stored in a database, spreadsheet (as in Figure 4.8) or even in a filing cabinet, is an invaluable resource. What data should be stored? It is not possible to give hard and fast rules, but consideration should be given to the following:

- actual effort (preferably broken down by phase);
- predicted effort (again, preferably broken down by phase);
- project size (could be LOC or FPs or similar);
- quality indicators (as minimum defect counts);
- characterize environment (for instance, methods used, languages, any atypical project characteristics);
- characterize product (application type, non-functional requirement levels);
- name of a contact for further information (possibly the project manager).

If possible, it can be very useful to break down actual and predicted effort by project phase, always assuming that the phases are well defined and standardized across projects. Since size is the key attribute to all the effort prediction models we have examined, this is a vital part of the database. Thought should be given to capturing size in a variety of ways, perhaps KDSI, the object code in bytes and function points. Where a structured specification or design notation is used, it can be possible to extract additional size indicators such as the number of functions from a data flow diagram or the number of states from a state transition diagram. Although seemingly trivial, this type of count can provide a good early indication of size.

proj history database

	A	B	C	D	E	F	G	H	I	J	K	L	M
1	Project	Date	Manager	Actual	Pred.	% err.	MRE	KLOC	KLOC	CPLX	RELY	SCED	etc.
2				PM	PM				/PM				
3	ATS1	Aug-87	DK	436	625	30%	30%	415	0.95	N	H	N	
4	DC6	Feb-89	MSJ	531	180	-195%	195%	186	0.35	N	N	VL	
5	CC3	Mar-89	PEB	504	290	-74%	74%	227	0.45	N	N	N	
6	CC4	Dec-90	OJ	21	19	-11%	11%	20	0.95	N	H	N	
7	CC5	Nov-91	MC	88	130	32%	32%	119	1.35	N	N	N	
8	OLH1	Feb-92	IKB	492	504	2%	2%	353	0.72	N	N	N	
9	OLH2	Jun-92	DCI	475	230	-107%	107%	152	0.32	EH	H	VL	
10	CC6	Aug-92	HM	682	745	8%	8%	359	0.53	H	H	L	
11													
12		Means		404	340	-39%	57%	229	0.7				
13													
14													

Figure 4.8 Historical project effort database

When using historical effort data it is also important to have some indication of the quality of the delivered product. A previous project may have been very productive in the short term, but at the expense of many post-release defects. We should be wary of using such a project for calibrating our model. Aspects of the development environment should also be recorded, especially any atypical features which, again, might make us cautious in using the data for calibration. In addition, we will need to document the product type, for instance embedded or management information system, together with any unusual non-functional requirements such as very high reliability.

No matter how meticulously a project is documented, there will always be questions; consequently, the name of a person associated with the project can be invaluable for locating additional details. A difficult design decision for the historical database is how much data to store. A high level of information can help to yield valuable insights and contribute to understanding why a particular project deviates from a generally stable pattern. But, there are other disadvantages associated with collecting a large number of project measures, apart from the basic collection costs. Staff may become alienated by the size of the form filling exercise. More definitions and counting rules will be required, not to mention checking procedures to validate the data collected. Analysis will be more complex, and often many of the measures are not independent of each other; so, for example, the COCOMO productivity drivers MODP (use of modern programming practices) and TOOL (use of tools) tend to be highly related. Arguably, the worst reason for collecting data for a historical database is that 'although it has no obvious application at present, it just might become useful one day'. The road to 'write only' databases is paved with such intentions! When in doubt err on the side of brevity.

The fictitious, spreadsheet[16] in Figure 4.8 shows an example of how even a quite simple database can be used to help calibrate an effort prediction model.

Third, use the historical database to derive values for the effort estimation model. From the above database of eight completed projects we can compute an average productivity level of 0.57 KLOC per person month.[17] The most straightforward use of this information would be to use it to find a value for the productivity coefficient of $p = (1/0.57) = 1.75$. Returning to effort prediction model we now have:

$$\text{effort (PM)} = 1.75 * \text{KLOC}$$

Comparing our model with the historical predictions in Table 4.16 we see that in terms of mean magnitude of relative error (MMRE) it performs a little better with a (MMRE) of 42% compared with 57% for the original predictions. This is not so impressive, however when it is recalled that we are able to use actual KLOC, which

[16] Spreadsheets are sadly underrated tools for the analysis of metrics, carrying out the percentage error, MRE and productivity calculations automatically. The majority of spreadsheets are also able to output basic graphs, scatter plots and so forth.

[17] The productivity is calculated as `(ΣKLOC)/(ΣPM)`, thereby weighting the larger projects more than the smaller projects.

Table 4.16 Comparison of historical and model predictions

Project	Actual PM	Pred. PM	Model PM	Pred. MRE (%)	Model MRE (%)
ATS1	436	625	726.25	30	40
DC6	531	180	325.5	195	63
CC3	504	290	397.25	74	27
CC4	21	19	35	11	40
CC5	88	130	208.25	32	58
OLH1	492	504	617.75	2	20
OLH2	475	230	266	107	79
CC6	682	745	628.25	8	9
			MMRE	57	42

would be unknown as the predictions are made. Furthermore, Conte *et al.* [17] suggest that a useful prediction system should have an MMRE ≤25%.

Why should an effort prediction model perform so poorly? There are a number of possible contributory factors.

First, eight projects represents quite a small data set.

Second, even with the limited information available from the two COCOMO products and the one project attributes, it is apparent that there is considerable variety between the projects. Lack of homogeneity is one of the great hindrances to accurate prediction systems. In this case product complexity ranges from nominal to extra high, required reliability ranges from normal to high and schedule compression ranges from very low to nominal. There is also more than an order of magnitude difference between the smallest and the largest projects. Possible solutions are either to develop a more sophisticated model using productivity drivers in a similar way to the intermediate and detailed COCOMO models, or to partition the data set in an effort to deal only with more comparable projects, such as excluding those having compressed development schedules, which reduces the MMRE to 32%. Partitioning data sets is frequently more straightforward, especially if there is a small data set. This is the approach recommended by Albrecht [4].

Third, timescales ought to be considered. Older data can be less valuable. Is productivity data from 1987 a good basis for calibrating today? One should at least be on the lookout for productivity trends – hopefully increasing – over time.

Last, our calibration has been very naïve in assuming that the best fit will go through the origin; that is, a hypothetical null project will have zero costs. In practice, a better predictive relationship may be found over a limited range of project sizes by relaxing this assumption.[18] Consequently, the normal approach is to

[18] Since companies rarely wish to predict effort for null projects, the hypothetical absurdity of such a project either incurring a large cost or, even more surprising, a negative cost, can be regarded as largely irrelevant.

use a linear regression technique to find the best possible relationship between size and effort. This yields a model:

$$\text{effort (PM)} = \text{FC} + (\text{p} * \text{KLOC})$$

where FC is the point at which the prediction or regression line crosses the effort axis of the scatter plot (see Figure 4.9) and notionally represents project fixed costs. In this instance a project delivering zero code would take 128 person months, so obviously this model has limitations for very small projects!

In this case the best fit linear model is:

$$\text{effort (PM)} = 128.7 + (1.2 * \text{KLOC})$$

and is indicated by the line on the graph. Table 4.17 summarizes the relative performances of the two models as predictors of software project effort.

Superficially,[19] it would seem that the linear regression approach is less effective. Closer inspection reveals, though, that the project CC4 is substantially smaller than any other project at 21 KLOC. Given the dominating influence of the 'fixed costs' component of the model when predicting for smaller projects, the magnitude of error value of 86% is hardly surprising. If this project were excluded from the data

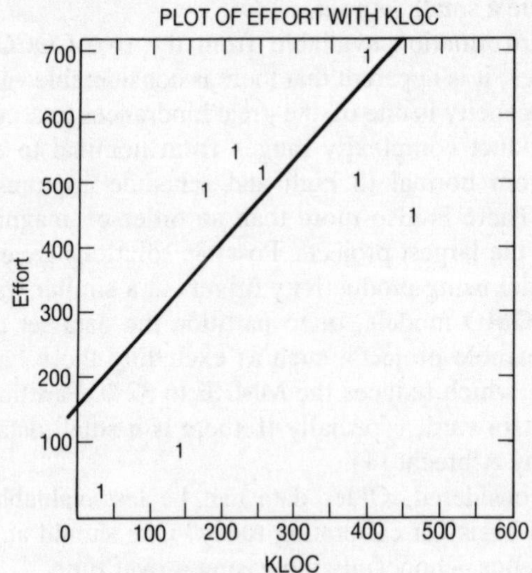

Figure 4.9 Linear regression for predictive models

[19] The other problem with using MMRE to evaluate the regression model is that the line of best fit is determined by attempting to minimize the sum of the squares of each $(E_{pred} - E_{act})$ term or residual. This strategy tends to produce a prediction model where there is less range in estimation error but the mean error could be greater than using an unweighted approach. Thus, the MMRE approach discriminates against least squares derived models. Chapter 7 discusses the statistical issues in rather more depth.

Table 4.17 Comparison of effort prediction models

Project	Actual PM	Pred. PM	Model PM	Regression PM	Pred. MRE (%)	Model MRE (%)	Regression MRE (%)
ATS1	436	625	726.25	626.70	30	40	30
DC6	531	180	325.5	351.90	195	63	51
CC3	504	290	397.25	401.10	74	27	26
CC4	21	19	35	152.70	11	40	86
CC5	88	130	208.25	271.50	32	58	68
OLH1	492	504	617.75	552.30	2	20	11
OLH2	475	230	266	311.10	107	79	53
CC6	682	745	628.25	559.50	8	9	22
				MMRE =	57	42	43

set, the model would have an MMRE of 32%. This improvement is roughly comparable to that obtained from our first model based on average productivity after the data set was reduced by excluding those projects with highly compressed schedules.

From these two examples it should be evident that calibration using smaller, but more homogeneous, data sets can often yield improved predictions. However, it should be emphasized that there must exist *a priori* grounds for this type of manoeuvre, as our main goal is prediction, not after the event manipulation of data.

Calibrating function points

Thus far we have only considered the calibration of highly simplistic and rather generalized models. We now turn to function point based prediction as an example of a more realistic application. Here the problems are a little more extensive than merely trying to derive a value for the productivity coefficient p. Recall that, in order to count function points, a large number of weights is required for the different function types and so forth. Values were supplied by Albrecht [5] from his original analysis of IBM projects and these have been codified by IFPUG [27] into a detailed set of rules. It would seem most unlikely that exactly the same values will be suitable for all software developers, and this is borne out by empirical studies such as that by Kemerer [33], where he found that the unadjusted FPs performed no worse than the adjusted FPs, where fourteen weighted general application characteristics are applied to modify the basic FP count.

So, strictly speaking, to calibrate FPs to a particular environment we should consider the following:

- five function types each with three complexity weights (contained in Table 4.2);
- four boundary values for assigning function types to a given complexity category (see Tables 4.2a and 4.3b);
- fourteen general application characteristics (see Table 4.4);

- the overall value adjustment factor (VAF) weight of ±35% to the unadjusted FP count;
- the value of the economies of scale exponent `e`, if a non-linear function is assumed;
- the productivity coefficient `p`.

If this is not daunting enough, the calibration exercise will have to contend with at least two other problems. First, there are measurement errors. Different studies have reported a range of counting variations, possibly as great as ±30% [40]. Given that this is the primary model input, this is significant. Consequently, full consideration should be given to training and very tightly defined counting rules. The second problem is that many of the factors we are concerned with are not independent. This makes many of the standard techniques for statistical analysis unreliable,[20] and, indeed, the usual strategy for dealing with this situation is to attempt to simplify the model using factor analysis (Chapter 7 gives a fuller explanation).

Given the enormous difficulties outlined above, a simpler approach to FP calibration is employed. The various weights are taken as given, and local adjustments are made via the productivity coefficient `p` and, on occasion, the economies of scale coefficient `e`. Unfortunately, it is not generally possible to compensate for inaccuracies in n ($n \geq 2$) model factors with a single calibration factor, in this case `p`. This is best illustrated by an example.

Assume an FP model based upon two function types only, inputs and outputs, and that the standard weights of 4 and 5 are applied. Assume also 'real' weights of 6 and 3, and a 'true'[21] productivity coefficient of $p = 10$. Even if this value is known, we cannot calibrate the model for the three projects in Table 4.18 properly on the basis of the 'inherited' weights of 4 and 5 see Figure 4.10. Although Project A would be correctly predicted using our FP model, this is entirely due to compensating errors, with an underestimate of input and an overestimate of output effort. Projects B and C cannot be predicted correctly as long as the inherited weights are applied and we attempt to correct solely by the use of `p`. Nor will, in general, the situation be improved by the introduction of the second coefficient `e`.

What should we conclude? First, that calibrating the more complex effort prediction models such as COCOMO, or those based upon function points, is a necessary, but well nigh impossible, task given the many different constants and coefficients that have to be determined. Second, that accepting the majority of values as 'industry standard' or pre-determined and focusing upon the local productivity coefficient is better than no calibration but will, almost by definition, mean that the model will contain many assumptions that cannot easily be verified. Ironically, more complex models may tend to give less exact predictions (see Figure 4.10).

[20] Briefly, a prediction model with a number of dependent inputs tends to be unstable, as the same underlying phenomenon will be captured more than once. Thus the model will amplify its response to the particular circumstance.

[21] True in the sense that for the domain of interest $p = \Sigma$ `effort (person hours)/` Σ`FP`.

Table 4.18 Calibration difficulties

Project	#inputs	#outputs	FP	'real' FP	Effort
A	2	2	(2 * 4) + (2 * 5)	(2 * 6) + (2 * 3)	180
B	4	1	(4 * 4) + (1 * 5)	(4 * 6) + (1 * 3)	270
C	3	6	(3 * 4) + (6 * 5)	(3 * 6) + (6 * 3)	360

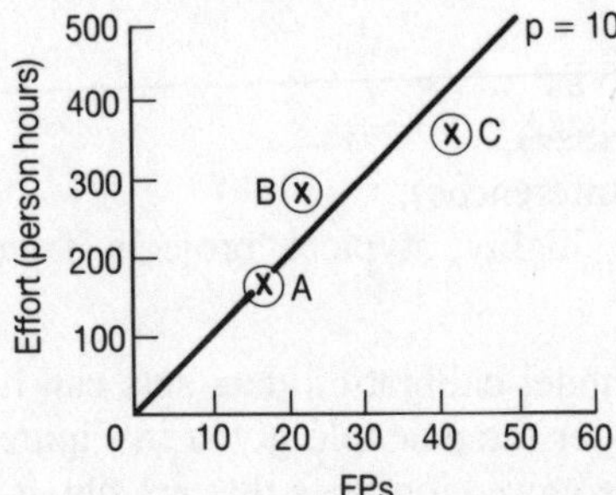

Figure 4.10 Calibration difficulties

Some remedies

Given that there are no universal effort prediction models for software projects, calibration is essential; consequently models should be designed with this end in mind. Wherever possible, the number of drivers, coefficients and constants should be minimized so as to facilitate calibration. Recent work by the Esprit project MERMAID [35, 37] has highlighted the fact that many of the environmental adjustment and productivity factors are redundant. A particularly surprising result was that staff capability factors seemed to have less impact than is generally presupposed by models such as COCOMO.[22] They also found that there is little evidence within an organization for either economies or dis-economies of scale and that e can reasonably be disregarded. The research team concludes that 'simple models are likely to be sufficient within a single environment' [35].

To support the move towards simpler prediction models, we need more homogeneous data sets. Calibration of data sets that include both small pay-roll projects developed using 4GLs, to time and safety critical, embedded control systems written in machine code will be difficult to calibrate! Such data sets would be better partitioned into two smaller sets, each being more similar internally. Just as Boehm recognized the need for three different models – organic, semi-detached and embedded – for different environments, so we should be prepared to develop and

[22] A likely explanation for the limited influence of staff capability is that, at *team* level, differences tend to even out; although, clearly, there are enormous variations between *individual* software engineers.

calibrate a range of simple prediction models. The outcome will be a separate model for each environment, but with the virtue of simplicity.

Deciding if, or when, to partition a historical data set is not always straightforward. Possible strategies are to partition using the following:

- gross domain or environment characteristics, for example information systems versus real time;
- organization structure, especially if the organization is large, so that project data from the head office systems group is kept distinct from the intelligent networks division;
- statistical classification techniques such as:
  - cluster analysis (looking for similarities),
  - discriminant analysis (looking for differences);
- outlier analysis to eliminate a few highly atypical projects from the calibration set.

Whatever strategy is applied, partitioning model calibration data sets can have a major impact upon prediction accuracy. Consider the example given in Figure 4.11 and Table 4.19. Figure 4.11 illustrates the three regression lines that are obtained by treating the data set as a whole, and by keeping projects of type `A` distinct from those of type `B`. Apart from the quite different slopes of the prediction lines and hence values for the `p` coefficient, justification for this manoeuvre can be obtained from the fact that the mean productivity for `A` is `0.52` person months per FP, for `B` `0.20` and for the combined set `(A+B)` `0.27`. As has already been stated, we must have a good basis for distinguishing between type `A` and `B` projects; furthermore, we must be able to do it at the time that the prediction is required, otherwise it will not be possible to decide whether to use a p_A or p_B productivity coefficient for the effort prediction model.

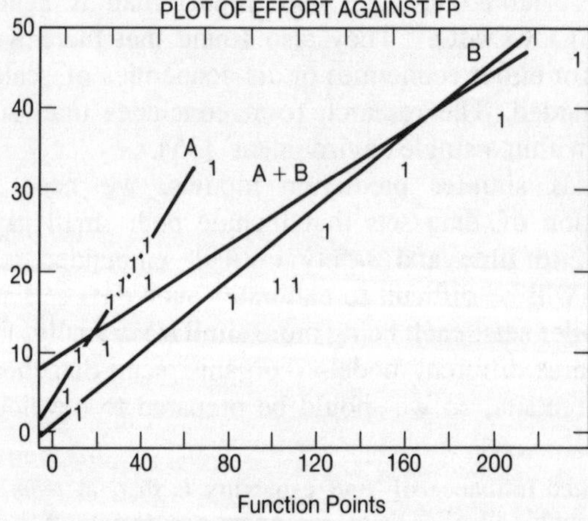

Figure 4.11 Effort prediction and partitioning the calibration data set

Table 4.19 Hypothetical data set for partitioning the calibration

Effort	FP	Data set
16.70	28.20	A
22.60	41.60	A
32.20	67.50	A
3.90	7.40	A
17.30	40.30	A
17.70	30.80	A
10.10	22.70	A
19.30	34.00	A
10.60	16.90	A
2.90	10.90	B
37.10	189.00	B
46.00	219.30	B
32.00	146.80	B
18.40	97.00	B
15.00	76.30	B
17.80	105.70	B
23.50	116.20	B

Calibration re-cap

Calibration is concerned with the fitting of a predictive model to a specific local environment so that it gives the best possible predictions. Since there is no evidence of a standard level of productivity across the industry the process is an essential one.[23] Calibration is accomplished by finding values for the model coefficients and constants based upon historical project data, and it is a continual process. To make calibration as effective as possible we need high quality historical data, preferably drawn from as near a homogeneous environment as possible. It is also helpful, as far as possible, to avoid complex, synthetic measures and models requiring many coefficients and constants.

Finally, we have made the implicit assumption that the software development organization has a certain minimum level of maturity,[24] that there are some procedures and standards and that these are generally adhered to. If this is not the case, and anarchy prevails, then each project will be more or less unique, adopting its own method of working and its own acceptable levels of quality. In such circumstances, calibration or any accurate prediction is extremely difficult.

[23] And even if there were standard levels of productivity they would, in all probability, be obscured by different counting conventions and measurement procedures, so calibration is still going to be necessary.

[24] In terms of the SEI process maturity model [26], this would be a level two organization where engineering processes are, at least in some sense, repeatable.

4.4 Summary

Effort prediction is an important part of a software project manager's job. Without a view of how much effort a project will take, delivery dates will be unknown, budgets will be out of control and the tendering for profitable contracts will be speculative. Given its central role, and the increasing scale and complexity of software projects, it is not surprising, then, that considerable effort has been devoted over the past twenty years to developing effort prediction models.

In this chapter we have covered two of the more important approaches – COCOMO and function points. There are a number of other models, but – excepting the resource constraint models [39, 44, 45] – they share the same general structure of estimated product size, coefficients for productivity and economy of scale, and range of productivity drivers to reflect local conditions such as product complexity and usage of tools.

We have aimed to show that, though frequently neglected, calibration is an essential part of using any quantitative model for prediction. Though much energy has been devoted to developing accurate effort prediction models, none can be 'taken off the shelf'. Historical data need to be collected to establish suitable values for the model coefficients and constants. Moreover, this calibration needs to be a continual process as software development environments undergo change over time.

Despite the comparative maturity of these models, their usage does not guarantee accurate effort prediction. Potential sources of difficulty are the calibration process and some of the assumptions that the models make, which do not always seem to hold. For example, there is evidence that, within a single environment, an economies of scale coefficient does not enhance model accuracy [35]. The model complexity also imposes a data collection burden, introduces additional uncertainty through problems of definition and complicates analysis of performance.

In the face of the mounting evidence that some of the traditional effort prediction models are unnecessarily complex, the good news is that the simpler models appear to be more effective for single environments.[25] Such models need to be targeted at as homogeneous an environment as possible, so it is quite possible that a large or disparate software developer will finish up with several models. Wherever possible, the size component of the model will be derived from a specific object, for example the size of the system requirements document in words, and will exploit any structure and standardization in requirements specifications. The use of productivity drivers should be kept to a minimum; initially two or three may be quite adequate. Complexity should only be introduced into a model when there is a demonstrable need.

Last of all we should not neglect to measure our measurements! In particular, we need to assess how well or badly the models are behaving. There is no possibility of improvement unless we have quantitative data concerning our present situation.

[25] A good example of a simple, yet effective, model is the Bailey and Basili meta model, which, for its own data set of eighteen NASA projects, had a MMRE of 18% [6].

4.5 Exercises and further reading

1. One of the problems of a project manager is dealing with very large amounts of information. Suggest three or four metrics which might act as key project indicators for our beleaguered manager. Devise some hypothetical project profiles to illustrate the metrics in action.
2. If you have access to suitable software, set up a spreadsheet for historical project productivity data you can collect: [8, 9, 11] are good starting points. Try to devise you own prediction model. Use the spreadsheet to perform the necessary calculations and to compare predicted with actual. How does your model compare with others? For the data to have much validity you will need to record local environmental factors. What extra spreadsheet columns will be needed to accomplish this?
3. Obtain a copy of the ISO 9000-3 standard. Section 6.4 deals explicitly with measurement. Attempt to apply it to a software project with which you are familiar. What metrics, if any, does it suggest should be collected and how should they be acted upon?
4. A potential weakness of function points lies in the subjectivity of the counting procedures, leading to the possibility that different analysts may derive markedly different scores from the same system specification. Several experiments have been conducted to explore the practical significance of these variations. Low and Jeffery [40] report within-organization variations of 0% to 360% and suggest that 30% was typical, whilst Kemerer [34] found much smaller discrepancies, usually of less than 10% between pairs of analysts. Can you explain the differences? Are both studies comparing like with like? What, if any, are the practical ramifications of these variations in FP counting?
5. It is generally agreed that function points are not well suited to real-time applications; however, there have been a number of adaptations and modifications, most notably [31], [47] and [24]. What do you consider to be the key aspects in which real-time systems differ from more conventional information systems and to what extent do you believe the modifications to FP analysis capture these aspects?
6. Abdel-Hamid and Madnick [1, 2] make an interesting observation that the predicted software project effort may have an impact upon actual project effort. For example, a high prediction may become self fulfilling as the software engineers may devote the surplus time to 'gold plating' activities, that is, building in additional functionality and quality over and above the customer's real requirements. This could lead one to the surprising conclusion that accurate effort estimates could actually be harmful! Do you agree? If not, why not?
7. As an alternative to statistically driven models, Karunanithi *et al.* [32] describe the use of neural networks to build prediction systems. They claim the approach to be quite effective for software reliability data. To what extent do you consider that their approach might be an effective means of predicting project effort.

Boehm, B., *Software Engineering Economics*, Prentice-Hall: Englewood Cliffs, NJ, 1981.

Despite its vintage this is a classic work, covering all aspects of productivity measurement and effort prediction using COCOMO. There is a wealth of detail and sound advice.

Londeix, B., *Cost Estimation for Software Development*, Addison-Wesley, Wokingham, 1987.

This text book describes in considerable detail a range of prediction models including a class of model not covered in this chapter on resource constraint. The best-known model of this type is Putnam's SLIM. More recently, however, some concerns have been expressed over the validity of some of the underlying assumptions for resource constraint models [29, 35].

McDermid, J.A., *Software Engineer's Reference Book*, Butterworth–Heinemann: Oxford, UK, 1991.

A very useful source when in a hurry or stuck! This book covers far, far more than just project management metrics, but nevertheless contains helpful chapters on project management, effort prediction, quality assurance and standards.

Rook, P. (ed.), *Software Reliability Handbook*, Elsevier Applied Science, London, 1990.

Chapter 11 and Appendix D provide authoritative coverage of the well-known effort prediction models. There is also much useful material on project management, quality assurance and measurement in general. Recommended.

Symons, C.R., *Software Sizing and Estimating. Mk II FPA*, John Wiley: Chichester, 1991.

This short book gives a detailed explanation of Mk II function points, a variant upon the original Albrecht approach. They are particularly well suited for entity–relationship analysis of information systems.

References

[1] Abdel-Hamid, T.K. and S.E. Madnick, 'A model of software project management dynamics', in *Proc. COMPSAC 82*. IEEE, 1982.

[2] Abdel-Hamid, T.K. and S.E. Madnick, 'Impact of schedule estimation on software project behaviour', *IEEE Softw.*, **3**(4), 70–5, 1986.

[3] Albrecht, A.J., 'Measuring application development productivity', in *Proc. SHARE-GUIDE Symposium*. Monterey, CA: IBM, 1979.

[4] Albrecht, A.J., AD/M Productivity Measurement and Estimate Validation. Report No. CIS & A Guideline 313, IBM Corporate Information Systems and Administration, 1984.

[5] Albrecht, A.J. and J.R. Gaffney, 'Software function, source lines of code, and development effort prediction: a software science validation', *IEEE Trans. on Softw. Eng.*, **9**(6), 639–48, 1983.

[6] Bailey, J.J. and V.R. Basili, 'A meta-model for software development resource expenditures', in *Proc. 5th Intl. Conf. on Software Eng.* IEEE, 1981.

[7] Banker, R.D., H. Chang and C.F. Kemerer, 'Evidence on economies of scale in software development', *Information and Softw. Technol.*, **36**(5), 275–82, 1994.

[8] Banker, R.D., S.M. Datar and C.F. Kemerer, 'A model to evaluate variables impacting the productivity of software maintenance projects', *Management Science*, **37**(1), 1991.

[9] Banker, R.D. and C.F. Kemerer, 'Scale economies in new software development', *IEEE Trans. on Softw. Eng.*, **15**(10), 1199–204, 1989.

[10] Basili, V.R. and B.T. Perricone, 'Software errors and complexity: an empirical investigation', *CACM*, **27**(1), 42–52, 1984.

[11] Basili, V.R. and D.M. Weiss, 'A methodology for collecting valid software engineering data', *IEEE Trans. on Softw. Eng.*, **10**(3), 728–38, 1984.

[12] Behrens, C.A., 'Measuring the productivity of computer systems development activities with function points', *IEEE Trans. on Softw. Eng.*, **9**(6), 649–58, 1983.

[13] Belady, L.A. and M.M. Lehman, 'The characteristics of large systems', in *Research Directions in Software Technology*, P. Wegner, ed., MIT Press: Cambridge, MA, 1979.

[14] Boehm, B.W., *Software Engineering Economics*. Prentice-Hall: Englewood Cliffs, NJ, 1981.

[15] Boehm, B.W., 'Software engineering economics', *IEEE Trans. on Softw. Eng.*, **10**(1), 4–21, 1984.

[16] Brooks, F.P., *The Mythical Man Month*. Addison-Wesley: Reading, MA, 1975.

[17] Conte, S., H. Dunsmore and V.Y. Shen, *Software Engineering Metrics and Models*. Benjamin Cummings: Menlo Park, CA, 1986.

[18] Cowderoy, A.J.C. and J.O. Jenkins, 'Cost estimation by analogy as a good management practice', in *Proc. Software Engineering 88*, ed. Pyle, I.C., Liverpool: IEE/BCS, 1988.

[19] Curtis, B. and N. Iscoe, 'Modeling the software design process', in *Empirical Foundations of Information and Software Science, V*, P. Zunde and D. Hocking, ed., Plenum Press: 1990.

[20] Davis, H.A., 'Measuring the programmer's productivity', in *Engineering Manager*. February 1985, 44–8.

[21] DeMarco, T., Yourdon project report: Final report. Technical Report No., Yourdon Inc., 1981.

[22] DeMarco, T., Controlling Software Projects. Management, measurement and estimation. Yourdon Press: NY, 1982.

[23] Duncan, A.S., 'Software development productivity tools and metrics', in *Proc. 10th Intl. Conf. on Softw. Eng.* Singapore: Computer Society Press, 1988.

[24] EFPUG, Function Point Analysis and Real Time Allocations. A Position Report No., European Function Point User Group, 1992.

[25] Fagan, M.E., 'Design and code inspections to reduce errors in program development', *IBM Syst. J.*, **15**(3), 182–211, 1976.

[26] Humphrey, W.S., 'Characterising the software process: a maturity framework', *IEEE Softw.*, **5**(2), 73–9, 1988.

[27] IFPUG, Function Point Counting Practices Manual: Release 3.4. International Function Point User's Group, 1992.

[28] IIT Research Institute, A descriptive evaluation of software sizing models. Data Analysis Center for Software, RADC/COED, Griffiths AFB, NY 13441, USA, 1987.

[29] Jeffery, D.R., 'Time-sensitive cost models in commercial MIS environments', *IEEE Trans. on Softw. Eng.*, **13**(7), 852–59, 1987.

[30] Jones, C., *Programming Productivity*. McGraw-Hill: NY, 1986.

[31] Jones, C., A short history of function points and feature points. Technical Paper, Software Productivity Research Inc., 1987.

[32] Karunanithi, N., D. Whiyley and Y.K. Malaiya, 'Using neural networks in reliability prediction', *IEEE Softw.*, **9**(4), 53–9, 1992.

[33] Kemerer, C.F., 'An empirical validation of software cost estimation models', *CACM*, **30**(5), 416–29, 1987.

[34] Kemerer, C.F., 'Reliability of function point measurements: A field experiment', *CACM*, **36**(2), 1993.

[35] Kitchenham, B.A., 'Empirical studies of assumptions that underlie software cost estimation models', *Information and Softw. Technol.*, **34**(4), 211–18, 1992.

[36] Kitchenham, B.A. and N.R. Taylor, 'Software cost models', *ICL Tech. J.*, **4**(3), 73–102, 1984.

[37] Kok, P., B.A. Kitchenham and J. Kirakowski, 'The MERMAID approach to software cost estimation', in *Proc. Esprit Technical Week*, 1990.

[38] Kuntzmann-Combelles, A., 'Metrics for management', in *Software Reliability and Metrics*, B. Littlewood and N.E. Fenton, ed., Elsevier Applied Science: London, 1991.

[39] Londeix, B., *Cost Estimation for Software Development*. Addison-Wesley: Wokingham, 1987.

[40] Low, G.C. and D.R. Jeffery, 'Function points in the estimation and evaluation of the software process', *IEEE Trans. on Softw. Eng.*, **16**(1), 64–71, 1990.

[41] Miyazaki, Y. and K. Mori, 'COCOMO evaluation and tailoring', in *Proc. 8th Intl. Softw. Eng. Conf.* London: IEEE Computer Society Press, 1985.

[42] Myers, W., 'Can software for the Strategic Defense Initiative ever be error free?', in *Computer*. November, 1986, 61–7.

[43] Myers, W., 'Allow plenty of time for large scale software', *IEEE Softw.*, **6**(4), 92–9, 1989.

[44] Putnam, L.H., 'A general empirical solution to the macro software sizing and estimating problem', *IEEE Trans. on Softw. Eng.*, **4**(4), 345–61, 1978.

[45] Putnam, L.H. and A. Fitzsimmons, 'Estimating software costs', in *Datamation*, September 1979, 189–98.

[46] Quantitative Software Management, Reference Notes for the DOD SLIM Software Cost Estimating Course. Quantitative Software Management, McClean, VA, 1983.

[47] Reifer, D.J., ASSET-R: A Function Point sizing tool for scientific and real-time systems. Technical Report No. RCI-TN-299, Reifer Consultants Inc., 1990.

[48] Rubin, H.A., 'Macroestimation of software development parameters. The Estimacs system', in *Proc. SOFTAIR Conf. on Software Development Tools, Techniques and Alternatives*. Arlington, VA: IEEE Press, 1983.

[49] Software Metrics Definition Working Group, Software size measurement with allocations to source statement counting. Draft for Review, Software Engineering Institute, Carnegie Mellon, 1991.

[50] Stevens, R., 'Creating software the right way', in *Byte*. August 1991.

[51] Vessey, I. and R. Weber, 'Research on structured programming: An empiricist's evaluation', *IEEE Trans. on Softw. Eng.*, **10**(4), 397–407, 1984.

[52] Walston, C.E. and C.P. Felix, 'A method of programming measurement and estimation', *IBM Syst. J.*, **16**(1), 54–73, 1977.

[53] Wingfield, C.G., USACSC experience with SLIM. Technical Report No. 360-5, U.S. Army Institute for Research in Management Information and Computer Science, 1982.

Chapter 5

Methods

Synopsis

In which it is argued that effective use of measurements from software engineering products and processes is a difficult undertaking. It needs the support of guidelines and methods. Consequently, there has been an upsurge of interest in what we shall call metric methods. This chapter examines a number of methods with varying emphases, including quality, measurement goals, process maturity, the organization and a combination of the above. Each method has merit but also aspects that are more problematic. Further evolution and development of metric methods is an active research area. The chapter concludes with some discussion of the management issues associated with the introduction and continued use of measurement on a software project.

5.1 Obstacles to software measurement

In the preceding chapters we have considered the importance of measurement. Measurement enables us to compare objectively the various methods, tools, techniques and designs available to software engineers. Measurement helps us to make objective statements concerning the quality of the software products that we claim to engineer. Measurement provides the analytical apparatus to understand the complex processes that make up a software project. And measurement provides quantitative feedback from software engineering processes: indicators of how well or badly they are faring, whether a project is on course or heading for disaster. We have encountered a wide range of software engineering applications for measurement. We have seen metrics used to review software design, assess software quality, productivity and form the basis for project effort prediction. So why should there be such limited use of software metrics in industry? What makes software measurement so problematic or unattractive?

The answer is, in brief, because software engineering is a highly complex process concerned with the construction of highly complex products. Such complexity is not easily reflected by a few simple measures; moreover, any analysis is forced to take into account a multiplicity of different factors. Suppose we wish to measure defect levels in software: to make sense of such a measure we would also need to take into account the size and type of software, the competence of those involved in its development, the type and cost-to-repair of the defects, the nature of any quality control procedures and how and when any defects were uncovered. The simple metric, nineteen defects, by itself is not very informative.

Second, each project tends to be something of a 'one off'; this is quite unlike the majority of other manufacturing processes. The result is that measures must be selected and tailored for each measurement environment. The use of fixed sets of metrics for all purposes seems neither realistic, nor has it been very successful in the past. Collection procedures cannot easily be standardized and analysis of the results will depend upon each individual circumstance.

There is also the issue of the scope of any software measurement exercise. Researchers such as DeMarco [18] and Kitchenham [13] have pointed out that successful measurement exercises must be sufficiently broad to provide a complete picture. This would normally include the collection of cost, duration and quality values; otherwise there is a danger that measuring one aspect, for example cost, may cause the problem to migrate to another area such as quality. Using a single metric in isolation can be both misleading and can cause unintended side effects.

A related problem is that the very act of measuring will disturb the system being measured. Staff may behave differently if they are under scrutiny, and the collection of a metric can be unintentionally interpreted as the setting of a goal.

Over recent years, in response to these difficulties, there have been various attempts at introducing a more systematic approach to software measurement. These we will term 'metric methods'. They are guidelines, procedures, techniques and tools to enable software measurement related work to be performed. As such they can be considered to be analogous to other software engineering methods such as those associated with requirements capture or system design. Successful software measurement requires an extensive range of skills so that any attempt to impose structure and provide a mechanism must be to the good. Methods also support the re-use, of and benefit from, past software measurement experience in a systematic fashion. Even at the outset, it is worth emphasizing that no method can be completely prescriptive and that there will always be a need for skill and judgement on the part of those involved in the measurement process. None the less, a method should indicate what steps should be taken, and in what order, together with advice as to how to evaluate the various alternatives if decisions need to be made.

Prior to considering metric methods we need to review briefly what is involved in software measurement and to break down the process into its constituent stages (as illustrated in Figure 5.1). Note that since we are concerned with the application of measurement, the measurement process is far greater in scope than the mere act of taking a measure. The stages are planning, collection and analysis, with validation as an on-going activity throughout. Despite the diversity of software measurement goals and environments, these three basic stages can encompass any software measurement related activity in a generic process. Given the importance of having a thorough understanding of this process we will consider each stage in a little more detail.

Planning. This stage involves activities such as identifying the business requirements for measurement, setting specific measurement objectives, identifying the metrics required and defining them in terms of the particular measurement environment. As an example, lines of code will frequently be interpreted differently between various software organizations: one environment might count delimiters, another the number of carriage returns and so forth. Whatever, decisions must be made. Planning will also include preparing for collection and so will also embrace education, setting up the actual measurement processes and any tool development that might be necessary.

Collection. This second stage is based upon the actual measurement process itself and will include all control activities to ensure that procedures are adhered to.

Analysis. This is the third stage, which is concerned with measurements once they have been obtained. Statistical analysis is important to help uncover patterns and anomalies. The results should provide feedback into the software process, at all levels from individual through team to organization. Clearly, there is no point in planning for, and collecting, measurements which then remain unused. Indeed, this topic is so important that Chapter 7 explores analytical techniques in some depth.

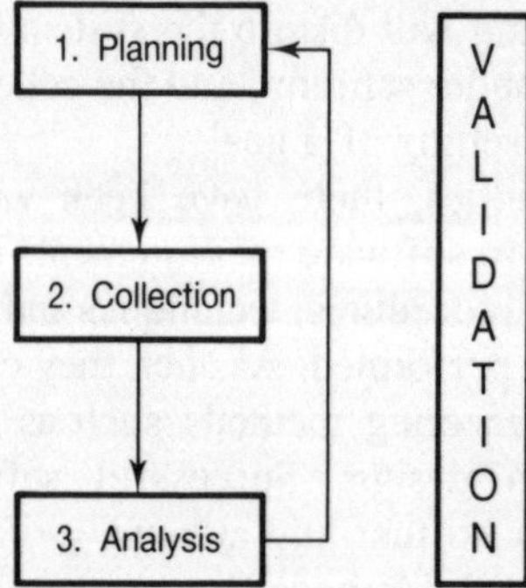

Figure 5.1 Stages for software measurement

In addition there is the frequently overlooked issue of *validation*. Basically, measurers need to ask themselves continuously whether the measurement is a true, or adequate, representation of whatever attribute they believe is being captured. Validation can take place throughout the measurement process. During the planning stage, a range of techniques is possible. These include measurement theoretic [20, 21, 34, 50], axiomatic [49] and algebraic [45] approaches. These all share the same basic aim of ensuring that the metrics and their underlying models behave as the measurer intends. They all have the advantage of being possible prior to the potentially costly, or unrepeatable implementation stages of the measurement process. Chapter 6 covers some of these theoretical techniques in detail. Validation for the collection stage includes procedures to assess the validity of the actual measurements, such as sampling and cross checking. Validation during the analysis stage is most common, usually being based upon the search for associations between the metric and other measures of the attribute in question, using historical data. Typically, association will be assessed in terms of the strength of the correlation coefficients.[1]

Aside from support for the whole measurement process, there are a number of other factors that must be borne in mind when judging the utility of a metric method. These include their ease of use, flexibility and track record, particularly in an industrial rather than an academic context.

We now examine the following metric methods:

- factor criteria metric [16, 38];
- quality function deployment [33];
- goal question metric [4, 5];
- ten step metric programme [24];
- application of measurement in industry (AMI) [35];
- process maturity based approach [41].

5.2 Early methods

Factor criteria metric

The earliest approach to software measurement that could reasonably be termed a method, comes from the mid-1970s and stems from the work of Boehm *et al.* [7, 8] on software quality. This was codified into the factor criteria metric (FCM) method by McCall *et al.* [16, 38]. The principal aim of FCM is not measurement as such,

[1] The correlation coefficient is a statistical test to measure the extent to which there exists a simple linear relationship between two variables. As values tend towards 1.0 or −1.0 the stronger is the relationship. A value of zero indicates no relationship whatsoever. Use and abuse of this coefficient has been a major feature of much metrics work over the past twenty years. See Chapter 7 for a discussion of the proper use of, and limitations to, correlation coefficients.

but, rather, to obtain a quantitative view of quality. It is also important to stress that FCM is very much oriented to the user's or customer's perspective of quality as encapsulated in the phrase 'fitness for purpose'. The method also emphasizes the need for an overtly quantitative approach to software quality.

The FCM method also recognizes explicitly that not all aspects of software quality are of equal concern to the user. Factor criteria metric handles this type of situation by breaking the overall concept of software quality down into eleven distinct quality factors. Examples of quality factors are reliability, efficiency and usability. Fixed sets of criteria are identified as influencing the quality factor, so, for example, the criteria, consistency, accuracy, error tolerance and simplicity are deemed to influence software reliability. Each criterion is, in turn, defined by a set of pre-determined metrics. The result is a hierarchy, as shown by Figure 5.2.

The criteria for each factor are evaluated subjectively on an ordinal scale of 1–10 using a checklist and a formula that enables a rating measure of software quality to be determined for each software quality factor of interest. This gives:

$$F_q = c_1 * m_1 + c_2 * m_2 \ldots c_n * m_n$$

where F_q is a quality factor of interest such as testability, $c_1 \ldots c_n$ are pre-determined regression coefficients and $m_1 \ldots m_n$ are the criteria measures that are considered to determine the quality factor. Effectively, the coefficients $c_1 \ldots c_n$ are statistically derived weights to model the relative importance of the different criteria upon the quality factor in question. The complete set of quality factors and criteria are given in Figure 5.3, from which it will be noted that all factors have at least two criteria and the majority of criteria are related to more than one quality factor. The meaning of the quality factors is in the main self-evident, with the possible exception of inter-operability, which is the ease with which a system may be linked to other systems.

Factor criteria metric has proved to be highly influential. McCall's type of structure and terminology has been accepted by the IEEE standard on software

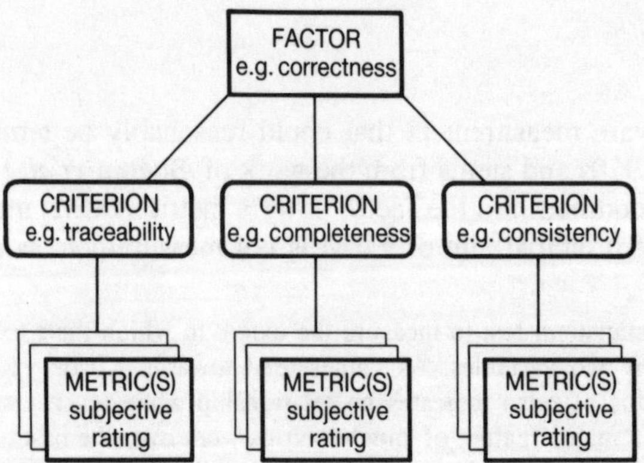

Figure 5.2 Hierarchy of quality factor, criterion and metric

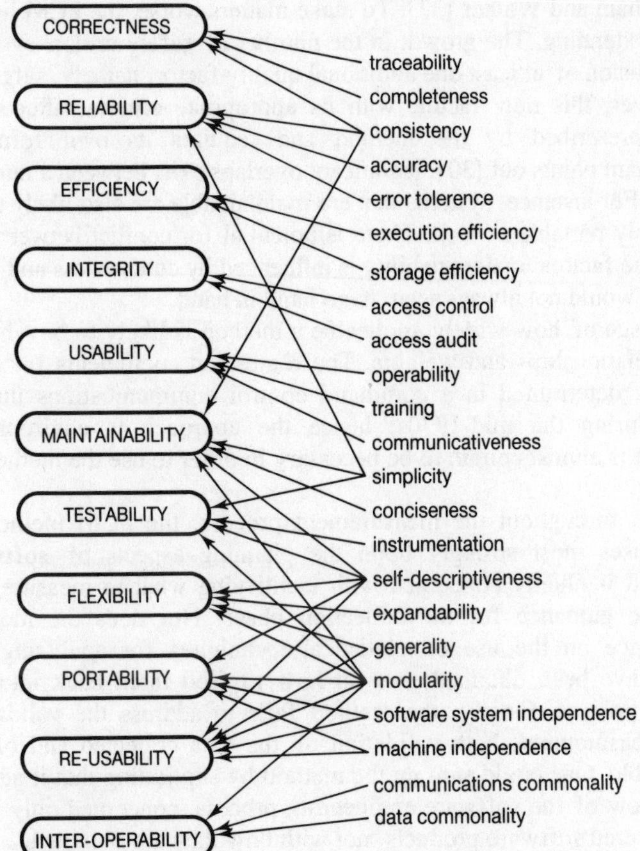

Figure 5.3 Quality factors and criteria of McCall *et al.*

quality metrics.[2] In addition, the method is simple to use. The criteria and their coefficients are already provided. All that is required of the software engineer is to determine, in conjunction with the user, which quality factors are considered to be of importance. This will highlight relevant criteria for which the associated metrics can be assigned ratings.

However, McCall's work has a number of drawbacks. First of all, FCM concentrates upon delivered product quality factors using pre-determined, fixed relationships between the factors, criteria and metrics. This is a major restriction, as it prevents us from considering the quality of intermediate products such as the design.

Another problem affecting how flexible FCM might be is that there is no consensus on the quality factor to criteria relationships. For example, see the variants offered by

[2] If forms part of the IEEE software quality metrics methodology standard IEEE P-1061-D2, and has been used in formulating the ISO 9126 Criteria for Evaluating Software.

Boehm [7] or Kitchenham and Walker [32]. To make matters worse, the FCM list of quality factors needs extending. The growth in the number of safety critical systems would suggest the inclusion of at least one additional quality factor, namely, safety or dependability.[3] However, this new factor, with its appropriate criteria, affects the original coefficients prescribed by the method and requires its own formula. Moreover, as Kitchenham points out [30], significant overlaps exist between a number of the quality factors. For instance, systems that are maintainable are also likely to be flexible, and presumably portable as well. There is potential for conflict between the various criteria for some factors: maintainability is influenced by conciseness and self-descriptiveness, which would not always seem to go hand in hand.

Next, there is the issue of how widely applicable a method is likely to be when it is based upon fixed relationships and weights. The regression coefficients for each factor's formula were determined in a command control communications intelligence environment during the mid-1970s; hence the approach is environment specific. Re-calibration is almost certain to be necessary in order to use the method in other environments.

In terms of support throughout the measurement process, the FCM method is rather patchy. It focuses most strongly upon the planning aspects of software measurement, in that it is chiefly concerned with identifying what to measure. By contrast, there is little guidance for the collection phase. Nor does the method provide much assistance on the use of statistical techniques for analyzing the measures once they have been obtained, nor on how to feed them back into the software engineering process. Finally, the method fails to address the validation issues of software measurement, both validation of the data collected and of its utility once it is available. One could sum up the method by suggesting that it adopts a rather 'black box' view of the software engineering process, concerned only with the quality of the delivered software products, not with how they are obtained.

Quality factor deployment

A related approach to the factor criteria metrics (FCM) method is the quality factor deployment (QFD) method, first proposed by Akao in the 1960s. It also focuses upon the quality of the delivered software. Originally it was aimed at controlling and improving quality for the manufacturing industry. Examples of users are car manufacturers such as Ford and General Motors, and major computer manufacturers such as IBM, Hewlett-Packard and DEC. However, more recently the method has been extended to cover software quality [33].

Quality factor deployment extends the ideas contained within the FCM method, in that it places more emphasis upon the manufacturing process; quality must be

[3] Note that reliability and safety cannot be considered to be synonyms. Bennett [6] gives the example of a railway signalling system. A safe system will be one that sets a red light to halt trains if a track sensor failure is detected. By comparison, a system might be reliable – in the sense of behaving as intended – but unsafe is such a circumstance has not been specified.

controlled throughout the development. Quality factor deployment relates quality requirements laid down by customers and developers to product characteristics that can be measured throughout the software development process. Throughout the development process, all requirements are tabulated and assigned priorities for monitoring purposes.

At the heart of QFD is the use of matrices to link customer quality requirements to design or technical solutions. Figure 5.4 illustrates a simplified matrix chart showing the basic components of a QFD matrix chart. These charts are often referred to as houses of quality, due to their rather characteristic shape. The areas of the chart are as follows:

- *what* product requirements the customer wants;
- *customer importance*, which indicates the relative value to the customer of the various software requirements;
- *how* the requirements will be met in terms of design requirements;

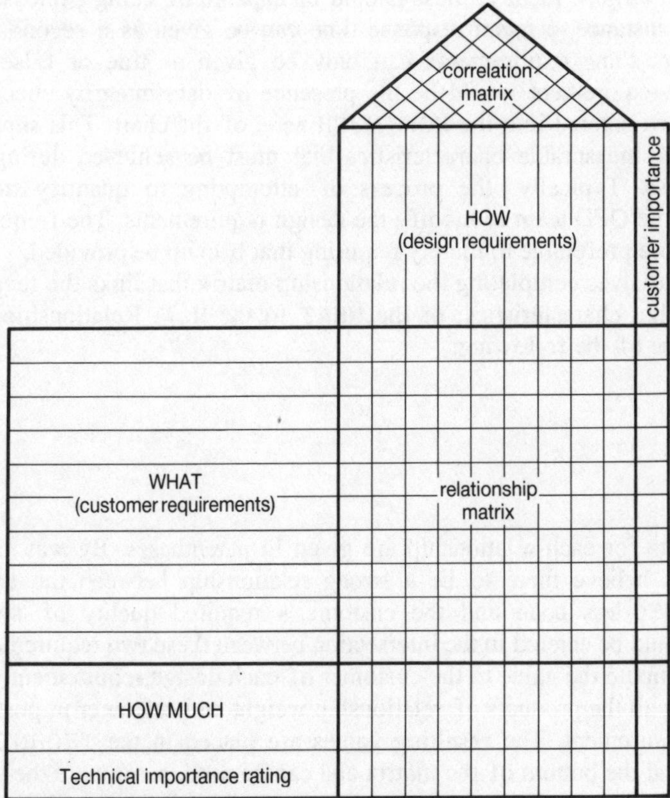

Figure 5.4 The structure of a QFD matrix

- *technical importance*, which indicates the value of each design requirement in terms of how much customer satisfaction it contributes;
- the *relationship matrix* between the customer requirements and the design requirements;
- the *correlation matrix*, which indicates any positive or negative interaction between the individual design requirements;
- *how much*, which provides quantitative target values for each design requirement or how we may determine that the target has been satisfied.

The first step is to tabulate the customer's quality requirements in the WHAT zone of the matrix, grouped by subject area. Quality factor deployment emphasizes the need to use the customer's own words to avoid subverting customer requirements into solutions that are technically attractive to the supplier.

Second, the product design requirements must be identified and entered into the HOW zone of the matrix. It is generally accepted that this is the most difficult step in the QFD method.

The third step is to quantify the design requirements as objectively observable thresholds or design targets. Ideally, these should be capable of being expressed in numeric form. For instance, a mean response time can be given as n seconds. On occasions, however, some requirements can only be given as true or false. An example of such a requirement would be the presence of data integrity checking. These values are then entered into the HOW MUCH zone of the chart. This supports the identification of measurable characteristics that must be achieved during the development process. Typically, the process of attempting to quantify design requirements leads the QFD team to modify the design requirements. The frequency of backup is therefore preferable to merely requiring that backup be provided.

The fourth step involves completing the relationship matrix that links the required qualities to the design characteristics, or the WHAT to the HOW. Relationships are assessed as being one of the following:

strong (9);
medium (3);
weak (1);
none (0).

The numeric weights for each relationship are given in parentheses. By way of an example, we might believe there to be a strong relationship between the design requirement of GOTO-less code and the customer's required quality of system reliability, so a 9 would be entered in the intersection between these two requirements.

The fifth is to compute the value to the customer of each design requirement. This is done by summing all the products of relationship weight and customer importance for each design requirement. The resulting values are placed in the TECHNICAL IMPORTANCE row at the bottom of the matrix and can be used to compare the value of the various design techniques, not from a software engineering but, rather, from a user perspective.

The sixth step is to look at the deployment of the design requirements and in particular their interactions. This is accomplished by completing the `CORRELATION MATRIX` (the 'roof' part of the chart). Note that correlation is not intended in the strict statistical sense, but merely indicates an association. The following types of correlation are recognized:

strong positive (9);
weak positive (3);
no interaction (0);
weak negative (−3);
strong negative (−9).

A positive correlation indicates that the design requirement or `HOW` supports the implementation of another design requirement. Conversely, a negative correlation implies that the design requirement hinders implementation of another design requirement. A significant number of negative correlations are indicative of a `HOW` that may prove to be difficult to carry out in practice. Such technologies will need very careful monitoring. Quality factor deployment enables these problem areas to be identified early on in a project.

The outcome of the above six steps is a matrix that can be used to guide the development process to build a high quality product that meets the customer's expectations. Once the matrix has been completed it can be validated. The QFD team should check for empty rows, which imply unfulfilled customer requirements because no technical solution has been identified. Likewise, empty columns suggest solutions for problems that are not of interest to the customer. Efficient charts will also tend to have a higher proportion of filled-in cells in the relationship matrix, indicating that many of the `HOWS` are relevant to more than one `WHAT`. The ideal situation would, of course, be one in which every cell was completed with a strong relationship (i.e. all nines).

There are many other aspects to the QFD approach, such as the use of multi-disciplinary teams and assessment of competitors' products and technology, which have not been described here. For a fuller account the reader is referred to [11, 33, 48].

We conclude this section with an example of a partial matrix given in Figure 5.5. This matrix shows the customer's requirements under the headings of RELIABILITY and PERFORMANCE. In reality, it is probable that the customer for a software system will have more extensive quality requirements than those shown in the `WHAT` section of Figure 5.5. However, in order to keep the example simple, we will ignore such a possibility. A major concern of QFD is to hear the 'voice of the customer'; consequently, the requirements are expressed in the customer's own words. Thus, we have requirements such as 'handles all finance dept data' as opposed to specifying storage capacities and transaction processing rates. The latter are design requirements which are actually means to accomplish the customer's requirements rather than ends in themselves. After entering these requirements on to the matrix it is next necessary to establish their relative value to the customer. In this

−1 −9 −3 −3 −9

Customer requirements	Backup frequency	Integrity checks	Computer availability	No. of transactions	Volume of data	No. of users	Av. response time		customer importance
RELIABILITY									
never loses data	9	3							5
available when needed			9						3
prevents inconsistent data	1	9							3
PERFORMANCE									
handle all finance dept data			1	9	9	9			2
fast response time							9		1
HOW MUCH	Once per day	YES	85%	500/hr	200 Mb	30	6 secs		
Technical importance rating	48	42	29	18	18	18	9		

Figure 5.5 An example QFD matrix

example, 'never lose data' is given as being the most, and a 'fast response time' the least, important requirement.

A total of seven design requirements is identified in the `HOW` part of the matrix as comprising a possible implementation strategy. These are linked to specific customer requirements by indicating the strength of the relationship in the matrix. In the example a strong relationship is identified between 'never loses data' (the `WHAT`) and 'backup frequency' (the `HOW`). The technical importance rating for each `HOW` is computed using the strength of the relationship and customer importance. The design requirement 'integrity checks' has a value of:

$$(3 * 5) + (9 * 3) = 42$$

which suggests that after 'backup frequency' (48) it will contribute the most to customer satisfaction.

From a software measurement standpoint, the most interesting aspect of QFD is the `HOW MUCH` or the quantification of the design requirements. Without such values it is difficult to be objective about the achievement, or non-achievement, of each of these HOWs. Note that, in this example, only the 'integrity checks' requirement is not expressed as a directly measurable property, but, rather, as a true or false value. Even here it might be desirable to re-state this as a probability of detecting inconsistent data.[4] The conflicts between the HOWs are also highlighted. For our example we note the weak negative correlation between 'integrity checking' and 'average response time', since one could reduce response time by cutting out integrity checks.

QFD evaluation

Quality factor deployment supports specification of the strength of association between the required qualities and the technical characteristics of the intermediate and final product throughout the software development process. This constructive view of product quality coupled with the use of tables enables the tracing of these requirements during production. There is no provision for ensuring the quality of the development process; achieving the desired product characteristic can take one or many attempts. This is because the technical characteristic measures are purely quality indicators; they only tell a developer when to progress onto the next stage. Once the required indicator value is achieved, the process is deemed to be successful and the developer may proceed to the next step. This mechanism is rather inflexible, however, since processes can only be satisfactory or unsatisfactory, with no possibility of any intermediate outcome.

The QFD method is strong in terms of its support for product quality, but weak for processes. It helps to define quality both in the final delivered software and in intermediate products. There is recognition of the fact that if quality is not measured until the product has been completed, this provides little scope for remedial action. Quality cannot easily be imposed, it must be built in throughout the construction process. On the other hand, it fails to provide guidance as to how these quality levels can be achieved. Indeed, it is possible to define quality levels that cannot be achieved within the time and budget constraints of a project. A project could become stuck in a loop in an early task, attempting to achieve an unattainable technical quality level, which, if the method is not employed in a flexible fashion, might jeopardize completion of the whole project. The better understood the process – as in traditional manufacturing – the less likely this is to happen.

Quality factor deployment is considerably more flexible than FCM since it allows the user to identify relationships, appropriate to their environment, between final and intermediate quality characteristics. However, the approach is still limited to quality related measurement and would not support, for instance, a project to investigate what aspects of software maintenance are most costly. There is also the potential danger of allowing the user to postulate relationships between the intermediate and final product. Software engineering has a well-developed mythology, much of which

[4] See the Section, p. 3.3, in Chapter 3 on measuring quality for a more detailed approach to quantifying data integrity.

is based upon supposition as opposed to empirical observation.[5] Consequently, one must beware of using technical characteristics that do not in reality support the desired, final quality characteristic.

Like FCM, Akao's QFD method has, as its principal concern, planning for measurement and, in particular, the selection of metrics to collect. There is no explicit support for the collection stage of measurement, and analysis is limited to indicating when an intermediate quality level has been achieved and the development process may proceed to the next stage. Similarly, there is no support for validation, and this is potentially the most dangerous aspect of QFD. None the less, when used with care, QFD could have much merit in helping to structure a quality measurement programme.

5.3 The goal driven method

The next major development in providing a systematic method for software measurement came in the mid-1980s from the University of Maryland, in the form of the goal question metric (GQM) method. This originated as a data collection technique and has evolved into a fully fledged method, which has proved to be highly influential upon subsequent software measurement thinking.

During the early-1980s a number of researchers, led by Basili, were heavily involved in a software measurement programme at the NASA Software Engineering Laboratory. This afforded them an important opportunity to conduct a whole range of empirical investigations into issues such as software reliability and the impact of various development methods using large scale, industrial software systems as their test bench. Given these circumstances, Basili [5] had certain concerns with the data collection process, chief of which were the needs (i) to clearly establish the data collection goals and (ii) to be able to validate the data. Without goals, patterns were unlikely to be visible, since the data collected would be unfocused and hence incomplete. Without data validation, Basili found that up to 50% of the data collected could be erroneous. In response to these concerns, a number of guidelines were developed to help researchers focus upon a goal and then refine it into a list of questions. In turn, these suggest specific measures to be collected. Other guidelines emphasized the importance of careful form design for the data collection and the need to validate the responses by means of a form reviewer and by interviews.

From this background the guidelines evolved into a generally applicable metrics method, known as GQM [3, 42]. The most notable feature of Basili's approach is

[5] A good example is module size. There have been many pronouncements upon maximum module size, in terms of lines of code, which could suggest an intermediate product or technical characteristic of `LOC` $\leq$ `n`, where `n` is an exact multiple of `50` and `n` $\leq$ `200`! Work by Bowen [10], Basili and Perricone [2] and Card *et al.* [15] casts considerable doubt over the existence of a simplistic relationship between module size and such quality factors as reliability.

the central role of a goal. There must always be a reason for measuring; otherwise why bother? He rejects the notion of fixed sets of metrics, such as maintenance metrics, but instead offers a method to assist tailoring sets of metrics to specific organizational goals and environments. Since these goals and environments will be extremely varied, so the metrics that are to be collected will necessarily be. Thus, the starting point for any measurement exercise should be 'What is the purpose of measurement?', and not 'What metrics should we use?'

There are four basic steps to GQM, which we will examine in turn.

1. Identification of goals
   - define goals
   - pose questions
   - derive metrics
2. Plan measurement process
   - identify hypotheses
   - plan measurement
3. Perform measurement
   - data collection
   - data validation
4. Analysis and interpretation

1. *Identification of goals*. As has already been stated, identification of the measurement goal is the linchpin to GQM. Possible informal measurement goals are to:

- improve the software project effort prediction;
- identify unreliable software modules at design time;
- classify software product maintenance behaviour.

PURPOSE

(i) measurement approach e.g. to understand, classify, compare
(ii) object, either a product (e.g. functional requirements) or a process (e.g. design inspection)
(iii) reason (e.g. improve, eliminate)

PERSPECTIVE

e.g. software engineer, customer, project manager

ENVIRONMENT

a description of the organization in which the measurement object is embedded

Given the importance of defining a measurement goal, Basili provides a template structure which divides a goal into three components.[6]

To illustrate use of the template to structure measurement goals, consider the following, informally stated measurement goal:

To improve the accuracy of software project managers' cost estimates at the specification stage of a project within the Telecommunication Systems Division at Aardvark International.

This can be restructured to yield:

PURPOSE

(i) understand
(ii) factors that influence project costs
(iii) to improve costs estimation accuracy at the specification stage

PERSPECTIVE

project manager

ENVIRONMENT

the Telecommunication Systems Division at Aardvark International

The measurement approach will be to characterize project cost estimates so as to determine which factors lead to accurate and inaccurate estimation. This information can then form the basis of a programme to improve estimation process at the Telecommunication Systems Division at Aardvark International. On occasions it can be quite difficult to specify the measurement approach at this early stage; consequently, there can be a tendency to retreat into the use of 'weasel' words such as 'analyze' and 'assess'. Still, it is always possible to return to a goal and refine it during the measurement process.

Having defined the goal or goals, these then suggest questions, so from the above example goal, we might wish to ask:

Q1: Is the 'size' of the specification the major determinant of project costs?
Q2: Does project personnel experience influence costs?

It is generally accepted that progressing from goal to question is the most difficult aspect of GQM. The method provides little guidance, relying instead upon the judgement, experience and insight of those involved with measurement to identify

[6] The goal template has evolved over time; earlier versions have a fourth heading of measurement object.

useful questions. There exists a multiplicity of questions that could be asked about virtually any goal. The problem is choosing those questions likely to shed light or to support achievement of that goal. The top–down nature of GQM can also lead to difficulties. A goal may be so ambitious – for instance to eliminate all software defects prior to release – that it cannot readily be addressed by a manageable number of questions. Another problem is fuzzy goals. Despite the template it is difficult to eradicate completely goals such as 'improve software quality from the perspective of the development organization'. In such circumstances it would be better to backtrack and refine the goal than to continue to try to identify measurement questions.

Once the questions have been chosen, they must be quantified, so the question Q1 requires metrics to accomplish the following:

M1: measure specification 'size' (e.g. function points);
M2: measure project costs (e.g. person hours and staff grade).

Although a less difficult step than devising questions, identifying metrics is not a mechanistic step. In the above example, one could list a considerable number of candidate metrics for specification 'size'. Possibilities are function points, size of the specification in pages or words, the number of symbols if using a diagrammatic notation, DeMarco's 'bang' metric [18] and so forth. Choice should be governed by a combination of 'best practice' and what is feasible on pragmatic grounds. The 'bang' metric might be highly regarded in the literature, but if neither data flow nor entity–relationship diagrams are used as development aids, then collection of this metric could prove to be prohibitively expensive.

The output, from this first step of the GQM method, is a hierarchy of goals, questions and metrics as shown by Figure 5.6.

In this example there are two goals, G1 and G2, which have a question, Q2, in common. Metric M2 is needed by all three questions. The strength of GQM is that each metric identified is placed within a context, so metric M1 is collected in order to answer question Q1 to help to achieve goal G1. This re-use of questions and metrics in particular is not uncommon.

In practice, it is often helpful to introduce additional layers into the hierarchy so as to reduce the size of each refinement step. Rombach [42] describes some rules for

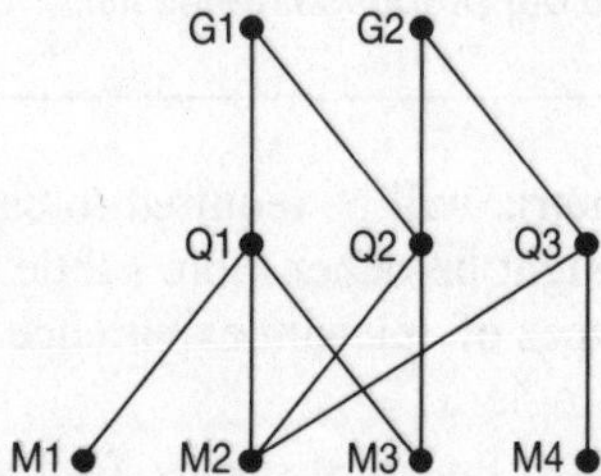

Figure 5.6 A GQM hierarchy of goals, questions and metrics

adding further levels into the hierarchy. He suggests that subgoals should address the following:

- the definition of the measurement object:
  - where the object is a *product* this should include quantitative characterization of both the product and the resources required to produce it,
  - where the object is a *process*, this should include quantitative characterization of the process and the process target;
- definition of the quality perspectives of concern, including the validity of any models employed and the data collected;
- feedback from these quality concerns to facilitate improvement, for example to find measurable early indicators of potential problems.

Another example of extending the GQM method to include subgoals and subquestions is to be found in the account of an experiment to validate some design metrics [44].

Given that metric collection may be difficult, unrepeatable or expensive, it is a good idea to validate the proposed metric set before proceeding to the next step of GQM. One effective way of accomplishing this is to build hypothetical profiles using the metrics that have been previously identified. The profiles can then be shown to an expert or target user, with a view to establishing whether they are able to interpret the data meaningfully without recourse to additional information. The outcome of this exercise will be to reveal whether the proposed metric list is inadequate or, conversely, contains redundant metrics. For instance, there may be little merit in collecting information on the number of years programming experience in C broken down by dialect, when the number of years of software development experience is sufficient.

Figure 5.7 shows hypothetical profiles of projects S1 and S2 based upon the metric list of function points and cost. One can imagine the following dialogue, based upon questions drawn from the GQM hierarchy:

Q: Why does project S2 appear to be more costly than project S1?
A: Well if the engineers were more experienced then....
Q: So you can't tell on the basis of function point size, alone?
A: Not really, because there's so much variation in the ability of our engineers.
QED: We need to add engineer experience as well to our proposed metric list.

It is evident from the responses that an additional metric will be required to capture average project experience. In reality, the problem might be rather more subtle since we would actually only be concerned about certain types of relevant experience.[7]

[7] Worse still, we might be confusing experience with ability. Empirical studies, for instance [46], suggest that the relationship between these two attributes is, at best, ill defined.

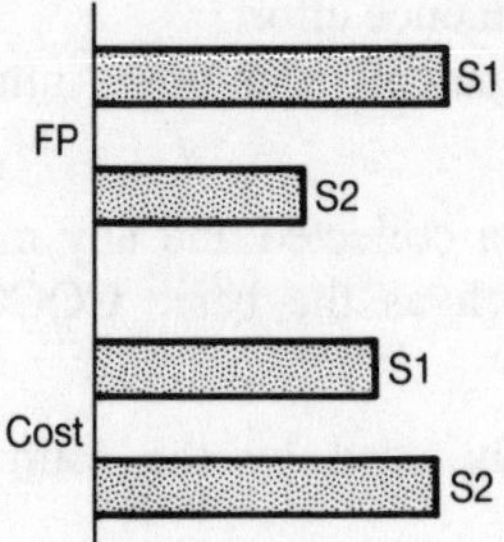

Figure 5.7 Hypothetical metrics profile

We conclude this first stage of the GQM method by returning to the cost estimation example in rather more detail.

G1: to understand factors that influence project costs in order to improve estimation accuracy at the specification stage from the perspective of project managers at the Telecommunication Systems Division of Aardvark International.

(Introduce subgoals.)

SG1.1: to establish the current accuracy of project cost estimates.

Q1.1.1 How are accurate are typical estimates at present?

Q1.1.2 Are estimates more accurate for new developments or for maintenance projects?

Q1.1.3 How does project manager experience in the group influence estimation accuracy?

(The aim here is for a quantitative characterization of the current process. The three questions are examples of the many questions that might be asked so as to better understand the current estimation process. Choosing pertinent questions is a skilful task and relies upon a detailed knowledge of the environment.)

SG1.2: to characterise the requirements specification documents used to estimate project costs.

Q1.2.1 Is the 'size' of the specification the major determinant of project resources?

(Supporting the aim to understand the process is the aim of a quantitative characterization of the object or objects upon which the process performs. In this case the main object will be the requirements specification document, although there could be other documents such as an invitation to tender and so forth.)

SG1.3: to determine the reliability of the historical data being used.

Q1.3.1 What is the likelihood of historical project estimation data being incorrect?

SG1.4: to determine the reliability of the estimation model currently used.

Q1.4.1 How accurately can managers estimate thousands of delivered source instructions (KDSI) at the specification stage of a project?

Q1.4.2 Does project personnel experience influence effort?
Q1.4.3 Does the choice of software development technology influence effort?

(It is also important to establish the validity of the data collected and any models employed, in this case a simple estimation model such as the basic COCOMO model,[8] with all development assumed to be embedded.)

SG1.5: to identify other factors, not presently used by the estimation process to improve accuracy.
Q1.5.1 Does project schedule compression influence effort?

(In addition this subgoal will share two of the questions linked to assessing the validity of the basic COCOMO model in this particular environment, namely Q1.4.2 and Q1.4.3.)

Having identified the various subgoals and questions, these must now be quantified. We discuss some of the issues for Q1.1.1 and then present the remainder of this worked example without further comment in Figure 5.7a.

Q1.1.1 How are accurate are typical estimates at present?
M1 Estimated project effort
M2 Actual project effort

(Metrics M1 and M2 make the assumption that there exists a single, well-defined point at which all project managers make their estimates. If this is not the case, one would need a series of estimates, dates and associated project milestones.)

Q1.1.2 Are estimates more accurate for new developments or for maintenance projects?
M1 Estimated project effort
M2 Actual project effort
M3 Project type (new or maintenance)

(Q1.1.2 re-uses the metrics M1 and M2 from Q1.1.1 and, in addition, requires the categorical measure of project type.)

The goal definition step of GQM is the most detailed and prescriptive part of the method. Subsequent steps rely increasingly upon the common sense, inter-personal and managerial skills of those involved in the measurement exercise.

2. *Plan the measurement process*. Having derived a GQM hierarchy, the second step in the method is to take this hierarchy and turn it into a detailed measurement plan specific to the environment of the measurement organization. This has two aspects: first it involves re-formulating the questions from the GQM hierarchy into hypotheses and second, planning for the measurement process. Typically, the GQM hierarchy produced out of the first step of the method will suggest many questions and a large number of metrics. It may well be impracticable to collect all these metrics at once, thus the second step is an opportunity to identify those parts of the

[8] Boehm's COCOMO effort estimation model is described in some detail in Chapter 4.

GQM hierarchy that are considered to be the most important. Even the simple example in Figure 5.7(a) has identified thirteen distinct metrics to collect. Factors to be taken into account include, cost, projected benefit and probability of success.

Plans for the measurement process must address both data collection, that is, how the measurements will be obtained, and data validation, or ensuring that the measurements are as accurate as possible. There exists a wide variety of data collection techniques which fall into two categories, manual and automated.

Manual techniques include form filling. Forms have the advantage that a number of pieces of information may be collected simultaneously and it is also possible to structure the responses, for instance by pre-defining categories or by influencing the order in which the data are entered. Form design is a highly skilled exercise and it is essential to have some form of trial before finalizing upon a particular design. Forms that are presented electronically can offer some benefits: they are more difficult to lose; validation rules can be built in; transfer of the information to other computer systems can be mechanized; and forms can be automatically presented at whatever time interval they are required so as to encourage their timely completion. Interviewing is the other commonly used manual technique. Its main strength is its flexibility; however, it is an extremely labour intensive technique, normally best suited to early or exploratory data collection.

Automated approaches include code analyers, CASE tools, audit and logging facilities of the kind often provided by operating systems and environments and custom built tools. Obviously, automation can greatly reduce collection costs and eliminate measurement error. Unfortunately, the scope of what can easily be automated is limited to computer based products and activities.

The importance of data validation can hardly be overstressed. As a minimum, we need to know how much reliance can be placed upon the measurement data; 200 hours ± 10 hours is hardly comparable to 200 hours ± 200 hours. Ideally, it is desirable to correct or filter out all erroneous data.

One validation technique is to sample. This involves random selection of a small percentage of the total population of measurement data to re-check, usually by interview, the validity of the data collected. If 20% of the sample prove to be inaccurate this implies that 20% of all the measurements taken are inaccurate. Hence we can determine how much confidence may be placed upon the data collected.

An alternative approach to data validation is to collect the data in two different ways and compare the results. For example, in a study to validate various design measures it was necessary to collect development effort in person hours. The subjects were requested to complete a simple form indicating how much effort had been expended. Effort was also measured, indirectly, by means of monitoring user connect time to the computer system via the operating system. The two sets of figures were compared. Interestingly, it was observed that, on a number of occasions, the connect time (comprising coding and test effort only) exceeded total reported development effort (comprising design and documentation time in addition to coding and testing effort). The explanation was that these developers tended to underrecord effort on the forms, since the actual effort required exceeded their

G1: To understand factors that influence project effort in order to improve estimation accuracy at the specification stage from the perspective of project managers at the Telecommunication Systems Division of Aardvark International

SG1.1 To establish the current accuracy of project effort estimates.

Q1.1.1: How accurate are typical estimates at present?

M1: Estimated project effort

M2: Actual project effort

Q1.1.2: Are estimates more accurate for new developments or for maintenance projects?

M1: Estimated project effort

M2: Actual project effort

M3: Project type (new or maintenance)

Q1.1.3: How does project manager experience in the group influence estimation accuracy?

M1: Estimated project effort

M2: Actual project effort

M4: No. of years as a project manager

SG1.2 To characterize the requirements specification documents used to estimate project effort.

Q1.2.1: Is the 'size' of the specification the major determinant of project effort?

M2: Actual project effort

M5: Requirements specification word count

SG1.3 To determine the reliability of the historical data being used.

Q1.3.1: What is the probability of historical project estimation data being incorrect?

M1: Estimated project effort

M2: Actual project effort

M6: 'Corrected'[9] estimated project effort

M7: 'Corrected' actual project effort

SG1.4 To determine the reliability of the estimation model currently used.

Q1.4.1: How accurately can managers estimate thousands of delivered source instructions (KDSI) at the specification stage of a project?

M8: Estimated KDSI

M9: Actual KDSI

Q1.4.2: Does project personnel experience influence effort?

M2: Actual project effort

M10: Median of project staff software development experience (years)

Q1.4.3: Does the choice of software development technology influence effort?

M2: Actual project effort

M11: Use of LOTOS (Y/N)

M12: Use of CASE tools (Y/N)

SG1.5 To identify other factors, not presently used by the estimation process to improve accuracy.

Q1.5.1: Does project schedule compression influence effort?

M2: Actual project effort

M13: Project duration

Q1.4.2: Does project personnel experience influence effort?

M2: Actual project effort

M10: Median of project staff software development experience (years)

Q1.4.3: Does the choice of software development technology influence effort?

M2: Actual project effort

M11: Use of LOTOS (Y/N)

M12: Use of CASE tools (Y/N)

Figure 5.7(a) A GQM example hierarchy

[9] It will be necessary to determine a method to correct for any inaccuracies in the data collection of these historical data. One possibility would be to use archived documents, another to interview staff from the projects concerned.

original expectations considerably. This additional effort was not thought to reflect very favourably upon their ability, and so the developers attempted to suppress this information.[10] The point of this anecdote is not to suggest that all developers behave in this fashion, but merely to highlight the value of measuring in two different ways. If it had not been for the connect time information, it would have been assumed that the data entered on to the forms was reliable.

Yet another validation technique is to use multi-variate outlier analysis. Although this sounds rather daunting, it simply involves looking for values that are unusual in the context of other variables for that particular observation. Consider the data set in Table 5.1.

At first glance it might appear that the values for project D are suspect. However, if we consider LOC in the context of effort expended,[11] project A would seem to be the most out of line and therefore worth re-examining. It may well be that the measurements are valid, albeit unusual; however, the technique at least enables the data to be highlighted and re-examined for validity.

3. *Perform measurement*. The third step for GQM is to actually perform the measurement process, as planned by the previous two steps. An important aspect is control. It is one thing to have a measurement plan; it is another to adhere to it. There are three reasons for departing from the plan – aside from the anarchic tendencies of a few.

First there is poor communication and training. It may be that staff are not fully aware of the planned measurement process, and therefore unintentionally deviate from it. The remedy is to incorporate training as an ongoing part of the measurement plan. Staff come and go, so it is seldom possible to see the training as a one-off exercise.

A second possibility is that under time and resource pressures – a common occurrence in software projects – short cuts are taken, or measurement is postponed,

Table 5.1 Project size and effort

Project	LOC	Effort
A	16	1
B	7	7
C	10	9
D	1278	1175
E	5	6

[10] This type of behaviour is an interesting example of the phenomenon that the psychologist Festinger termed 'cognitive dissonance'. The dissonance arises between the belief that the task is simple and ought to be completed in a given time period by any competent software developer and the reality that it is proving to be intractable and taking a great deal of effort. Subjects attempted to reduce their dissonance by reporting lower effort levels.

[11] In other words, we examine the ratio of the factors. In this case we have a LOC/effort ratio of approximately 1 for projects B to E, and 16 for project A.

thereby impacting the timeliness and almost certainly the accuracy of the data. This is really a management issue. Measurement has costs associated with it, and an effective measurement process must be adequately funded, a point that we will return to in Section 5.6.

The third reason why a measurement plan may not be fully adhered to is that there may be scope for improving the plan. It is an often overlooked possibility that the initial measurement plan may be impracticable or cumbersome in certain aspects. Those staff encountering such difficulties may choose to 'fix' the measurement plan by deviating from it. Clearly, this is a dangerous situation as it may lead to a whole range of local 'fixes', many of which could conflict. On the other hand it is important to acknowledge that plans can be improved and that the planning step of GQM may be highly iterative. Prototyping or pilot studies can help to limit the size of such changes.

4. *Analysis and interpretation*. The fourth and final step for GQM is to make use of the metrics that have been collected.The method supports this stage to the extent that any analysis will be in the context of a goal or objective. Moreover, the method requires the re-formulation of the questions from the GQM hierarchy as hypotheses, which again supports the analysis step, since a large number of statistical techniques are concerned with hypothesis acceptance or rejection at a given level of confidence or probability. Clearly, there exists an enormous variety of analysis techniques, not all of which will be appropriate for any given situation. Despite these difficulties, one cannot avoid the feeling that GQM – and other metrics methods – tend to side-step these issues. Chapter 7 describes a range of analytical techniques in detail.

Finally, whilst looking at the GQM method, we should note the related work of Basili on the improvement paradigm [1]. He argues that measurement and analysis should be a long term issue and must therefore extend throughout the entire software lifecycle. Figure 5.8 shows the four basic steps in the paradigm. In effect the GQM method is embedded into Steps 2(a), 3 and 4, within the overall context of the improvement paradigm. This is partly the result of GQM having originally been concerned with single projects, whilst the improvement paradigm represents an attempt by Basili to scale the method up to organizations over long timescales.

1. Characterizing the environment
2. Planning
   (a) using GQM to define goals for the software process and product
   (b) choosing and tailoring the process model
3. Analysis using GQM to relate measurements to questions and hypotheses
4. Learning and feedback, relating measurements to goals from GQM

Return to Step 1

Figure 5.8 The improvement paradigm

GQM Evaluation

The GQM method is without doubt the most influential metrics method presently in existence. Despite the deceptive simplicity of the GQM hierarchy it offers useful guidance, especially in the early stages of measurement. The emphasis upon goals and goal driven measurement has provided a necessary check against some earlier metrics work which gave all the appearance of metrics searching for a purpose,[12] rather than the other way around. Under GQM, metrics can only be collected for the purpose of supporting a clearly articulated goal. The method is also much more flexible than either FCM or QFD since it can address other measurement issues aside from the quality of the delivered product. It can be applied to small or large scale measurement problems, in the laboratory and in the workplace and it is as applicable to process measurement as to products.

Nevertheless, certain difficulties remain. Referring back to the generic measurement process portrayed by Figure 5.1, it will be seen that GQM provides strong support for the planning aspect of measurement. By contrast, there is little guidance for the collection and analysis aspects. This is unfortunate, as analysis, in particular, is a highly skilful part of the measurement process. The method emphasizes validation during the planning stages – and to some extent during collection – but, again, it does not feature prominently within the later stages of the measurement process. Up to a point, this lack of support for the collection and analysis of metrics is to be expected; collection processes depend intimately upon local details and vagaries; analysis depends upon the specific features of the measurement goals and data sets under scrutiny. None the less, given the importance of analysis, and the rather weak work carried out in this area by some software engineers in the past, this is a natural area for extension of a metric method and would seem to be a valuable research topic.

Other concerns with GQM relate to its top–down approach. This can be difficult for exploratory analysis, where establishing the relevance of questions, or even posing the questions in the first place, can be quite problematic. There is also the danger of setting overambitious goals. When working in a top–down fashion, the cost or the consequence of a decision is not always apparent. If we start with a seemingly modest goal, such as to reduce software maintenance costs, this can multiply down through the GQM hierarchy into an impracticably large number of metrics. Grady [22] describes how the use of GQM at Hewlett-Packard led to the identification of thirty-one questions and a list of thirty-five distinct metrics, clearly

[12] The problems of metrics without goals are typified by much of the complexity metric research over the past twenty years. Complexity can then be interpreted to mean one of a wide range of attributes for an equally wide range of purposes. The enormous range of applications proposed for Halstead's software science metrics [25] is a good example of this type of problem. In the end the wisdom of this type of approach depends upon one's belief in the existence of a universal measure suitable for all software development environments and objectives. Chapter 1 discusses the matter in more depth, with particular respect to modelling.

too many. And although the second step of the GQM method provides an opportunity to prune the tree, or at least to aim for phased implementation, it can still be too easy for questions and metrics to proliferate. The problem then emerges of how we decide which areas of the hierarchy to focus upon. Which avenues will be the most fruitful to pursue? Again, GQM provides no direct help.

An inevitable feature of a top–down approach to measurement is a certain degree of backtracking. A frequent occurrence is the modification of a goal in the light of the subsequent analysis. Questions, metrics, the planning and execution of measurement may all conspire to modify a measurement goal. Although we may not always work in a strictly top–down manner – as GQM might seem to imply – it at least provides a coherent framework to structure and document measurement work, even if this turns out to be a rather retrospective affair.[13]

Another area of concern is that the method has no formal concept of model building. This might appear somewhat academic, but, as this book has tried to show, model building is an integral part of measurement, and although GQM does nothing to prevent the development and use of models, it is arguable that this should be made a more central part of software measurement.

Lastly, the GQM method could be criticized on the grounds that it has a very weak view of process. By this it is meant that it is important not only to consider what is being measured, but when during the software engineering process it is being measured. Consider design measurement. The metric will have an entirely different meaning if it is collected during the initial, first cut design, as opposed to either subsequent optimization in order to enhance execution performance or to re-engineer an elderly system experiencing maintenance difficulties. The relationship between measurement and process is so important that Chapter 8 is entirely devoted to this topic.

Despite these various concerns, GQM is a highly important metrics method, which can provide much useful guidance to the would-be software measurer. Moreover, many of the concerns above could be incorporated into the basic GQM framework without undue difficulty.

5.4 Process based methods

At the same time as Basili was working on goal centred measurement, the Software Engineering Institute at the University of Carnegie-Mellon began to consider the role of process within a software development organization. In other words, it is important not only to consider measurable attributes of software products but also the methods and techniques that lead to their construction. The work, led by Humphrey [26, 28], was driven by the needs of the US Department of Defense to evaluate the capability of their various software suppliers. A five level process

[13] For a brilliantly argued case for this type of approach to software design see the paper by Parnas and Clements [39].

maturity model, shown by Figure 5.9, was used as a basis for the assessment. However, the process maturity model can be used aside from capability assessment[14] for process improvement purposes.

Maturity is assessed by a questionnaire containing questions, such the following:

- Is there a software engineering process group or function?
- Are code and test errors projected and compared to actuals?
- Are statistics gathered on software design errors?
- Does senior management have a mechanism for the regular review of the status of software development projects?
- Is a mechanism used for ensuring compliance with the software engineering standards?

The yes/no responses are then analyzed, leading to the classification of the organization by maturity level.[15] This can be backed up by either an SEI assisted inspection team or by an internal inspection by the software development organization only. At its inception in 1987, more than 80% of all software organizations were classified as level one and no organization exceeded level three. Since then there has been a phenomenal growth of interest in this approach to process assessment. Recently it has been reported that a couple of US and one Japanese software developer have attained level five [27]. Humphrey *et al.* [29] describe in some detail the work at Hughes Aircraft to progress from a maturity level of two to three.

The attractions of process maturity model are two-fold. First, it helps software development organizations to establish – albeit in a very simplistic fashion – where

1. *Initial*: characterized by *ad hoc* processes and a lack of control.

2. *Repeatable* : overall processes controlled by basic management mechanisms, but with a lack of internal visibility (i.e. a black box view of software projects).

3. *Defined*: here activities within a process are known and intermediate products well defined (i.e. a move towards a glass box view of software project processes).

4: *Managed*: processes are measured; however, they make only restricted use of the measurement.

5. *Optimizing* : such processes are dynamic and are characterized by their use of measurement for process feedback and improvement.

Figure 5.9 Five level process maturity model

[14] The term capability is used by the SEI in the specific sense of assessing the reliability of software contractors from a procurement point of view.

[15] Each maturity level is further subdivided into quartiles, giving a rise to a twenty-point weak order.

they and their competitors are. Second, it clearly defines an improvement path so that software developers are guided as to where to focus their attention at each level of maturity. So, despite some criticism[16] it is a highly influential model of software development processes.

As it stands the process maturity approach is not – and was not intended to be – a method to support software measurement. However, it has some significance for measurement, in that it recognizes that not all software development organizations have the necessary infrastructure to support complex measurement programmes. A level one organization – one characterized by out of control processes differing from project to project in an unpredictable fashion – will have difficulties with almost all aspects of measurement. It is arguable that only the most basic types of measure can be useful in such circumstances and that effort would be better devoted to improving processes and making them more stable.

Because of this relationship between the maturity of an organization's process and its ability to support and benefit from software measurement, there have been several recent efforts to integrate data collection into software development, such as the work by Pfleeger and McGowan [41]. They argue that metrics collection should be tied to the process maturity level of an organization, as shown in Table 5.2.

As well as suggesting suitable metrics for each level of process maturity, Pfleeger and McGowan also outline nine steps that form a necessary part of any measurement programme. These include assessing the process, determining and collecting the metrics and constructing a project database.

Table 5.2 Pfleeger and McGowan process level metrics

Process level	Metric type	Example metrics
1. Initial	baseline	product size, staff effort
2. Repeatable	project	function points, actual and reported person months of effort
3. Defined	product	number of modules, cyclomatic complexity, number of object interfaces to test
4. Managed	process and feedback for control	level of component re-use, module completion rate over time
5. Optimizing	process and feedback for modifying process	no specific recommendations at present

[16] Most criticisms centre around the fact that the model is vulnerable to manipulation, does not take into account the negative impact of bad practice and is somewhat hypothetical regarding the higher levels, since no level four or five organizations existed when it was defined [9]. See Card [13] for a balanced summary of the arguments for and against process maturity.

Although the linkage between process maturity is a useful idea, there is a danger that rigid adherence to the Pfleeger and McGowan hierarchy of metric type may prove inflexible. Even within a level one organization there can exist considerable variations in process maturity. Some processes can be stable and well defined, despite an organizational backdrop of *ad hoc* and out of control processes. As a result, this approach can impose unnecessary limitations on the metrics that may be used effectively. More serious is the way in which they advocate a base set of metrics for each level without any consideration of needs and objectives. Whether a particular metric, or metric set, is useful depends not only upon the maturity level of the organization, but even more upon why it wishes to measure in the first place. Metric types for process levels are therefore best treated as a heuristics, as opposed to a full blown method for software measurement.

5.5 European approaches

The importance of measurement for the software industry, and especially the need for a transfer of measurement technology, has been recognized by the European Union ESPRIT Research Programme. As a result, there have been a number of research projects in the general area of software metrics, including MUSE, METKIT, COSMOS, MERMAID and SCOPE. The application of measurement in industry method (AMI) is another such project specifically concerned with producing a method to support the industrial use of software metrics. It is a collaborative project involving a consortium of nine organizations from France, Germany, Italy and the UK. The chief output from the project is a handbook [35] that describes the AMI method.

The AMI method is somewhat eclectic in its approach to software measurement. It has flavours of Deming's plan–do–check–act cycle [19], GQM combined with use of the SEI process maturity model and Fenton's metric classification [20]. The basic structure of AMI is indicated by Figure 5.10, which shows the four basic stages.

1. *Assessment* is the starting point for the AMI method. The aim is to better understand the organization or measurement environment using the SEI process maturity model (described in the preceding section). From this understanding we can derive the primary goals for measurement. These goals must be consistent with the process maturity of the organization. The goal to produce zero defect software might be considered ambitous for an organization characterized by *ad hoc* processes.
2. *Analyze* is in some ways a misleading name for the second stage of AMI, as it is really concerned with deriving metrics. This takes the primary goals and applies a GQM-like technique to derive a hierarchy or goals tree of goals, questions and metrics. To support the derivation of metrics the AMI handbook provides lists of 'well-tried metrics' which should be used whenever possible. Clearly, benefiting from past experience is good advice, though the question must remain as to how arbitrary is the process of approving metrics.

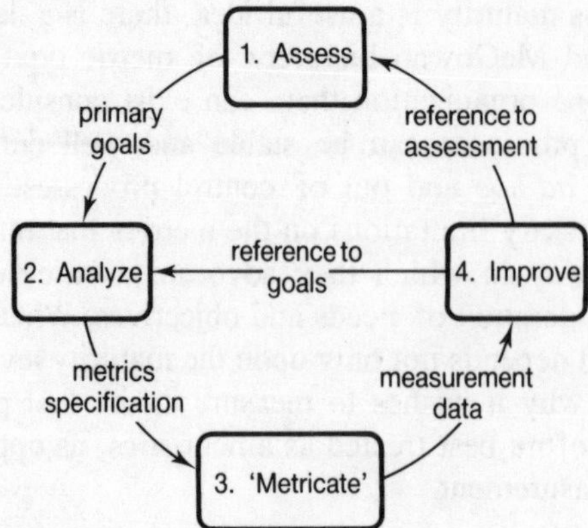

Figure 5.10 The AMI measurement method

3. '*Metricate*' is the step concerned with producing the measurement plan and collecting and verifying the metrics. The plan includes details of the measurement objectives, metric definitions, responsibilities and support material for each step. An independent check of the plan is advised to eliminate any unforeseen planning errors. The actual implementation stage of the method is only given cursory treatment; the handbook indicates design guidelines for data collection forms and gives recommendations on the use of testing, project management, spreadsheets and testing tools for data collection, and data verification activities.
4. *Improve*: is the final stage of the AMI method and deals with the analysis, interpretation and application of the measurement results. The use of basic exploratory data analysis techniques and simple graphical displays is recommended for statistical analysis.

Is the method of value? Basically as an extension of Basili and Rombach's GQM approach it takes more account of the organizational infrastructure and process maturity. It has the merits of clarity and simplicity. And, significantly, it is presented in a manner that renders it more accessible to software practitioners. Like the other metric methods, most attention is focused upon choosing and defining metrics; yet, again, analysis seems to be the poor relation. This is unfortunate, as elsewhere the AMI handbook is full of useful practical advice for any organization contemplating using software metrics.

5.6 People and measurement

Software measurement methods are developed to produce a structured, orderly approach to the utilization of metrics, typically for staff who have not previously been involved. Unfortunately, most metric methods do not directly address the human and political implications of introducing measurement into a software development organization. Senior management must be persuaded that the costs associated with any measurement programme represent a wise investment. Cynicism must be overcome. Champions must be found. Those collecting the measures must be certain that the results will not be used unfairly against them. Staff in positions of authority must appreciate the need not to appraise individuals using simplistic and arbitrary metrics. And so on.

A notable exception to this tendency to overlook the people actually involved in a software measurement is the ten step or company-wide metric programme, developed at Hewlett-Packard by Grady and Caswell [24]. Although their approach is founded upon statistical process control,[17] it does emphasize many of the non-technical aspects of using metrics within a organization, and, in particular, the concept of 'selling' software metrics.

The Grady and Caswell method involves the steps shown by Figure 5.11. Grady and Caswell advocate starting with a base set of metrics to get statistical quality control established, followed by adapting or developing alternative metrics specific to the company. Emphasis is placed on studying in order to improve company processes and reduce negative deviations of product characteristics from statistical baselines. However, what makes this method of particular interest is the way in which measurement is explicitly placed in an organizational context and attention is paid to promoting measurement. It is an unfortunate fact that there exists considerable resistance to software metrics within the software engineering community. Some of this can be justified by the relatively poor track record of

Determine the who, what and why of measurement
1. Define company objectives
2. Assign responsibilities

Find useful metrics
3. Do research
4. Define initial set of metrics

Do measurement
5. Sell the collection
6. Get tools for collection and analysis consistency

Promote continued measurement
7. Establish a training class
8. Publish success stories and exchange ideas
9. Create a metrics database
10. Establish a mechanism of change in an orderly way

Figure 5.11 Company-wide metric programme

[17] Statistical process control (SPC) is the application of statistics to determine limits within which a process should operate. Such ideas have been widely applied to manufacturing, where outputs should ordinarily fall within certain tolerances. A major implication is that repeating the process should lead to a similar outcome. It has been argued that this is often not the case for software production, and this is enshrined in the chaotic/repeatable process philosophy of the SEI process maturity work [26]

metrics in the past and the tendency to promote each new software technology as a panacea. Other, less well-justified, causes for resistance are poor communication, organizational inertia and the dislike by some individuals of change. The company-wide method seeks to overcome these problems by education, exhortation and good example.

More recent developments in the use of the programme at Hewlett-Packard are described by Cox [17] and Grady [23]. Like any method, it is capable of improvement. Cox notes certain areas of deficiency, including the lack of information available from the central software metrics database. Users have reported that it contains insufficient descriptive data to fully understand the 'whys and wherefores' of individual projects. Without this information it was difficult for the database users to have confidence in the applicability of the historical data.[18] Another difficulty is the inability of the metrics database to support the needs of senior management, whose concerns are with entire product lines and the productivity of whole departments rather than counts of non-commented lines of code. These observations reinforce the need to ensure that measurement is goal centred. Despite these technical difficulties, it is clear that the major contribution to the effective use of measurement at Hewlett-Packard has been the creation of a measurement culture. This is in no small part due to company-wide awareness of software metrics and their value and the creation of an organizational infrastructure to underpin software measurement.

Finally, reported usage of the method in other organizations suggests that it may be too specific to Hewlett-Packard's management environment and rather less effective as an 'off the shelf' method. Some tailoring to suit different organizational cultures and needs may therefore be necessary. One situation where this is likely to be the case is when the scope is less than companywide. On many occasions, measurement will only concern a single project or department, whereas the company-wide approach – as the name suggests – is concerned with whole, or at least significant parts, of organizations.

In addition to those issues highlighted by Grady and Caswell at Hewlett-Packard, there remain many other non-technical issues which ought to be considered when implementing measurement. We will briefly consider four such issues which can have a major bearing upon any software measurement exercise. These are migrating costs, the Hawthorne effect, the Kelvin syndrome and the cost of measurement.

(i) Migrating costs

As DeMarco states 'rational, competent men and women can work effectively to maximise any single observed indication of success' [18]. The software industry is full of such people so one needs to be extremely careful about setting partial targets.

[18] It is interesting to note that some other methods, such as GQM, overcome this particular problem by requiring the user to document the measurement environment as part of the goal template.

If we monitor one aspect of a software process or product in great detail and fail to measure other areas, then costs will have a tendency to migrate to those areas that are least well monitored. The most common example is delivery date and overall software quality. Delivery date is a high profile success indicator whilst quality may not be formally observed, or at least not in any quantitative sense. The upshot will be much energy devoted to meeting a delivery deadline but at the expense of the quality of the product. Another area that is extremely difficult to measure is maintainability, so, again, there is a tendency for costs to drift from areas such as effort expended to future maintenance costs.

A related problem is that of perceived goals. There is a danger that the mere act of measuring a particular attribute will convey the impression that it has become an objective. The potential influence of imputed goals can be seen from an experiment conducted by Weinberg and Schulman [47]. Five software development teams were each given a different goal, for instance to write the system in the shortest possible time or to minimize the program size. Next, the performance of each team was compared to that of the other teams and it was found that each team rated best at its own goal, despite variations in overall team ability.

The moral is clear. Educate staff and be very wary of single measures of software quality.

(ii) The Hawthorne effect

Another phenomenon sometimes associated with measurement is that of the Hawthorne effect, so called because it was first reported after an empirical study conducted at the Hawthorne Plant in the US. The study into the impact of lighting levels upon productivity was confounded by the discovery that making changes – both increasing and decreasing lighting levels – caused productivity to increase. The generally accepted explanation is that the investigation itself, and the attendant variations to normal work patterns, caused an increase in motivation and hence productivity [36]. The basic principle is that the act of measuring or observing can cause the process to behave differently than if no measurement or observation had taken place. Some potential examples as follows

- Measuring software designs may create variety and stimulation, thereby causing software engineers to improve their productivity.
- Collecting McCabe's metric v(G) [37] could cause programmers to partition modules in order to reduce v(G), even if the aim of the exercise is merely to see if any relationship exists between v(G) and reliability.

There is no simple solution, although involving staff in the measurement process and explaining its purpose may help. Sometimes it is possible to be unobtrusive so that staff are unaware that they are being measured. However, secrets are not always well kept, so there is a risk of creating resentment once staff realize that they have been under surveillance. Failing this, measurement analysts should at least be aware of this phenomenon and take it into account both when designing collection procedures and when analyzing the resultant data.

(iii) The Kelvin syndrome

> When you can measure what you are speaking about, and can express it in numbers, you know something about it; but when you cannot measure it, when you cannot express it in numbers, then your knowledge is of a meagre and unsatisfactory kind.

This quotation, from a public address by Lord Kelvin in 1889, is rightly famous for emphasizing the important role of measurement in understanding and analysis. However, the conclusion that therefore all metrics must always be useful is a *non sequitur*. Likewise, measurement might give an appearance of control but it is not necessarily the case. Metrics based upon flawed, incomplete or inappropriate models are not only of no value; they can be positively misleading. In the quest for a software engineering panacea it is essential that any measures used are carefully validated.

(iv) Cost of measurement

You get the quality of measurement that you pay for. It may be an obvious point but measurement programmes cost money. Costs that can easily be overlooked include the following:

- education and training;
- consultancy;
- tool development;
- learning and improvement.

The last point requires special emphasis. Mistakes can and will be made, especially during the early stages of a measurement exercise. It is difficult to set an exact figure on the costs of measurement since it will be so dependent upon the exact nature of the measurements required and the environment from which they must be collected. None the less, authorities such as DeMarco suggest costs as high as 10% [18], whilst Card and Glass report 7–8% of total project costs at the NASA Software Engineering Laboratory [14]. This reinforces the need for careful cost–benefit analysis (see e.g. Grady [23]). Conversely, if budgets are pre-determined, then it is important to ensure that measurement goals are appropriate to the available resources.

5.7 Summary

In this chapter we have seen the need for structure and discipline in the complex process of applying measurement to software engineering. Using metrics successfully is difficult; hence it is hardly surprising that there has only been limited adoption by the software industry. The result has been the recognition of the need for methods in order to guide people in the use of software measurement, to codify good practice and to support the re-use of successful measurement experiences.

The earliest methods such as factor criteria metric (FCM) and quality factor deployment (QFD) were based upon the desire to quantify software quality. This is useful, but fairly restrictive. The goal question metric (GQM) approach was the first truly general measurement method, and its importance in ensuring that any measurement exercise is firmly tied to specific objectives can hardly be underestimated. Other approaches have emphasized the role of the development process (SEI and process maturity) and organizational and human issues (the company-wide programme at Hewlett-Packard).

Despite this progress, there remain parts of the measurement process for which these methods provide little support, in particular the analysis stages. This is clearly an area for further work.

Methods are intended to be our servants, not our masters. Hence, one should not be hesitant about following only those parts that appear useful for a particular measurement task and environment. In other situations, more than one approach could be beneficial. It is naïve to expect a single 'best' method to exist. Which is the 'best' method critically depends upon the exact nature of the measurement exercise and measurement environment. Also, methods evolve. As lessons are learnt through using methods so these can be fed back into improving and extending methods. Thus, it would seem highly likely that the measurement methods in use ten years hence will not be those described in this chapter. None the less, it is probable that their lineage will be apparent.

5.8 Exercises and further reading

1. Use the quality factor deployment (QFD) approach for a management decision support system. Assume that the customer has the following quality requirements (the priorities are given in parentheses):

   'quick to learn' (2)
   'easy to use' (3)
   'gives helpful advice' (4)
   'makes few mistakes' (3)

   Complete a QFD matrix identifying appropriate design requirements which should be measurable. Validate your matrix.
2. Using the GQM approach, suggest a measurement based solution for the following, sadly not fictitious, example.

   Soft Touch Systems supply 'off the shelf' PC-based software to small businesses to handle accounts, stock control and so on. They have been in the business for only three years but, thanks to aggressive marketing, have attained a significant market share. However, they are now experiencing severe problems. The company has found that the software, which was originally developed rather hurriedly, contains many faults leading to increased numbers of customer problems. The software is also poorly structured and very badly documented.

In common with similar businesses, they find it necessary to provide customers with telephone support (a 'hot-line') to help them deal with problems they encounter. (If they did not, they would not be able to sell so much.) Customer numbers have increased dramatically during the past eighteen months – presently there are about 4000 – and the customer support (CS) department has expanded to nine full time staff, out of a total of 48.

Most of the customer support staff are recently recruited and inexperienced (they tend not to stay long!). They are under intense pressure from the very high volume of customer telephone calls – often desperate and angry – and, hence, have no time to learn about the products.

When faults in the software are found to be responsible for the problems, the CS staff usually find it impossible to fix them and they have to call upon the software development (SD) staff (who originally wrote it). This prevents the SD staff from getting on with the task of upgrading the software and developing new products (which is jeopardizing future business). The user manual has also proved poor and gives users insufficient guidance. It is difficult to keep track of customer problems since one problem may result in several telephone calls, and these are often handled by different CS staff and there is a lack of communication within the CS department because they are all on the phone much of the time.

The CS manager is trying to monitor the situation and has implemented a system of customer record cards upon which each telephone call is recorded, assuming that the card can be found! He is also trying to keep a record of all the software faults discovered (about 1000 in the last year), but categorization and filing is very problematical.

At the eleventh hour there has been a friendly takeover of Soft Touch Systems with the possibility of an injection of capital. However, the parent company requires objective evidence to support any new investment.

You have been called in as an independent software measurement consultant, to advise the managing director regarding the best course of action.

[Hint: There may be more than one goal.]

3. To what extent do you consider the packaging or presentation of a method to facilitate its uptake? Contrast the approach of GQM with AMI.
4. 'Measurement technology is especially difficult to transfer because its proper use will affect the entire organisation.' (Rombach [43].) From your experience, list areas of difficulty and, for each one, indicate how it could be overcome.
5. Cost–benefit analysis (CBA) can be used to support decision making. In order to conduct such an analysis, identify what measurements would be required for the following scenario.

   Albatross Software is a medium-sized software house specializing in the development of real-time control systems, typically using Ada and Unix based workstations. The structured development method of RT/SASD is adhered to. A recent internal process assessment has determined that the software house is operating at the repeatable level (2) of process maturity. Presently, the company employs approximately fifty software engineers working on eight projects.

The company is operating in an increasingly competitive market and is seeking a marketing edge over its rivals. The marketing department has suggested that using object-oriented technology would be attractive to customers and increase sales by an estimated 10% or £5m. The company tenders with a profit margin of 10%, assuming of course that costs are estimated correctly. Project managers can estimate accurately since the organization has a stable process and is developing very similar software products.

Should Albatross Software adopt object-oriented development methods?

[Hint: Grady [23] suggests using the headings of training, management, engineering, capital expenses, time to market, job complexity, customer-satisfaction and sales to structure a CBA. For further background information on OO technology transfer see [12]].

Basili, V.R. and H.D. Rombach, 'The TAME project: Towards Improvement-oriented software environments', *IEEE Trans. on Softw. Eng.*, **14**(6), 758–71, 1988.

An important paper crammed with insights concerning the successful application of metrics. Included is a brief account of both the GQM and the improvement paradigms.

Grady, R.B., *Practical Software Metrics for Project Management and Process Improvement*, Prentice-Hall: Englewood Cliffs, 1992.

An excellent book containing many valuable insights, derived from the author's experience at Hewlett-Packard, into the practical aspects of software measurement in an industrial context.

Kitchenham, B.A., 'Towards a constructive quality model Part I : Software quality modelling, measurement and prediction', *Softw. Eng. J.*, **2**(4), 105–13, 1987.

COnstructive QUAlity MOdel (COQUAMO) is another quality based metrics method which was developed under the ESPRIT project REQUEST. It focuses upon software quality throughout the construction process. Petersen *et al.* [40] provide another, more recent, account.

Kuntzmann-Combelles, A. *et al.*, eds., *Handbook of the Application of Metrics in Industry: A quantitative approach to software management*. AMI ESPRIT Project: 1992.

This handbook is a highly readable reference source for the AMI metrics method. Essential reading for anybody considering following the AMI approach for using software metrics in earnest.

Rombach, H.D. and V.R. Basili, 'Practical benefits of goal-oriented measurement', in *Proc. Annual Workshop of the Centre for Software Reliability: Reliability and Measurement*, eds. Fenton, N.E. and Littlewood, B. Garmisch-Partenkirchen, West-Germany: Elsevier, 1990.

Gives a short comparison of three metrics methods, FCM, QFD and GQM before describing in some depth the advantages of top–down and goal driven software measurement.

References

[1] Basili, V.R., 'Software development: a paradigm for the future', in *Proc. COMPSAC, 13th Annu. Compute Softw. and Applications Conf.* IEEE, 1989.

[2] Basili, V.R. and B.T. Perricone, 'Software errors and complexity: an empirical investigation', *CACM*, **27**(1), 42–52, 1984.

[3] Basili, V.R. and H.D. Rombach, 'The TAME project: Towards improvement-oriented software environments', *IEEE Trans. on Softw. Eng.*, **14**(6), 758–71, 1988.

[4] Basili, V.R. and D. Selby, 'Data collection and analysis in software research and management', in *Proc. American Stat. Assoc. and Biomedical Soc. Joint Statistical Meeting*. Philadelphia, PA: 1984.

[5] Basili, V.R. and D.M. Weiss, 'A methodology for collecting valid software engineering data', *IEEE Trans. on Softw. Eng.*, **10**(3), 728–38, 1984.

[6] Bennett, P.A., 'Safety', in *Software Engineer's Reference Book*, J.A. McDermid, ed., Butterworth-Heinemann: Oxford, 1991.

[7] Boehm, B.W. *et al.*, *Characteristics of Software Quality* North-Holland: Amsterdam, 1978.

[8] Boehm, B.W., J.R. Brown and M. Lipow, 'Quantitative evaluation of software quality', in *Proc. 2nd Intl. Conf. on Softw. Eng.* IEEE Computer Society Press, 1976.

[9] Bollinger, T.B. and C. McGowan, 'A critical look at software capability evaluations', *IEEE Softw.*, **8**(4), 25–41, 1991.

[10] Bowen, J.B., 'Module size: a standard or heuristic?', *J. of Syst. and Softw.*, **4**, 327–32, 1984.

[11] Brown, P.G., 'QFD: echoing the voice of the customer', *AT & T Tech. J.*, **70**(2), 18–32, 1991.

[12] Capper, N.P. *et al.*, 'The impact of object-oriented technology on software quality: three case histories', *IBM Syst. J.*, **33**(1), 131–57, 1994.

[13] Card, D., 'Understanding process improvement', *IEEE Softw.*, **8**(4), 102–3, 1991.

[14] Card, D. and R. Glass, *Measuring Software Design Quality*. Addison-Wesley: Reading, Mass., 1990.

[15] Card, D.N., G.T. Page and F.E. McGarry, 'Criteria for software modularization', in *Proc. 8th Intl. Softw. Eng. Conf.* London: Computer Society, 1985.

[16] Cavano, J.P. and J.A. McCall. 'A framework for the measurement of software quality', in *Proc. Softw. Quality Assurance Workshop*. San Diego, Calif.: 1978.

[17] Cox, G., 'Sustaining a metrics programme in industry, in *Software Reliability and Metrics*, B. Littlewood and N.E. Fenton, eds., Elsevier Applied Science: London, 1991.

[18] DeMarco, T., *Controlling Software Projects. Management, measurement and estimation.* Yourdon Press: NY, 1982.

[19] Deming, W.E., *Out of the Crisis*. MIT Press: Cambridge Mass., 1986.

[20] Fenton, N.E., *Software Metrics: A rigorous approach.* Chapman & Hall: London, 1991.

[21] Finkelstein, L. and M.S. Leaning, 'A review of the fundamental concepts of measurement', *Measurement*, **2**(1), 25–34, 1984.

[22] Grady, R.B., 'Measuring and managing the software maintenance process', *IEEE Softw.*, **4**(5), 35–45, 1987.

[23] Grady, R.B., *Practical Software Metrics for Project Management and Process Improvement*. Prentice-Hall: Englewood Cliffs, N.J., 1992.

[24] Grady, R.B. and D.L. Caswell, *Software Metrics: Establishing a company wide program*. Prentice-Hall: Englewood Cliffs, N.J. 1987.

[25] Halstead, M.H., 'Advances in software science', in *Advances in Computers*, M. Yovits, ed., Academic Press: NY, 1979.

[26] Humphrey, W.S., 'Characterising the software process: a maturity framework', *IEEE Softw.*, **5**(2), 73–9, 1988.

[27] Humphrey, W.S., D.H. Kitson and J. Gale, 'A comparison of US and Japanese software process maturity', in *Proc. 13th International Conference on Software Engineering*. IEEE Computer Society Press: Austin, Texas: 1991.

[28] Humphrey, W.S., D.H. Kitson and T.C. Kasse, The state of software engineering practice: a preliminary report', in *Proc. 11th International Conference on Software Engineering*. IEEE Computer Society Press: Pittsburg, 1989.

[29] Humphrey, W.S., T.R. Snyder and R.R. Willis, 'Software process improvement at Hughes Aircraft', *IEEE Softw.*, **8**(4), 11–23, 1991.

[30] Kitchenham, B.A., 'Towards a constructive quality model Part I: Software quality modelling, measurement and prediction', *Softw. Eng. J.*, **2**(4), 105–13, 1987.

[31] Kitchenham, B.A., 'An introduction to software metrics', in *PC Business Software*. vol. 16(4), April 1991, pp. 6–9.

[32] Kitchenham, B.A. and J.G. Walker, 'The meaning of quality', in *Proc. Software Engineering '86*. eds. Barnes, D. and Brown, P., Southampton, UK: Peter Peregrinus, 1986.

[33] Kogure, M. and Y. Akao, 'Quality function deployment and CWQC in Japan', *Quality Progress* (October), pp. 25–9, 1983.

[34] Krantz, D.H. *et al.*, *Foundations of Measurement*. Vol. 1. Academic Press: London, 1971.

[35] Kuntzmann-Combelles, A. *et al.*, eds., *Handbook of the Application of Metrics in Industry: A quantitative approach to software management*. AMI ESPRIT project: South Bank University, London, 1992.

[36] Mayo, E., *The Human Problems of an Industrial Civilisation*. Macmillan: 1933.

[37] McCabe, T.J., 'A complexity measure', *IEEE Trans. on Softw. Eng.*, **2**(4), 308–20, 1976.

[38] McCall, J.A., P.K. Richards and G.F. Walters, Factors in software quality. Report No. NTIS AD/A-049 014 015, US Rome Air Development Center, 1977.

[39] Parnas, D.L. and P.C. Clements, 'A rational design process: How and why to fake it', *IEEE Trans. on Softw. Eng.*, **12**(2), 251–7, 1986.

[40] Petersen, P.G. *et al.* 'Software quality drivers and indicators', in *Proc. Hawaii Intl. Conf. on Systems Science*. Hawaii, 1989.

[41] Pfleeger, S.L. and C. McGowan, 'Software metrics in the process maturity framework', *J. of Syst. Softw.*, **12**, 255–61, 1990.

[42] Rombach, H.D. and V.R. Basili, 'Practical benefits of goal-oriented measurement', in *Proc. Annual Workshop of the Centre for Software Reliability: Reliability and measurement*. eds. Fenton, N.E. and Littlewood, B. Garmisch-Partenkirchen, Germany: Elsevier, 1990.

[43] Rombach, H.D. and B.T. Ulery, 'Improving software maintenance through measurement', *IEEE Proc.*, **77**(4), 581–95, 1989.

[44] Shepperd, M.J., 'An empirical study of design measurement', *Softw. Eng. J.*, **5**(1), 3–10, 1990.

[45] Shepperd, M.J. and D.C. Ince, 'The algebraic validation of software metrics', in *Proc. 3rd European Softw. Eng. Conf*. Milan: Springer-Verlag, 1991.

[46] Shepperd, M.J. and D.C. Ince, 'Design metrics and software maintainability: An experimental investigation', *J. of Softw. Maint.*, **3**(4), 215–32, 1991.

[47] Weinberg, G.M. and E.L. Schulman, 'Goals and performance in computer programming', *Human Factors*, **16**(1), 70–7, 1974.

[48] West, M. 'Quality function deployment in software development', in *Proc. Colloquium on Tools and Techniques for Maintenance and Traceability*. Savoy Place, London: IEE, 1991.

[49] Weyuker, E.J., 'Evaluating software complexity measures', *IEEE Trans. on Softw. Eng.*, **14**(9), 1357–65, 1988.

[50] Zuse, H., *Software Complexity. Measures and methods*. de Gruyter: Berlin, 1991.

Part 2

Supporting topics

Chapter 6

Building rigorous models

Synopsis

Although the role of models or prediction systems has been stressed, their treatment has, thus far, been relatively informal. The disadvantage is that any reasoning and evaluation about these models must, therefore, also be conducted on an informal basis. This chapter provides the apparatus to specify models more rigorously. This is done algebraically, with intended model behaviours defined as sets of axioms, from which it is possible to prove that a given model does indeed exhibit the desired behaviour in terms of satisfying its axiom set. This approach is illustrated with reference to the architectural models of software design taken from the chapter on architectural design. Finally, some of the limitations of rigorous treatment are outlined, especially the problem of selecting an appropriate set of axioms for a particular model.

6.1 Why formal models?

Throughout this book we have stressed the relationship between measurement and models: in particular the role of explicit prediction systems, a specialized class of model that has as its output one or more predicted quantitative entity attributes. However, there are other aspects of measurement that we might wish to model. For example, the measurement rules of how we assign symbols to represent entity attributes, to analyze the entity to be measured more carefully or to formalize our intuitions concerning the empirical properties of the entity being measured.

Models are useful because, as abstractions, they enable us to deal with complex situations and to focus upon, and reason about, aspects of interest. An advantage of formal models is that this reduces ambiguity and enhances precision. This can be very useful when considering measurement, as we can then address such questions as exactly what is being measured, how it is to be measured and how we can utilize the results. There is one danger, though, and that is that formal systems can represent a retreat from reality in that they can only deal with known factors: they are closed systems. In this sense they contrast with stochastic or probabilistic models that deal explicitly with uncertainty, but at the expense of determinism.

One of the difficulties with measurement in a comparatively new field such as software engineering is that much work is still at a very tentative stage and hence there is a great need for validation work. This takes two forms: either theoretical or empirical, and both are important. Empirical validation helps to address the question of how useful a prediction system is in practice within a particular measurement environment. Clearly, it is very important to be able to answer this type of question. However, empirical validation can be costly and time consuming, hence preparatory theoretical analysis can prevent effort being devoted to fundamentally flawed measures and prediction systems.

Other reasons for building formal models include the removal of ambiguity from the counting rules, so that different workers can have greater confidence that they are measuring the same thing. Incidentally, this is also a useful precursor to any tool development. Also, a formal model can help us to better understand, or even simulate, the behaviour of a measurement system when dealing with complex entities such as software architectures.

6.2 The algebraic approach

The modelling approach used in this chapter is known as algebraic specification. The use of algebra as a specification technique was first proposed by Guttag and others [2]. It is chosen because the notation is simple, it focuses upon the construction of the entities being measured and the semantics are fully defined, that is, it is a formal notation.

An algebraic specification is based around the concept of functions, where a function will take an arbitrary number of argument types and yield a *single* result type. This rules out the possibility of side effects since the only thing that can change is the result. Examples are:

double: integer → integer

which is a function that takes an integer, doubles it and returns the result, which will also be an integer. Another example is:

today's_date: → date

which has no arguments. Note that the example given below is not a valid function due to the fact that it has two results:

not_a_function: employee_id → salary AND tax_code

There are two parts to an algebraic specification:

- *syntax*, which describes the form of all the functions (this is called a function signature);
- *semantics*, which describes the behaviour of each function.

The syntax, then, lists all functions, with their signatures, which make up the specification of the model. Consider a very simple situation of wishing to measure (count) the number of modules within a system architecture or design:

new: → design
add: mod × design → design

We start off by considering the constructor functions – those functions that enable designs to be built. In this case there are two constructors, `new`, which defines an empty or null design which in effect is the base case, and `add`, which takes an existing design and adds a module, in other words a composition operation. From these two constructor functions we can define all possible designs by their successive application, for example:

add(file_handler, add(main, new))

defines a design with two modules, `main` and `file_handler`. This very simple example does not describe any relationship between these two modules; however, for the purposes of defining a measure of the number of modules this is irrelevant. The next operation we require is the measurement function itself:

metric: design → nat

This takes an arbitrary design and yields a natural (i.e. non-negative) integer indicating the count of modules.

So far, we have only considered the syntax or form of these operations. More interesting is to address their semantics or meaning. Meaning is defined in terms of equations or re-write rules. That is, if we can match the term on the left hand side of the equation it can be substituted by the right hand side. The process of substitution or term re-writing continues until no further substitutions are possible. In order to define the behaviour of the measurement operation metric we have:

m: mod
D: design

1. metric(new) = 0
2. metric(add(m,D)) = 1 + metric(D)

In this case there are two equations or rules. The first rule states that if the design is empty – where the only constructor that has been applied is `new` – then the count of modules must be zero, by definition. The other case, that of a non-empty design, is covered by the second rule, which can be matched whenever a module has been added to an arbitrary design `D`. This rule states that we add to the result value and strip away the last module that has been added to the design. The process continues until there are no more modules left and we can apply the first rule, which is the boundary condition.

In the following example we wish to measure the design comprising the modules `file_handler` and `main`. This is formally represented as:

metric(add(file_handler, add(main, new)))

This states that the measurement operation metric is applied to the design that obtains from adding twice to a new design. To find the meaning of this expression we search the set of rules to see if any substitutions are possible. In this case Rule 2 can be applied twice, followed by Rule 1, yielding:

= 1 + metric(add(main, new)) – Rule 2
= 1 + 1 + metric(new) – Rule 2
= 1 + 1 + 0 – Rule 1
= 2

At this stage there are no further rule matches so the re-writing process terminates with a result of `2`. So, we can formally show that our metric function gives a result of `2` – as we might expect – for the design containing two modules. This might not appear to be very useful; however, with more sophisticated measurement functions this more formal approach can yield interesting insights about the measurement behaviour. It also provides an unambiguous definition which could be useful for the construction of automated measurement tools.

6.3 A model of a system architecture

In this section we develop a detailed model of software system architecture and then illustrate how it can be used to reason about various design measurements. The preceding section showed how designs could be defined in terms of sets of modules – this view, however, doesn't incorporate any notion of connections between modules. To overcome this we introduce two more constructor operations `rd` and *`wr`* to define read and write relationships from modules to data structures. Modules are then linked or coupled when one module writes to a data structure and another module reads from it, since the first module can influence the behaviour of the second module. The operations have the following signatures:

rd: mod × ds × design → design
wr: mod × ds × design → design

Note that both operations have three arguments, the module name, the data structure that is accessed and the design within which they are contained. The result is an updated design. For example, Figure 6.1 shows a simple architecture which can be described algebraically as:

rd(B,cust_tab, rd(A,cust_tab,wr(A,cust_tab, add(B, add(A, new)))))

As can be imagined such expressions can become quite complex for large designs; they do, however, have the benefit of being easy to manipulate and reason about.

The first complication that we need to deal with is that not all objects that we can define are meaningful to measure. For instance, we might wish to impose the restriction that a design should not contain modules with duplicate names since this could cause an ambiguity with respect to module couplings, as we would not be able to determine which instance of the module we were referring to. This may be accomplished as follows. The `add` operation is modified so that the result depends upon whether the module to be added already exists within the architecture:

add: mod $\times$ design $\rightarrow$ design $\cup$ {duplicate_module}

From the signature we see that the result is either an updated design or an error type, a special set with a single member `duplicate_module` to indicate that the module name is not unique and therefore the `add` operation cannot succeed. Error types have the effect of halting the term re-writing process because they cannot match the left hand side of any equation in the semantics part of the model specification.

3. add(m,D) = IF exists(m,D) THEN (duplicate_error} ELSE add′(m,D)

Note that a new operation `add'`, known as an internal operation,[1] will be invoked if module `m` does not exist. `Add'` is identical to the original `add` operation and so always succeeds, which is a desirable property of a constructor. We also require the definition of a further operation `exists`, which is an example of an interrogator operation. Given the name of a module, `exists` simply returns true or false to indicate whether there is another occurrence of the name within the design. The signature is shown below:

exists: mod $\times$ design $\rightarrow$ Boolean

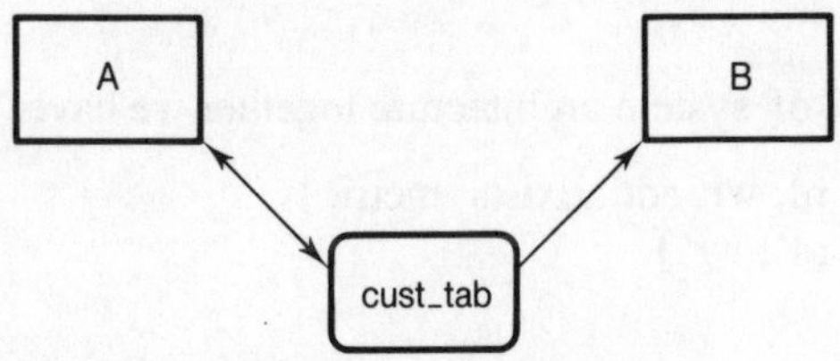

Figure 6.1 An example architecture

[1] Note that all internal operations are denoted ⟨`name`⟩′. They are so called because the operation is not externally visible to the user of the specification; its presence is merely required in order to write the specification.

The semantics are defined by the following two equations. Equation 4 deals with the boundary case, that of an empty design where, by definition, there cannot be a duplicate module name. Equation 5 defines all other cases, that is, non-empty designs, as an arbitrary design, `D`, to which at least one module has been added, `m`. If this module matches the value `n` which we are looking for, the search succeeds and the result `TRUE` is returned, otherwise the operation is recursively called (with the outermost `add'` stripped away) until the search terminates on the boundary condition defined by Equation 4.

4. exists(m,new) = FALSE
5. exists(m,add' (n,D)) = IF m = n THEN TRUE ELSE exists(m,D)

In general, operations fall into two categories, external and internal, the latter from now on being denoted by a prime. Internal operations are required in order to restrict the range of the constructor operations, although their presence is transparent to the behaviour of the model, hence their name. Equation 5 defines the relationship between the external, unrestricted `add` module operation and its internal, restricted counterpart. The latter is guaranteed to succeed because we have already tested for the possibility of duplicate modules.

A similar argument can be made for the two other constructors `rd` and `wr`. In practice, we don't wish to consider designs that contain reads or writes by non-existent modules; hence we modify the signature as follows:

rd: mod × ds × design → design ∪ {missing_module}
wr: mod × ds × design → design ∪ {missing_module}

Both constructors test that the module already exists or returns the error type `{missing_module}` in order to restrict the range of the constructor so that we only deal with meaningful designs. This requires two internal operations `rd'` and `wr'`, which only take as their arguments module names that have been previously defined. This is defined by two further equations:

6. rd(m,d,D) = IF exists(m,D) THEN rd' (m,d,D) ELSE {missing_module}
7. wr(m,d,D) = IF exists(m,D) THEN wr' (m,d,D) ELSE {missing_module}

Putting the specification of the model of system architecture together we have:

external operations (new, rd, wr, add, exists, metric)
internal operations (add', rd', wr')

new: → design
rd: mod × ds × design → design ∪ {invalid_module}
wr: mod × ds × design → design ∪ {invalid_module}
add: mod × design → design ∪ {duplicate_module}
exists: mod × design → Boolean
metric: design → nat

add′: mod × design → design
rd′: mod × ds × design → design
wr′: mod × ds × design → design

m,n: mod
D: design

1. metric(new) = 0
2. metric(rd′ (m,d,D)) = metric(D)
3. metric(wr′ (m,d,D)) = metric(D)
4. metric(add′ (m,D)) = 1 + metric(D)
5. add(m,D) = IF exists(m,D) THEN (duplicate_error} ELSE add′ (m,D)
6. exists(m,new) = FALSE
7. exists(rd′ (m,d,D)) = exists(D)
8. exists(wr′ (m,d,D)) = exists(D)
9. exists(m,add′ (n,D)) = IF m = n THEN TRUE ELSE exists(m,D)
10. rd(m,d,D) = IF exists(m,D) THEN rd′ (m,d,D) ELSE {missing_module}
11. wr(m,d,D) = IF exists(m,D) THEN wr′ (m,d,D) ELSE {missing_module}

So far, the only metric that we have defined is a simple count of the number of modules within a system design: hardly worth all the effort! For this reason we will move on to some more complex measures.

An interesting property of a system design is the extent to which there are connections or couplings between the components. The reader will recall that this characteristic is a major component or influence for many of the design measures – in particular the information flow ones – discussed in Chapter 2. We formally define two measures, C_i, which is the count of the number of couplings between module i and its environment and C, which is the total number of module couplings within an entire system architecture. Interestingly, the latter metric immediately raises a question as to the meaning of the number of couplings since for every coupling there must be two participatory modules. Summing C_i will not be the same as counting the number of couplings in the system. It all depends on what we mean by 'the total number of module couplings within an entire system'. This reinforces the need for careful thought and unambiguous definitions, even when dealing with seemingly simple metrics. In this case we will count the total number of module coupling participations,[2] so C is given as:

$$C = \sum_{i=1}^{i=n} C_i$$

[2] One reason for the decision to count module coupling participations as opposed to a simple count of couplings is that this is the approach adopted by all the major coupling measures. By following suit we will be building a model that may be more easily adapted to reason in a rigorous fashion about such metrics.

where there are n modules in a system. In terms of the algebraic model the operations have the following signatures:

$$C_i: mod \times design \rightarrow nat^3$$
$$C: design \rightarrow nat$$

These are both external operations. We turn now to their semantics, starting with C_i since this can then be used as a basis to define C. From the constructor operations it can be appreciated that in order for there to be a coupling between modules A and B we need either:

> A to write to, and B to read from some common data structure which can be expressed algebraically as: wr(A,d,rd (B,d,D))[4]

or for

> B to write to, and A to read from some common data structure where the equivalent algebraic statement is: wr (B,d,rd(A,d,D)).

In either case, the two modules are coupled together by a potential information flow via the data structure d. Note that, in this model, because there is no constructor to represent module parameters, our model cannot address any issues relating to parameter based couplings. This simplification is addressed in [7].

Equation 12 shows that the metric C_i is the sum of the fan_in (flows into) and fan_out (flows out of) of each module. Note that this differs from some of the information flow metrics published in the literature and described in Chapter 2, where the product of the fan_in and fan_out is employed.

12. $C_i(m,D) = fan\_in(m,D,D) + fan\_out(m,D,D)$

The fan_in operation is given as:

m.n: mod
D,E: design

fan_in: mod × design × design → nat

13. fan_in(m,new,D) = 0
14. fan_in(m,add' (n,E),D) = fan_in(m,E,D)
15. fan_in(m,wr' (n,d,E),D) = fan_in(m,E,D)
16. fan_in(m,rd' (n,d,E),D) = IF m = n THEN #wr(d,n,D) + fan_in(m,E,D) ELSE fan_in(m,E,D)

[3] Strictly speaking, C_i should have the form: C_i: mod × design → nat ∪ {missing_module} since in principle one could supply a module name that is not contained within the system design. For reasons of brevity we will side-step the issue.

[4] Note that rd (B,d,wr(A,d,D)) is equivalent to wr(A,d,rd(B,d,D)) because an important property of a valid algebraic specification is that its meaning should be independent of the order in which the operations are applied.

Starting with the boundary case we note in Equation 13 that a new or empty design will not have any couplings at all so the `fan_in` will be zero. Equation 14 merely states that for the purposes of identifying couplings we ignore the module defining constructor `add'`: it is stripped away in the term re-writing process. Likewise, for the purpose of determining the `fan_in`, writes to data structures are ignored (see Equation 15). So, the problem becomes one of determining which, if any, data structures the module reads from and, wherever a read is found, determining how many other modules write to that data structure. Equation 16 states that for any data structure read operation where the module is the one for which we are trying to compute C_i (i.e. m = n), the function `#wr` returns a natural number which represents the number of modules that write to the data structure `ds` – excluding the module itself, because a coupling must be between two distinct modules.

d,e : ds

#wr: ds × mod × sys → nat

17. #wr(d,n,new) = 0
18. #wr(d,n,add′(m,S)) = #wr(d,n,S)
19. #wr(d,n,rd′(e,m,S)) = #wr(d,n,S)
20. #wr(d,n,wr′(e,m,S)) = IF d = e AND m ≠ nTHEN 1 + #wr(d,n,S)
    ELSE #wr(d,n,S)

Note that Equations 18–19 merely indicate that the constructors `add'` and `rd'` can be ignored whilst we are searching for data structure writes. Equation 20 increments the count every time the data structure is matched and the module writing is not the module for which we are trying to compute the `fan_in` value (i.e. `m≠n`). Lastly, Equation 17, the boundary case, provides the termination condition for the recursion when the design is empty.

The `fan_out` operation is similar to the `fan_in` other than the direction of the flow, hence:

fan_out: mod × design × design → nat

21. fan_out(m,new,D) = 0
22. fan_out(m,add′(n,E),D) = fan_out(m,E,D)
23. fan_out(m,rd′(n,d,E),D) = fan_out(m,E,D)
24. fan_out(m,wr′(n,d,E),D) = IF m = n THEN #rd(d,n,D)
    + fan_out(m,E,D) ELSE fan_out(m,E,D)

and the `#rd` operation, which returns the number of modules that read from *ds* other than excluding the module itself:

#rd: ds × mod × sys → nat

25. #rd(d,n,new) = 0
26. #rd(d,n,add′(m,S)) = #rd(d,n,S)

27. #rd(d,n,wr′(e,m,S)) = #rd(d,n,S)
28. #rd(d,n,rd′(e,m,S)) = IF d = e AND m ≠ nTHEN 1 + #rd(d,n,S)
    ELSE #rd(d,n,S)

We now illustrate how these equations can be applied to formally define the C_i metric value for a given system design. Recalling the architecture shown by Figure 6.1, we will try to find C_i, where i = A.

The architecture in terms of our model is:[5]

rd′(ct, B, rd′(ct, A,wr′(ct, A, add′(B, add′(A, new)))))

where the types of the variables are:

ct: ds
A,B: mod

and D is treated as a constant with the value rd′(ct,B,rd′(ct,A,wr′(ct,A,add′(B,add′(A,new))))).

To find C_i for module A we have:

C_i(A,rd′(ct,B,rd′(ct,A,wr′(ct,A,add′(B,add′(A, new))))),D)

which, by Equation 12, becomes:

fan_in(A,rd′(ct,B,rd′(ct,A,wr′(ct,A,add′(B,add′(A, new)))))D)
+ fan_out(A,rd′(ct,B,rd′(ct,A,wr′(ct,A,add′(B,add′(A, new))))),D)

Dealing with the `fan_in` first, we substitute as follows. By Rule 16, since m ≠ n (m = A and n = B) we obtain:

fan_in(A,rd′(ct,A,wr′(ct,A,add′(B,add′(A, new)))),D)

and then by the same rule as m = n (m = A and n = A):

#wr(ct,A,D) + fan_in(A,wr′(ct,A,add′(B,add′(A, new))),D)

Solving `#wr(ct,A,D)` and expanding D yields:

#wr(ct,A,rd′(ct,B,rd′(ct,A,wr′(ct,A,add′(B,add′(A, new))))))	
#wr(ct,A,rd′(ct,B,wr′(ct,A,add′(B,add′(A, new)))))	Rule 19
#wr(ct,A,wr′(ct,A,add′(B,add′(A, new))))	Rule 19

By Rule 20 we note that d = e(d = ct and e = ct) but that m ≠ n is false (m = A and n = A), so:

#wr(ct,A,add′(B,add′(A, new)))	Rule 20
#wr(ct,A,add′(A, new))	Rule 18
#wr(ct,A, new))	Rule 18
0	Rule 17

[5] Note that the data structure `cust_tab` is rendered `ct` for the purposes of brevity in this example.

So we now have:

0 + fan_in(A,wr′(ct,A,add′(B,add′(A, new))),D)
0 + fan_in(A,add′(B,add′(A, new)),D)   Rule 15
0 + fan_in(A,add′(A, new),D)   Rule 14
0 + fan_in(A, new,D)   Rule 14
0 + 0   Rule 13

The term re-writing now terminates and we find that the `fan_in` for module `A` is zero, which can be confirmed by re-examining Figure 6.1. To complete this example we look at the `fan_out`:

fan_out(A,rd′(ct,B,rd′(ct,A,wr′(ct,A,add′(B,add′(A, new))))),D)
fan_out(A,rd′(ct,A,wr′(ct,A,add′(B,add′(A, new)))),D)   Rule 23
fan_out(A,wr′(ct,A,add′(B,add′(A, new))),D)   Rule 23

Since m = n (m = A and n = A) we obtain from Rule 24:

#rd(ct,A,D) + fan_out(A,add′(B,add′(A, new)),D)   Rule 24

Solving #rd(ct,A,D) yields:

#rd(ct,A,rd′(ct,B,rd′(ct,A,wr′(ct,A,add′(B,add′(A, new))))))

From Rule 28, d = e(d = ct and e = ct) and $m \neq n$ (m = B and n = A):

1 + #wr(ct,A,rd′(A,ct,wr′(ct,A,add′(B,add′(A, new)))))   Rule 28

Again from Rule 28, d = e(d = ct and e = ct) but m = n (m = A and n = A):

1 + 0 + #wr(ct,A,wr′(ct,A,add′(B,add′(A, new))))   Rule 28
1 + 0 + #wr(ct,A,add′(B,add′(A, new)))   Rule 27
1 + 0 + #wr(ct,A,add′(A, new))   Rule 26
1 + 0 + #wr(ct,A,new)   Rule 26
1 + 0 + 0   Rule 25
1

Substituting back into our `fan_out` expression we have:

1 + fan_out(A,add′(B,add′(A, new)),D)
1 + fan_out(A,add′(A, new),D)   Rule 22
1 + fan_out(A, new),D)   Rule 22
1 + 0   Rule 21
1

So we can see that the `fan_out` of module `A` is 1, which again can be confirmed by reference to Figure 6.1.

Although this may seem long winded, it is unambiguous and can easily be automated using any term re-writing system such as OBJ [1] or even a functional language. Problems of ambiguity with counting rules have long beset workers in the metrics field and for this reason alone more rigorous definitions are valuable. Having said this, it must still be pointed out that difficulties remain. For example, what constitutes a module? What is a data structure? None the less, the discipline of having to define a metric more formally, such as in the algebraic fashion described in this chapter, forces the measurement workers to address questions that might otherwise be side-stepped.

The other design metric, C, is based upon the sum of module coupling participations across the entire system. Defining this metric does expose a problem with the algebraic approach that we have been using. In general, the lack of state, and hence the absence of side effects, results in very compact and elegant specifications. However, in this instance we require both a destructive search and an intact copy of the system design. The solution is to mimic a state by making a copy of the design and using it as a second argument by means of an internal operation C′:

$$C': \text{design} \times \text{design} \rightarrow \text{nat}$$

29. C(D) = C′(D,D)

Equation 29 defines the relationship between C and C′: essentially the argument D is duplicated in order to mimic a state. After this our definition of the metric C′ takes the familiar pattern, with Equation 30 using the boundary case of an empty design having a metric value to terminate the recursion of Equations 31–33:

30. C′(new,D) = 0
31. C′(add′(m,E),D) = C_i'(m,D) + C′(E,D)
32. C′(rd′(m,d,E),D) = C′(E,D)
33. C′(wr′(m,d,E),D) = C′(E,D)

and

D,E: design

Equation 31 defines C′ as being the sum of C_i of module m plus C′ applied to the remainder of the system architecture. This recursion continues until every module has been stripped from the design and the term re-writing halts when the design is empty (E = new). Equations 32 and 33 are merely present to discard read and write operations which are not directly needed when searching for each module in the design.

This completes our specification of a model of system design and three design metrics. The full algebraic model may be found in the appendix at the end of this chapter.

Although this coupling metric could be extended, for example it ignores parameterized communication between modules, it is still potentially useful for software designers, and in fact forms a major subset of system architecture metrics as IF_4 [5] and the information flow metric due to Henry and Kafura [3].

An advantage of a formal model definition is that it removes all ambiguity, so in this instance it is clear that a global flow is not counted when a module both reads and writes to a data structure itself, since the operation explicitly tests for $m \neq n$. It is also evident that this metric will count duplicate flows between modules, either via more than one shared data structure or, by means of multiple reads and writes, to the same data structure. One might debate the desirability of such a counting strategy but at least it is made explicit.

Such formal models can also be validated by means of axioms. This approach involves stating the required behaviour of the metric mathematically in terms of one or more axioms. As an example we might require the property of monotonicity, so that as additional global flows or couplings are introduced to an arbitrary software design, this must increase the value of the C metric. This may be stated more formally as:

$$\forall D{:}design;\ d{:}ds;\ m,n{:}mod \cdot C(D) < C(wr'(n,d,D)) \text{ where } \#rd(m,d,D) \geq 1 \text{ and } m \neq n$$

and

$$\forall D{:}design;\ d{:}ds;\ m,n{:}mod \cdot C(D) < C(rd'(n,d,D)) \text{ where } \#wr(m,d,S) \geq 1 \text{ and } m \neq n$$

Once the axioms have been determined the next step is to show that the axiom holds for all possible inputs over the model. Such proofs, although not necessarily difficult to construct, tend to be lengthy and are omitted from this text. For further work in this area see [6, 7].

Choosing the properties that we wish to represent as axioms is not always straightforward. Pioneers in this field, such as Prather [4] and Weyuker [8] tended to search for fixed sets of axioms which they considered should be true for all metrics. The problem with this approach is that one either finishes up with a general and rather undemanding set of axioms, as in the case of Prather, or a highly inflexible set, as in the case of Weyuker. To compensate for this, Zuse [10] and subsequent workers have customized the axioms to suit the particular metric in question. This Zuse terms a viewpoint.

Where it cannot be shown that a model satisfies such an axiom, two conclusions are possible. First, one might infer that the model is deficient in some respect, or, second, that the axiom itself is inappropriate. Whatever, this axiomatic method at least draws the attention of the metrologist to such potential problem areas. It does not necessarily provide an answer.

6.4 Summary

In this chapter we have looked at a constructive or algebraic way of specifying the semantics of a metric and its underlying model formally. Although this appears to lead to a great deal of work – and is more likely to be the province of the researcher than the practitioner – there are many real benefits, which include the following:

- to be able to define the metric counting rules formally, so that researchers are able to compare like with like;

- identification of those structures which we do not wish to measure because they have no meaning, for example data structures that are accessed by modules that do not exist;
- formal demonstration that a metric always possesses a particular property, thereby complementing any empirical validation.

As with many other areas the introduction of rigour into the process forces metrics workers to deal with difficult questions and makes it that much more difficult to shelter behind a few vague examples and general appeals to one's intuition.

6.5 Exercises and further reading

1. Produce an algebraic model of the Yin and Winchester C metric (see Chapter 2 or [9]). [Hint: you will need the following constructors:

   new: →design
   addmod: mod × design → design
   calls: mod × mod × design → design

   and assume that no constructor will lead to an error condition.]
2. Using the above model demonstrate that adding additional module calls must increase the Yin and Winchester graph impurity metric for all valid designs. [Hint: you should use the following axiom:

   $$\forall D{:}design;\ m,n{:}mod \cdot Y\&W(D) < Y\&W(calls(m,n,D))$$

   and try to construct an inductive style proof.]

Ehrig, H. and B. Mahr, *Fundamentals of Algebraic Specification*. Springer-Verlag, Berlin: 1985.

The definitive work on algebraic specification for those wishing to pursue the technique beyond the usual plethora of stacks and queues!

Gehani, N.H., 'Specifications formal and informal – a case study', *Softw. Pract. and Experience*, **12**, 433–44, 1982.

This short tutorial paper offers a very accessible introduction to algebraic specification via several examples including a simplified relational database management system.

Shepperd, M.J. and D.C. Ince, *The Derivation and Validation of Software Metrics*, Oxford University Press, Oxford: 1993.

This monograph contains a number of algebraic models of design metrics including information flow and the work measures. It also describes in detail the use of axioms to validate models prior to empirical analysis.

Appendix – An algebraic model of system design

external operations (new, rd, wr, add, exists, metric, Ci, C, fan_in, fan_out, #rd, #wr)
internal operations (add′, rd′, wr′, C′)

m.n: mod
D,E: design
c, d, e: ds

new: $\rightarrow$ design
rd: mod × ds × design $\rightarrow$ design $\cup$ {invalid_module}
rd′: mod × ds × design $\rightarrow$ design
wr: mod × ds × design $\rightarrow$ design $\cup$ {invalid_module}
wr′: mod × ds × design $\rightarrow$ design
add: mod × design $\rightarrow$ design $\cup$ {duplicate_module}
add′: mod × design $\rightarrow$ design

exists: mod × design $\rightarrow$ Boolean

metric: design $\rightarrow$ nat
C_i: mod × design $\rightarrow$ nat
C: design $\rightarrow$ nat
C′: design × design $\rightarrow$ nat

fan_in: mod × design × design $\rightarrow$ nat
fan_out: mod × design × design $\rightarrow$ nat
#wr: ds × mod × sys $\rightarrow$ nat
#rd: ds × mod × sys $\rightarrow$ nat

1. metric(new) = 0
2. metric(rd′(m,d,D)) = metric(D)
3. metric(wr′(m,d,D)) = metric(D)
4. metric(add′(m,D)) = 1 + metric(D)

5. add(m,D) = IF exists(m,D) THEN (duplicate_error) ELSE add′(m,D)

6. exists(m,new) = FALSE
7. exists(rd′(m,d,D)) = exists(D)
8. exists(wr′(m,d,D)) = exists(D)
9. exists(m,add′(n,D)) = IF m = n THEN TRUE ELSE exists(m,D)

10. rd(m,d,D) = IF exists(m,D) THEN rd′(m,d,D)
    ELSE {missing_module}
11. wr(m,d,D) = IF exists(m,D) THEN wr′(m,d,D)
    ELSE {missing_module}

12. C_i(m,D) = fan_in(m,D,D) + fan_out(m,D,D)

13. fan_in(m,new,D) = 0
14. fan_in(m,add′(n,E),D) = fan_in(m,E,D)
15. fan_in(m,wr′(n,d,E),D) = fan_in(m,E,D)
16. fan_in(m,rd′(n,d,E),D) = IF m = n THEN #wr(d,n,D) + fan_in(m,E,D) ELSE fan_in(m,E,D)
17. #wr(d,n,new) = 0

18. #wr(d,n,add′(m,S)) = #wr(d,n,S)
19. #wr(d,n,rd′(e,m,S)) = #wr(d,n,S)
20. #wr(d,n,wr′(e,m,S)) = IF d = e AND m ≠ n THEN 1 + #wr(d,n,S) ELSE #wr(d,n,S)

21. fan_out(m,new,D) = 0
22. fan_out(m,add′(n,E),D) = fan_out(m,E,D)
23. fan_out(m,rd′(n,d,E),D) = fan_out(m,E,D)
24. fan_out(m,wr′(n,d,E),D) = IF m = n THEN #rd(d,n,D) + fan_out(m,E,D) ELSE fan_out(m,E,D)

25. #rd(d,n,new) = 0
26. #rd(d,n,add′(m,S)) = #rd(d,n,S)
27. #rd(d,n,wr′(e,m,S)) = #rd(d,n,S)
28. #rd(d,n,rd′(e,m,S)) = IF d = e AND m ≠ n THEN 1 + #rd(d,n,S) ELSE #rd(d,n,S)

29. C(D) = C′(D,D)

30. C′(new,D) = 0
31. C′(add′(m,E),D) = C_i'(m,D) + C′(E,D)
32. C′(rd′(m,d,E),D) = C′(E,D)
33. C′(wr′(m,d,E),D) = C′(E,D)

References

[1] Futatsugi, K. *et al.* ‘Principles of OBJ2’, in *Proc. 12th ACM Symp. on Principles of Programming Languages*. Computer Society Press, 1987.

[2] Guttag, J.V. and J.J. Horning, ‘The algebraic specification of abstract data types’, *Acta Informatica*, **10**, 27–52, 1978.

[3] Henry, S. and D. Kafura, ‘The evaluation of software systems’ structure using quantitative software metrics’, *Softw. Pract. and Experience*, **14**(6), 561–73, 1984.

[4] Prather, R.E., ‘On hierarchical software metrics’, *Softw. Eng. J.*, **2**(2), 42–5, 1987.

[5] Shepperd, M.J., ‘An empirical study of design measurement’, *Softw. Eng. J.*, **5**(1), 3–10, 1990.

[6] Shepperd, M.J., ‘Algebraic models and metric validation’, in *Formal Aspects of Measurement*, T. Denvir, R. Herman and R.W. Whitty, eds., Springer-Verlag: London, 1992.

[7] Shepperd, M.J. and D.C. Ince, *The Derivation and Validation of Software Metrics*. Oxford University Press: Oxford, 1993.

[8] Weyuker, E.J., 'Evaluating software complexity measures', *IEEE Trans. on Softw. Eng.*, **14**(9), 1357–65, 1988.

[9] Yin, B.H. and J.W. Winchester, 'The establishment and use of measures to evaluate the quality of software designs', in *Proc. ACM Softw. Qual. Ass. Workshop*, 1978.

[10] Zuse, H. and P. Bollmann, 'Software metrics: using measurement theory to describe the properties and scales of static complexity metrics', *ACM SIGPLAN Not.*, **24**(8), 23–33, 1989.

Chapter 7

Experimentation and empirical analysis

Synopsis

Having argued for the importance of formal model building for software measurement in the preceding chapter, we now proceed to describe the equally important need of empirical corroboration: that the two forms of model evaluation are complementary. However, this appeal to the empirically observable domain must be firmly grounded on sound analytic and statistical principles. Throughout, examples are provided of how abuse of these principles can lead to erroneous conclusions.

This chapter commences by emphasizing the importance of data analysis and the use of appropriate techniques. There is a discussion of the common problems associated with the analysis of software metrics and reviews of some simple techniques for the presentation and interpretation of data. These fall into the categories of exploratory and inferential statistics and are followed by a brief account of analyzing data sets in order to develop effective prediction systems. Emphasis is given to more robust statistics that make fewer assumptions concerning the nature of the data under scrutiny. The chapter then concludes with an outline of some of the factors that ought to be taken into account when designing software engineering experiments.

7.1 Statistics and software engineering

There is little doubt that empirical analysis, be it through case study, industrial data collection or experimentation in the laboratory, is an essential form of enquiry. Such analysis enables us to test theories, explain phenomena and predict future events, and this is just as important in the domain of software engineering as in any other discipline.

We use the term 'empirical analysis' to embrace all forms of data collection and analysis of observable phenomena. This includes passive investigation of products and processes in the workplace, frequently by means of case study and experimentation where a controlled situation is created in which the data collection can be carried out. The glossary below introduces some of the more important terminology for empirical analysis.

A glossary of empirical analysis terms

Mean: the average of a set of observations. The mean of n observations of x is $(\Sigma x_i)/n$. Note that this is only a meaningful statistic when dealing with interval or higher scales (see Table 7.5).

Median: the middle value (or the boundary between the second and third quartiles) when the observations are ranked; it is useful for giving a robust indication of a typical value. This statistic may be used for ordinal scale measurements as well as for interval and higher scales.

Mode: the most frequently occurring value or class in a set of observations. Some datasets may contain more than one mode. The mode may be used for any scale of measurement.

Case study: an empirical enquiry into phenomena within their real life context using multiple sources of evidence. The main disadvantage is not knowing how representative the results are as there is no replication.

Experiment: a systematic empirical investigation involving a number of subjects assigned to at least one of a minimum of two contrasting treatments. The main difficulty is in constructing an experiment that is representative of the 'real world'.

Population: the entire group of people or objects of interest, for example all software engineers or all Cobol programs.

Sample: a subset drawn from its underlying population. Typically, the sample is much smaller than the population as the population is too large to examine every member. If the sample includes all the population it is known as a *census*.

Dependent variable: a variable influenced by changes in other variables.

Independent variable: a variable unaffected by changes in other variables.

Statistical significance: the probability, usually denoted p, of an effect occurring due to chance rather than as a result of the factors being studied. By convention, the effect is said to be statistically significant if p is less than 5%.

As has already been suggested by measurement methods such as Basili's GQM [1], interpretation of the measurement data, once it has been collected, is an essential part of the technology. It is all too easy to be preoccupied by the process of collecting and defining numbers, at the expense of giving consideration as to how we can learn from them, find patterns, make inferences, dispel misconceptions and compare techniques. Why should this be so? Firstly, perhaps because not many software engineers are statisticians and, secondly, because the data are frequently both extensive and complex. Although techniques to support these data analysis activities are comparatively widespread, software engineering data sets frequently possess a number of characteristics that render this a less straightforward exercise than one might presuppose. Many statistical tests make a number of assumptions concerning the underlying data set, which, if violated, can make the results unreliable. Thus, it is important to be aware of these restrictions if statistical investigation is not to lead analysts to the wrong conclusions.

We now review briefly some of the principal characteristics of software engineering data sets.

Distribution. First, there can be the problem of distribution of observed variable values. This might seem rather arcane but they can, in actual fact, have a considerable impact upon the way a data set should be analyzed. Data is said to be normally distributed if it displays the characteristic bell-shaped pattern when values are plotted against the number of occurrences. Deviations from this type of distribution can cause difficulties because many statistical tests make assumptions that the data are normally distributed. Where this assumption is violated this can give rise to deceptive results. Unfortunately, skewed distributions are commonplace within the world of software engineering. A good example is defects per module, where the majority have zero defects, a few one and a diminishing number more than one. Although various transformation techniques, such as logarithms, square roots and reciprocals exist in order to derive an approximately normal distribution, these are not always effective. Section 7.2.1 re-visits the topic of distribution in greater depth.

Multiple variables. Due to the complex nature of modern software, and software development processes, software engineering data sets are generally characterized by the need for many independent variables. As an example, defects may have a number of explanatory factors including system size, module size, age of the system and experience. This renders analysis more difficult and conventional display techniques such as scatter plots and histograms less useful.

Multicollinearity. A common feature of multivariate data analysis is lack of independence[1] between the explanatory or independent variables, for instance the use of structured design methods and the use of CASE tools may well be associated – CASE tools support structured methods whilst the use of the methods fuels demand for automated support. This lack of independence leads to models that are

[1] This lack of independence is significant where it is due to underlying functional relationships.

overly complex with more independent variables than there are underlying dimensions but, more significantly, to models that are extremely unstable and as a consequence extremely difficult to calibrate. The problem is compounded by the fact that such associations are not always self evident. Consider the strong relationship between cyclomatic complexity [18] and lines of code, despite the claims to the contrary by its originator [13]: here the underlying dimension is size, but this is not obvious without careful analysis. Kitchenham reviews this problem in the context of cost estimation models [9]; however the principles are equally applicable to defect analysis. The normal solution to such a situation is to employ one of stepwise regression, factor analysis or principal component analysis. These will be discussed in more detail in a later section of this chapter (7.2.2).

Heteroskedasticity. A widespread assumption for many forms of statistical analysis is equal variance of the error terms. This is particularly critical to linear regression [5]. Unfortunately, this assumption is frequently invalid for software engineering data sets.

Figure 7.1 indicates a situation where the variance increases with the value of `Y`, whilst Figure 7.2 shows a time dependency for the variance. The latter suggests either that the model is decreasing in its suitability or that the ordering of the measurements influences their outcome.

Ties. Another frequent occurrence for software engineering data is its tendency to have many tied values. Defect data is a particular case in point, as many modules will contain zero defects (or so one hopes!). This can be a problem as many non-parametric tests are based upon ranked data, for instance the Spearman correlation coefficient.

Measurement error. Another typical feature that needs to be taken into consideration whilst analyzing data is the accuracy and reliability of the measurement process itself. Various techniques exist to either improve, or at least identify, the level of measurement error. Automated collection is always to be preferred when possible. Otherwise, collection by more than one method, education of the collectors, sanity checks and cross checks can all be used to reduce error. The use of sampling to re-check a certain proportion of measurements for accuracy

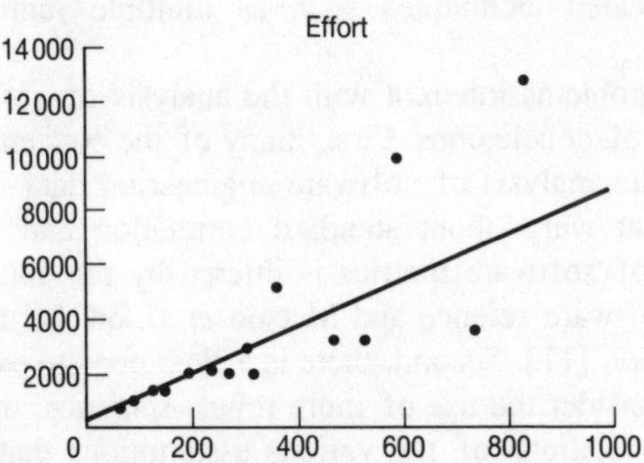

Figure 7.1 Variance increases with size

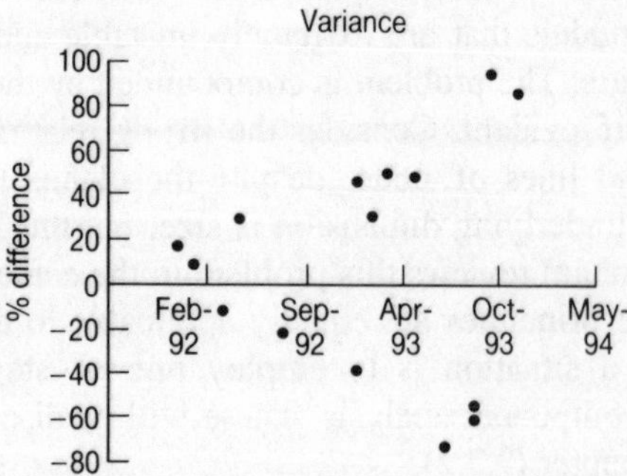

Figure 7.2 Variance increases with time

helps to determine the level of accuracy and reliability of the measurements. As a general principle it is always better to exclude suspect data – in the sense of there being doubt over the accuracy of the measurement – from an analysis as a single rogue data point can have a significant effect, especially on a small data set.

External variation. The last feature of software engineering data sets is that there is the problem of variation from outside the model. For example, if we are interested in predicting development effort it is clear that a number of factors will have a bearing upon effort, such as the size of the specification and the experience of the developers. Not all these factors may be known or incorporated into our model. An example is that a major explanatory variable for defects in software could be programmer ability; however, this is quite difficult to measure and indeed may vary from time to time, for instance due to minor illness, time of the day and so forth. This problem is exacerbated when dealing with only a few data points, thus the greater the number of factors the greater the need for more data points. Solutions include conducting controlled experiments where all factors, other than the one of interest, are held constant; and normalization, so that in the above example one might try to conduct the analysis in terms of unit size of specification or more sophisticated techniques such as multiple regression analysis.

The above list of some of the problems inherent with the analysis of software engineering data suggests a number of conclusions. First, many of the conventional techniques are not well suited for the analysis of software engineering data – as a minimum, one should be somewhat wary about standard correlation and linear regression techniques. The history of software metrics is littered by the abuse of statistics. See [26] on Halstead's software science and Matson *et al.* on the use of regression analysis for effort prediction [11]. Second, there is a clear need to explore less conventional approaches and consider the use of more robust statistics, that is, statistics that are less sensitive to violations of the various assumptions that they make [8].

7.2 Empirical analysis

The following is a short review of some of the simpler and more effective techniques to aid the analysis and interpretation of software measurement data. We will explore two categories of statistics: those suitable for exploratory analysis and those suitable for examining associations between variables. The section concludes by considering how to deploy these techniques in order to develop prediction systems.

7.2.1 Exploratory analysis

Generally the first step when trying to understand a data set is to study the distribution of values for each variable. Data is said to be normally distributed if they display the characteristic bell-shaped pattern when values are plotted against the number of occurrences. Figure 7.3 shows a normal distribution for the variable person hours of effort per design inspection. We see that eighteen hours is the most popular, or modal, value, with nine observations, and that the two tails are equal in size, with the number of observations decreasing with distance from the central point.

Sometimes, however, we may have to deal with data that are not normally distributed due to a few exceptionally high, or low, values. Such distributions are often referred to as skewed and these cause difficulties because many statistics, for instance means and correlation coefficients, make assumptions that the data are normally distributed. Where this assumption is violated it can give rise to deceptive results. Unfortunately, skewed distributions are commonplace within the world of

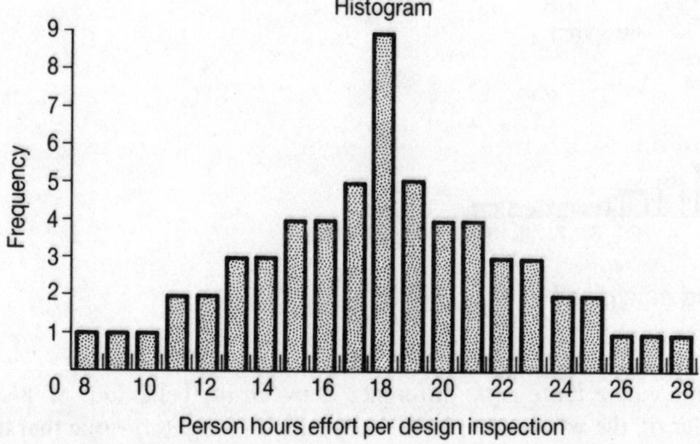

Figure 7.3 A normal data distribution

software engineering. Figure 7.4 gives an example of two skewed distributions: the top one with the lower tail skewed, sometimes referred to as negatively skewed, and the lower one with the upper tail skewed (positively skewed).

Almost invariably, defect data exhibit a tendency to be positively skewed, that is, an elongation of the upper tail. Software cannot contain a negative number of defects, the majority of modules will contain zero defects, some modules have one defect and a very small proportion contain a considerable number of defects. A simple indication of skew is when the median substantially deviates from the mean. Another measure of skew is Pearson's skew measure:

(mean – mode) / standard deviation

where a value of zero indicates a normal distribution, a negative value a negative skew and a positive value a positive skew. A skewed distribution severely limits the number of statistical tests available since all parametric tests make the assumption that the underlying distribution is normal or Gaussian. Unfortunately, the non-parametric tests tend to be more conservative in that they are more likely to accept a null hypothesis erroneously.[2] Various transformation techniques, such as logarithms, square roots and reciprocals exist in order to arrive at an approximately normal

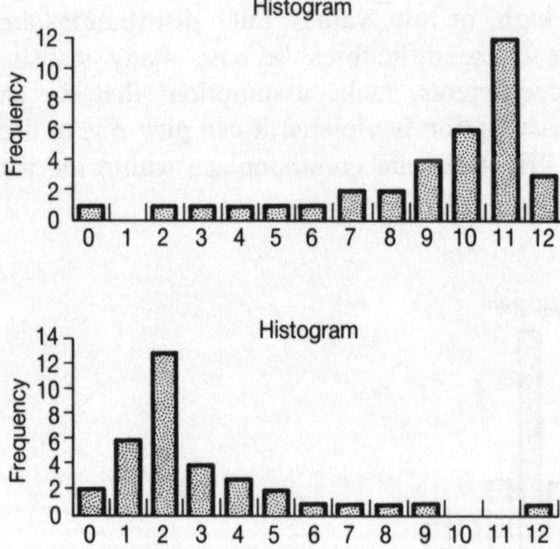

Figure 7.4 Skewed data distributions

[2] A null hyppothesis is one where there is no difference between the behaviour of a specific treatment and the behaviour of the whole sample. Usually, the investigators hope that the null hypothesis is overturned and that there is some significant effect.

distribution.[3] None the less, in many circumstances it may not be possible to transform the distribution into a sufficiently normal distribution for our purposes, and it may have undesirable side effects such as destroying linear relationships – a problem described by Mayer and Sykes in their analysis of size, defects and cyclomatic complexity data for the VME operating system [12].

When studying a distribution, one of the things which is useful to know is its central tendency. There are three relevant measures: the mean, median and mode. The mean or average is the best known and much abused statistic. Unfortunately, means are inappropriate for measurements based on the ordinal or nominal scales and can also be quite misleading for skewed distributions. The median indicates the middle value if all the observations are ranked in order and is therefore more representative of a typical value, whereas the modal class is the most common class frequency for discrete data and the mode the point of maximum frequency density for continuous data.

Another characteristic of a distribution is its spread. In terms of a normal distribution how wide is the bell? It is measured by the standard deviation statistic, σ, which is defined as:

$$\sigma = \sqrt{\left(\frac{\sum (x - \bar{x})^2}{n}\right)}$$

where n is the number of observations, x the observation value and $\bar{x}$ the mean.

The next set of examples is based upon the following, fictitious, module error and length data (see Table 7.1).

Both the error and the length data can be displayed graphically (Figure 7.5) using simple histogram techniques. This has the advantage of being much easier to

Table 7.1 Module data

Module	Errs.	Len.
A	0	30
B	0	20
C	1	30
D	1	30
E	12	80
F	0	35
G	2	10
H	0	25
I	0	30
J	0	50

[3] For further information see Myrvold's [16] short article on transformational techniques applied to software engineering data sets, including Tukey's ladder and Box–Cox methods.

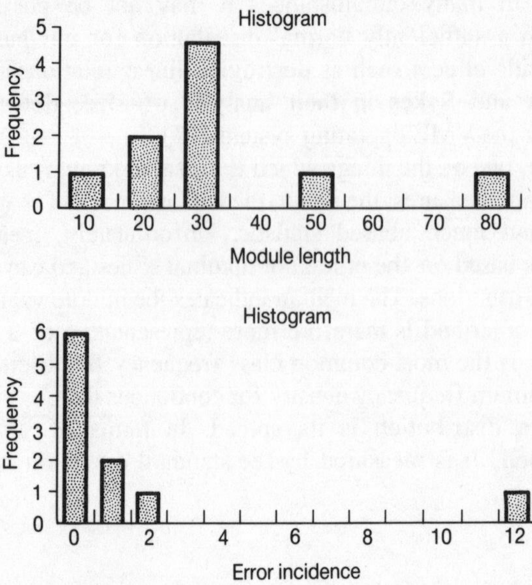

Figure 7.5 Histograms of module length and error incidence

interpret by eye than are columns of data, with the module with a length of eighty lines of code standing out. Similarly, the module with twelve errors is immediately apparent as being atypical.

Other statistics that can help to describe and compare data sets include means, medians and quartiles (see Table 7.2). Although the mean is probably the most widely used statistic, it can often be misleading, for example the mean number of errors per module is 1.6 but this is largely the consequence of a single outlier value of twelve for module E. Where the distribution is skewed the median may well give a better insight into the typical module. In this instance the typical module contains zero errors. Note that for the module length data the mean and median are much closer – an indicator that the data distribution is much nearer to normal.[4] The use of quartiles is a simple method for isolating abnormal or outlier values in an objective fashion. For these data, modules E and G have an unusually high incidence of errors since they both exceed 1.25.

Table 7.2 Means, medians and quartiles

	N	Mean	Median	Q1	Q3
Errs.	10	1.60	0.00	0.00	1.25
Len.	10	34.00	30.00	23.75	38.75

[4] Indeed, for a perfect normal distribution the mean and median values would be coincident.

The next step is to assess the relationship between the two factors, for which a scatter plot can be very effective (see Figure 7.6). This suggests that no simple linear relationship exists between length and errors; however, it does reinforce the impression that module `E` appears to be quite unlike other modules and should therefore be subjected to closer scrutiny as to why this should be. For instance, it may have been implemented by a novice or it may have been unusually complex. Whatever, the explanation, the metrics are highlighting it as an abnormal module within this data set.

Another powerful technique, which has the slightly daunting name of multivariate outlier analysis, is simply the means of identifying data points that are abnormal in the context of more than one variable. So far, we have only considered modules to be outliers in terms of a single variable, either length or error incidence. Now we turn to the issue of whether any modules have an abnormal level of errors, taking their length into account. This can be accomplished by considering the ratio of errors to length which is given in Table 7.3.

The interesting observation is that, now, module `G` may be seen to be the least typical of all the modules, something that was previously masked due to its unusually short length. This suggests that this module is most worthy of attention.

7.2.2 Association between variables

The techniques described up to now might be regarded as descriptive or designed to highlight anomalous data values. Another major area is the search for well-defined relationships between a dependent variable, say error incidence, and the independent variable, say module length. If the relationship is a strong one, this can be very useful as it enables predictions to be made, so in this instance if one knows the module length then the number of errors can be predicted effectively. The test for such a relationship is known as a correlation test, where a value of plus or minus one indicates an exact linear relationship, and zero suggests an entirely random relationship.

There are two common tests of correlation. The Pearson product moment is a parametric test that is suitable for data that is normally distributed, whereas the

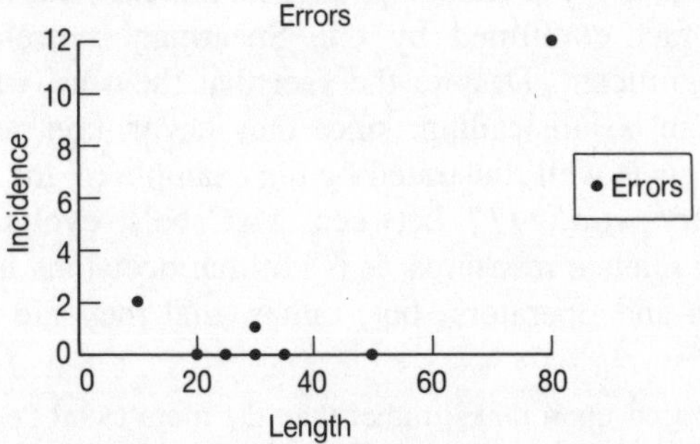

Figure 7.6 Scatter plot of module length versus error incidence

Table 7.3 Multi-variate outlier analysis of module data

Module	Errs.	Len.	Errs./Len.
A	0	30	0.000
B	0	20	0.000
C	1	30	0.033
D	1	30	0.033
E	12	80	0.150
F	0	35	0.000
G	2	10	0.200
H	0	25	0.000
I	0	30	0.000
J	0	50	0.000

Spearman test is based on ranks of values rather than absolute values and is a non-parametric test that should be used whenever data are skewed or violate assumptions of normality. Both tests are available in most statistics packages. Along with the correlation coefficient we also need an indication of its statistical significance, which is determined from the number of data points and the goodness of fit. Correlations with less than five chances in 100 of occurring randomly ($p < 0.05$) are generally regarded as statistically significant. It is important to take this into consideration, otherwise we might be deceived by a correlation coefficient of $r = 1.0$ but obtained from just two data points! Another statistic deriving from correlation analysis is the R^2 or coefficient of determination. This indicates how much variation in the dependent variable can be 'explained' by variation in the independent variable. This is useful, especially when trying to find predictive relationships. A situation of many data points might lead us to conclude that there exists a highly significant relationship between two variables, but a comparatively low correlation coefficient and an even lower R^2 would mean that there is little possibility of an accurate prediction system.

One glance at the scatter plot in Figure 7.4 is enough to suggest that no clear linear relationship exists and this is in fact confirmed by one Spearman[5] correlation coefficient $r_S = 0.064$, which is insignificant. Despite the fact that they are widely employed, correlation coefficients can be misleading, since they never, contrary to the popular view, imply causality. This is well illustrated by the example of the very high correlation reported by Henry *et al.* [7] between McCabe's cyclomatic complexity and Halstead's software science measures. It is not that decisions in the code cause an increase in operands and operators, but, rather, that they are both

[5] Note that the Spearman test is used, based upon ranks, rather than the more usual Pearson product moment, since the data are not normally distributed. This can be slightly suspect in the case of a large number of ties.

related to a third factor, namely, program size. Larger programs tend to contain more decisions *and* more operators and operands.

7.2.3 Building predictive systems

This section reviews some of the more conventional approaches to building prediction systems for multivariate data. Typically, use is made of regression methods in order to identify a linear relationship between a single dependent variable and a number of independent variables.

At its simplest, regression analysis (Figure 7.7) involves the determination of the best fit straight line between the independent variable and the dependent variable (the factor we are trying to predict). This is usually done by minimizing the sum of the squares of the deviation between actual and predicted (i.e. the perpendicular distance from the data point to the regression line).

In general, the better the correlation, in this case between FPs and LOC, the better the predictive relationship and the closer the data points will be to the regression line. When carrying out regression analysis it is important to check that the relationship is actually significant and also to examine the R^2 as an indicator of the predictive power of the regression equation. Finally, it is important to be aware of the impact of outliers upon the regression line. One or two data points can have an extremely disruptive effect, so the technique should be used with extreme caution on skewed data. As an example of the impact of outliers on regression analysis, see Matson *et al.* [11].

Most statistics packages also support more sophisticated methods, such as multiple regression analysis, where more than one independent variable is used. The reader should be aware of the fact that for such models to have predictive power it is very important that these variables are indeed, independent. However, as discussed in the introduction, software engineering data sets frequently exhibit the phenomenon of multicollinearity, which can lead to severe difficulties with regression methods. The normal approach is to attempt to reduce the number of underlying dimensions to arrive at a set of independent variables that are orthogonal. Such multivariate

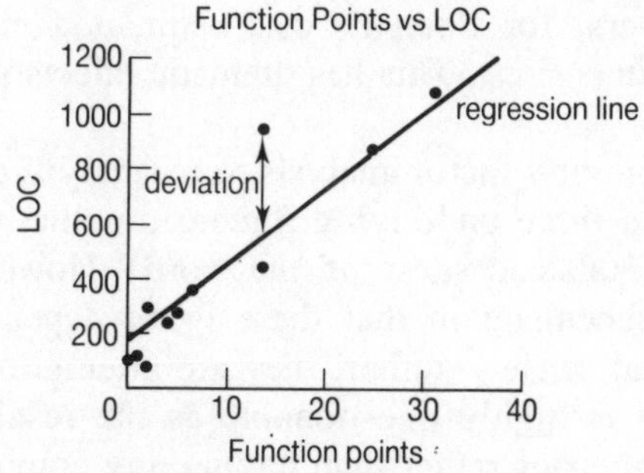

Figure 7.7 An example linear regression analysis

statistical techniques are collectively known as factor analytic methods, whose aim is to attempt to simplify complex models with large numbers of explanatory variables into separate dimensions and determine the factor loading of each variable on each factor. For further details, the reader is referred to [14] or [5].

There are a number of techniques, the two in most widespread use being (i) *common factor analysis* and (ii) *principal component analysis*. Common factor analysis is based upon common variance only, and is useful when we wish to identify underlying dimensions that are otherwise not very apparent. A good example would be the analysis of questionnaire responses containing 100 questions, where it is not obvious how the questions are related or what the fundamental factors are. However, in a situation of defect analysis it is less likely that these underlying factors will be so obscured; consequently principal components analysis will usually be more appropriate. Here the aim is to capture maximum variance with the minimum number of factors for prediction purposes.

Factor analysis also requires a decision on whether to seek an orthogonal solution – the normal approach – or an oblique factor solution. The former assumes that the factors identified are completely independent of one another, that is, there is zero inter-correlation. This is computationally more tractable and facilitates subsequent regression analysis and the construction of predictive models. The oblique approach is best suited when the analyst wishes to construct a more realistic model which reflects the fact that in the real world factors are seldom completely independent. However, the resulting model, although much simplified, will still suffer from problems of multicollinearity and, consequently, is unlikely to be appropriate for defect analysis.

Kitchenham [10] describes the application of principal components analysis to data collected from the ICL VME operating system, including a number of the better-known code metrics such as McCabe's metric and various of Halstead's measures, together with a number of module changes. Her table of cross correlations indicates a high level of dependence between many of the variables and hence that the number of underlying dimensions is less than the number of explanatory variables. Principal components analysis can be used to highlight the fact that there exists an underlying dimension that corresponds to our notion of program size, behind the code metrics. Elsewhere, she has reported on the use of this technique to reduce the fifteen cost drivers, for Boehm's cost estimation model COCOMO, to three or four underlying dimensions. This has dramatic effects upon the stability of the model.

Munson and Khoshgoftaar [15] use common factor analysis to re-analyze code data comprising eleven code metrics into three underlying dimensions that they term volume, control and effort (in the Halstead sense of the word). However, their approach differs from that of Kitchenham in that there is no dependent variable – at least not in the conventional sense – rather, they are attempting to infer a relative complexity metric. This is highly questionable as the resultant metric is an artificial amalgam of other metrics rather than having any empirical substance.

Factor analysis yields a number of benefits. First, it leads to models that are inherently more stable and that may be more easily calibrated either over time or between environments. This will lead to better prediction. Second, it can simplify data collection. When many variables are highly correlated there may be little benefit in collecting them all. Third, it can improve our understanding of complex systems and help analysts to observe underlying patterns.

Despite the many useful benefits, factor analytic techniques are not without problems. First, they do not work well with very small sample sizes. Hair *et al.* [5] suggest that, ideally, n should be four to five times the number of explanatory variables and that twice the number should be regarded as an absolute minimum. Furthermore, correlation coefficients become highly suspect when n is very small irrespective of the number of variables. Second, it is often unclear which of the many techniques will perform the best. Third, a subjective decision must be made as to how many factors are required. Too few factors means more unexplained variance and poorer prediction. Too many means excessive complexity. Last, is the stability of the model. When n is small, changes in the sample may lead to significant changes to the factors and hence to the model.

Notwithstanding these problems, using factor analysis, and principal components analysis in particular, can make a useful contribution to the analysis of defect data since many explanatory variables are potentially dependent. This will facilitate the development of more stable and better predictive models.

7.2.4 A data analysis example

We conclude this section with a simple example drawn from an analysis of real-time function points (FPs) carried out by the author and more fully described in [21].

Table 7.4 shows, in an abbreviated form, the set of data collected from an empirical investigation into the use of real-time FPs to predict development effort for twenty-one projects. Variables collected included the following:

- *estd. hours* (EST_HRS): the project manager's estimate of project effort made at the specification stage of the project;
- *actual hours* (ACT_HRS): the actual number of hours of effort for the project;
- *actual dur. weeks* (ACT_DUR): the project duration in weeks;
- RTFP: a measure of project size based on the number of real-time FPs derived from the project specification.

In this investigation ACT_HRS and ACT_DUR are the dependent variables and RTFP is the independent variable. In this example we will focus upon ACT_HRS. The first step is to examine the relationship between RTFP and ACT_HRS by means of a scatterplot (see Figure 7.8). Although there appears to be some visual evidence for a positive relationship between RTFP and ACT_HRS there is also a great deal of scatter which does not bode well for a prediction system based upon simple linear regression.

Table 7.4 Real-time function point analysis

Project	Estd. hours	Actual hours	Actual dur. weeks	RTFP
1	691	670	10	27
2	902	912	14	21
3	274	218	9	59
4	479	595	17	10
5	308	267	6	10
6	301	344	14	13
7	590	1044	23	8
8	234	229	3	8
9	172	190	2	29
10	334	870	9	49
11	159	109	5	2
12	239	289	8	4
13	373	616	8	6
14	308	557	8	3
15	588	416	10	6
16	861	578	13	7
17	104	98	4	0
18	424	439	6	27
19	232	99	6	0
20	218	75	3	4
21	505	1076	36	62

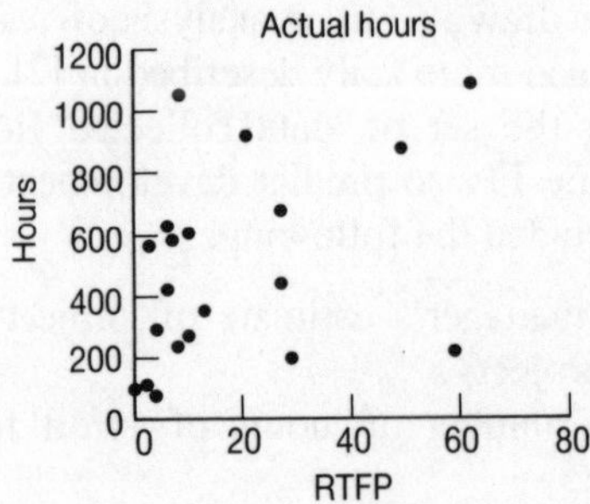

Figure 7.8 Actual hours effort against RTFP

Figure 7.9 shows that the distribution of RTFP values is somewhat skewed, so we proceed with the non-parametric correlation test, Spearman's rank correlation coefficient.

```
RTFP
ACT_HRS    .508
N(         21)
SIG        .009
```

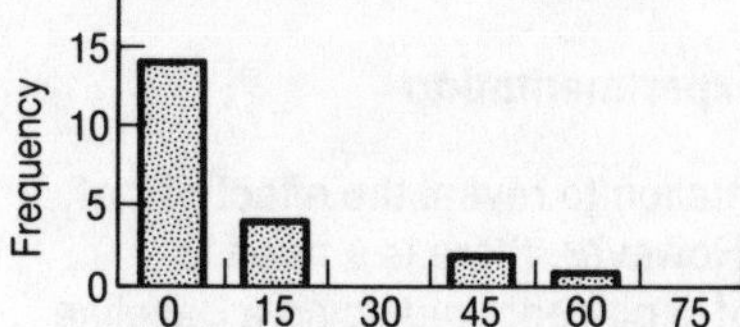

Figure 7.9 Histogram of RTFP frequencies

The r_s value of .508 is significant at $p \leq 0.05$ but, given that the R^2 is only .258, this means that less than 26% of the variation in ACT_HRS can be explained by RTFP, hardly a strong basis for prediction. A linear regression model of the form:

ACT_HRS = 357.02 + 8.56 * RTFP

can be derived, although it leads to a poor predictive model with an MMRE of 99% (see Chapter 4). It should be noted that such a prediction model performs markedly worse than EST_HRS made by the project managers (MMRE = 39%).

The next step is to inspect the scatterplot visually (Figure 7.8) and search for the gross outliers to see if there are any peculiar factors, for instance a weak project manager, that might explain the deviation from the normal relationship. The conclusion from this analysis is that there must be other factors that significantly influence ACT_HRS and that are not presently being captured.

7.3 Experimental design

Experiments are an important form of empirical enquiry since they allow us more control, though sometimes at the expense of realism. Work in the laboratory is usually small scale. At the beginning of this chapter we noted that the defining characteristics of an experiment were a minimum of two treatments, in order to make some comparison and replication through the use of many subjects, the aim being to discover if there is a significant causal relationship between the independent and dependent variables. This putative relationship is expressed in terms of the experimental hypothesis. The glossary on the next page introduces some of the basic terminology.

It is very important when considering experimentation to be clear what the aim of the experiment is and to express it as a hypothesis. Failure to do so can lead to hundreds of variables being collected and false relationships (Type II errors) being detected [3]. The following is an example of an experiment conducted by the author with the aim of better understanding of the relationship between software architecture and maintenance behaviour [20].

> HYPOTHESIS: that software engineers were more likely to make maintenance errors in modules with high levels of coupling as measured by the design metric IIF4.

Glossary of terms in experimentation

Control: a special treatment used in experimentation to reveal the effect of not applying the method or technique of interest. However, there is a need to distinguish between null treatment by means of a placebo and using a baseline treatment. For example, in an experiment to determine the impact of formal methods on software development productivity, some subjects would be allocated to the control treatment (i.e. not using formal methods) but these subjects would still be applying some sort of software development.

Null hypothesis: a hypothesis H_0 stating that there is no statistically significant difference or contradiction between the effect under investigation and the behaviour of the entire sample. Normally, experimenters expect the null hypothesis to be overturned and H_1 (that there is a significant difference) is accepted.

Type I error: the error of rejecting a hypothesis when it is true.

Type II error: the error of accepting a hypothesis when it is false.

NULL HYPOTHESIS: the `IF4` value of a module does not have a statistically significant impact upon maintenance errors.
DEPENDENT VARIABLE: number of maintenance errors per module.
INDEPENDENT VARIABLE: `IF4` for each module.
TREATMENTS: there were four versions of a system with the same underlying functionality and four different maintenance changes to be made, giving a 4×4 experimental design.
SUBJECTS: it was hoped to see sixty-four subjects so that four could be randomly assigned to each treatment. Unfortunately, a number of the subjects either failed to follow instructions correctly or to complete the task, so in the end we were left forty-nine useful results.[6]

Many difficulties can be encountered when conducting experiments. Perhaps the most problematic is that of *external variation*. This is variation in the dependent variable not accounted for by the experimental design. For example, in the experiment described above, one source of variation is differences in the ability of the subjects as maintenance programmers. This can be very considerable, as evidenced by the fact that one subject made zero errors whilst another made twenty-one for the same maintenance task on the same software. Moreover, the subjects had studied on the same degree course and had had the same industrial experience.

Techniques to deal with external variation include the following:

- pre-screening of subjects, for example by an aptitude test;

[6] Lessons to be learnt include the need for more extensive pilot studies to evaluate such things as the clarity of instructions and the duration of tasks for weaker subjects.

- standardizing the environment by use of laboratory conditions;
- random assignment of a sufficient number of subjects to each treatment so that variations counteract each other;
- use of a within-subject experimental design so that each subject has all treatments, though one has to be careful of learning effects and so the ordering of treatments is important.

The next difficulty with experimental design is one of *representativeness*. To what extent can one make general inferences regarding the whole population on the basis of the sample used in the experiment? The size of the task and the type of subject are the most controversial areas for software engineering experiments. Due to time and resource constraints experimental tasks are often far smaller than equivalent industrial tasks. At its extreme a so-called confirmation of Halstead's software science family of metrics was conducted based upon a FORTRAN program of seven lines of code [4]. Other researchers have been sceptical as to how representative this is of the general population of FORTRAN programs. The other problem has been the tendency to use computer science students, as opposed to professional programmers, as subjects, on the grounds of availability and cost. Although far from ideal, this may be less problematic. Analysis, by the author, of the performance of students with and without industrial experience has shown little significant difference.

A final area of difficulty is the choice of suitable tasks and materials for each treatment for an experiment. The author was involved in an experimental validation of various design metrics that failed to reveal any significant results, despite the use of over 600 subjects, due to there being an insufficient range of values for the independent variables, in this case design metrics, to expose any causal relationships. The problem was that the designs the subjects were working with were too small and too similar. The moral is again that better pilot studies would have revealed this problem at an earlier stage.

Despite these potential pitfalls, experiments have been an important and powerful tool of enquiry for the discipline of software engineering. Their great advantage is that the experimenter has a great deal of control, unlike case studies and passive observation, and they also have the benefit of replication of findings. This helps us to deal with the question of how representative findings really are.

7.4 Summary

From the above, it may be deduced that the statistical analysis of metrics is not always a straightforward process. Nevertheless, there exist many powerful and simple techniques that, if properly used, can yield useful insights into what may otherwise appear to be a morass of measurement data. However, a danger lurks in the form of abuse of statistics and the consequent drawing of inappropriate conclusions. For this reason alone, those involved in software measurement are

Table 7.5 Meaningful statistical operations by scale

Scale	Meaningful statistical operations[7]
Nominal	mode, frequency
Ordinal	median, percentile, Spearman ranked correlation
Interval	mean, standard deviation, Pearson product moment correlation
Ratio	geometric mean, coefficient of variation

strongly advised to ensure access to the necessary statistical expertise. We conclude this chapter with Table 7.5, which summarizes the appropriate statistical test for each type of measurement scale.

7.5 Exercises and further reading

1. Compute the mode, median and mean for the following dataset on module defect rates. Why might the mean be misleading when it comes to describing a typical module?

$$0, 0, 3, 1, 0, 0, 1, 4, 1, 0, 1, 0, 17, 2, 1, 0, 1, 0, 0, 1, 1, 0, 7$$

2. A golfer hits a ball which then lands on a blade of grass. The blade of grass is one of a million blades of grass on the fairway. Is the golfer right in stating that there was a one in a million chance of this event occurring? Are there any lessons to be drawn for the design of experiments?

Module	$Work_i$	Mean errors per maintenance change	Module	$Work_i$	Mean errors per maintenance change
1	21.3	3.5	15	4.3	1.7
2	3.3	1.0	16	1.7	2.7
3	1.7	2.0	17	24.7	3.8
4	1.7	0.3	18	2.7	2.0
5	6.3	2.2	19	1.7	1.0
6	5.7	2.3	20	1.7	1.0
7	1.3	0.2	21	3.0	1.0
8	1.3	0.0	22	24.3	4.4
9	1.3	0.0	23	4.3	1.2
10	1.7	0.0	24	1.7	0.0
11	1.7	2.0	25	3.3	2.0
12	1.7	3.0	26	1.7	0.3
13	1.7	3.0	27	1.7	0.0
14	3.3	2.0	28	3.0	0.0

[7] For an in depth account refer to Seigal and Castellan [17] as Table 7.5 only includes statistics referred to in the text.

3. The table on p. 208 provides the raw data from an empirical study into the relationship between module size as measured at design time by the work metric (see Chapter 2 and [19]). Analyze these data and determine if there is the basis for predicting the error proneness of modules using this measure.

Brooks, R.E., 'Studying programmer behaviour experimentally: the problems of proper methodology', *Communications of the ACM*, **23**(4), 207–13, 1980.

A straightforward introduction to designing and conducting experiments.

Conte, S., H. Dunsmore and V.Y. Shen, *Software Engineering Metrics and Models*. Benjamin Cummings: Menlo Park, CA, 1986.

An authoritative, if slightly dated, book on software metrics with a commendable emphasis upon statistical analysis.

Kitchenham, B.A. and L. Pickard, 'Towards a constructive quality model. Part II: Statistical techniques for modelling software quality in the ESPRIT REQUEST project', *Software Engineering Journal*, **2**(4), 114–26, 1987.

An accessible account of statistical analysis tailored to the needs of software engineering data sets. There is useful section on robust statistics.

Tiller, D.K., 'Experimental design and analysis', in *Software Metrics: A rigorous approach*, Fenton, N.E., ed., Chapman and Hall: London, 1991.

This chapter is a short, but highly informative, introduction to experimental design for the non-statistician.

References

[1] Basili, V.R. 'Software development: a paradigm for the future', in *Proc. COMPSAC, 13th Annu. Computer Softw. and Applications Conf.* 1989.

[2] Card, D.N. and W.W. Agresti, 'Resolving the software science anomaly', *J. of Systems and Software*, 7, 29–35, 1987.

[3] Courtney, R.E. and D.A. Gustafson, 'Shotgun correlations in software measures', *Softw. Eng. J.*, **8**(1), 5–13, 1993.

[4] Gordon, R.D. and M.H. Halstead. 'An experiment comparing Fortran programming times with the software physics hypothesis', in *Proc. Annu. AFIPS Conf.* 1976.

[5] Hair, J.F., R.F. Anderson, and R.L. Tatham, *Multivariate Data Analysis*. 2nd ed. Macmillan: 1987.

[6] Hamer, P.G. and G.D. Frewin. 'M.H. Halstead's Software Science – A Critical Examination', in *Proc. 6th Intl. Conf on Softw. Eng.* Tokyo: IEEE, 1982.

[7] Henry, S., D. Kafura, and K. Harris, 'On the relationship among three software metrics', *ACM SIGMETRICS Performance Evaluation Review*, **10**(Spring), 81–8, 1981.

[8] Huber, P.J., *Robust Statistics*. Wiley: 1981.

[9] Kitchenham, B.A., 'Empirical studies of assumptions that underlie software cost estimation models', *Information and Softw. Technol.*, **34**(4), 211–18, 1992.

[10] Kitchenham, B.A. and L. Pickard, 'Towards a constructive quality model. Part II: Statistical techniques for modelling software quality in the ESPRIT REQUEST project', *Softw. Eng. J.*, **2**(4), 114–26, 1987.

[11] Matson, J.E., B.E. Barrett, and J.M. Mellichamp, 'Software development cost estimation using function points', *IEEE Trans. on Softw. Eng.*, **20**(4), 275–87, 1994.

[12] Mayer, A. and A. Sykes, 'A probability model for analysing complexity metrics data', *Softw. Eng. J.*, **5**(4), 254–58, 1989.

[13] McCabe, T.J., 'A complexity measure', *IEEE Trans. on Softw. Eng.*, **2**(4), 308–20, 1976.

[14] Mosteller, F. and J.W. Tukey, *Data Analysis and Regression.* Addison-Wesley: 1977.

[15] Munson, J.C. and T.M. Khoshgoftaar. 'The relative software complexity metric: a validation study', in *Proc. BCS/IEE Software Engineering '90 Conf.* Brighton, UK: Cambridge University Press, 1990.

[16] Myrvold, A., 'Data analysis for software metrics', *J. of Systems & Software*, **12**, 271–5, 1990.

[17] Seigal, S. and N.J. Castellan Jr., *Nonparametric statistics for the behavioural sciences.* 2nd ed. McGraw-Hill: 1988.

[18] Shepperd, M.J., 'A critique of cyclomatic complexity as a software metric', *Softw. Eng. J.*, *3*(2), 1–8, 1988.

[19] Shepperd, M.J., 'Measuring the structure and size of software design', *Information and Softw. Technol.*, **34**(11), 756–62, 1992.

[20] Shepperd, M.J. and D.C. Ince, 'Design Metrics and Software Maintainability: An Experimental Investigation', *J. of Softw. Maint.*, **3**(4), 215–32, 1991.

[21] Shepperd, M.J. and R. Turner, 'Real-time Function Points: an industrial validation', in *Proc. European Software Cost Modelling Meeting*. Bristol: ESCOM, 1993.

Chapter 8

Process models and metrics

Our failure to highlight process modelling as the essential first step meant that often the people we persuaded to join the collection scheme began eagerly to customise our data model, halted when they discovered the lack of their own process model and remained halted.

(Linkman, Pickard and Ross [14].)

Synopsis

Thus far, our focus has been on software engineering products. We now turn our attention to the processes that have engineered these products, and consider how these may be depicted and reasoned about most effectively. The chapter discusses how metrics can be integrated into software process models and how such instrumented models can facilitate the introduction and application of metrics within the software industry.

8.1 Introducing process modelling

With the advent of quality standards and defined quality management systems (QMS) there has been an appreciation of the need to study process as well as product. This emphasis has been further fuelled by the work of the Software Engineering Institute from the late-1980s onwards, on process and capability maturity (see Chapter 5 or [9]). Consequently, there is considerable interest in the emerging subject area of software process modelling.

Process modelling is concerned with abstract representations of processes, in this case associated with manufacturing software related artefacts, although in principle most of the techniques could equally well apply to any other process.[1] The analogy of the process model being the recipe as opposed to cooking is apt. We are interested in developing a model of how a process behaves rather than just the outcome of the process.

As Curtis *et al.* [6] remark, what makes process modelling different from other types of modelling in computer science is that many of the phenomena modelled must be performed by a human rather than a computer. This introduces a degree of non-determinism into the models and demands a degree of subtlety hitherto unknown in computer science.

The basic principles of process modelling are best illustrated by a simple example. Consider the process of coding and testing a piece of software. We might identify the basic tasks of coding, unit testing and debugging, from which we can construct a simple model along the lines of Figure 8.1(a) or (b).

The pictorial model in Figure 8.1(a) is a gross simplification of the actual process of coding and testing. None the less, it conveys certain ordering information which is more concise than a traditional text based document, and more readily understood. For instance, coding precedes unit testing and debugging precedes coding and unit testing. An area that is excluded from the model is decision making: all that we can determine from the model is that unit testing involves some unspecified decision, resulting in the choice between ending the process and debugging.

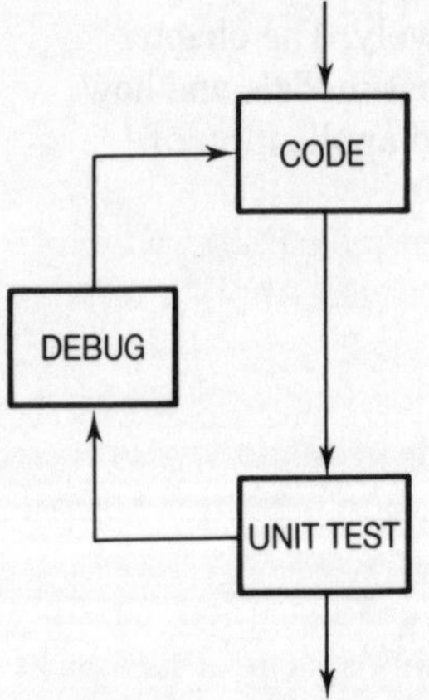

Figure 8.1(a) A simple process model

[1] In other disciplines the same underlying process technology is known by a variety of other names, including business process re-engineering and process improvement.

```
REPEAT
    code software
    unit test software
    IF code fails unit test THEN
        debug software
UNTIL NOT code fails unit test
```

Figure 8.1(b) A language based process model

Figure 8.1(b) shows the same coding and debugging process as the graphical model in Figure 8.1(a) but using different notation. This notation makes it clearer when the debugging activity is performed but gives no information as to what inputs and outputs are required or generated by each activity. Choosing the appropriate level of granularity and what to exclude from the model are important decisions, irrespective of the type of modelling notation, which depend upon the modelling goal. The key point, however, is that the model is of the process; it is not the process itself.

There is a wide range of potential benefits from process modelling, with modelling purpose dictating the approach to modelling. Applications include the following:

- understanding and communication;
- process improvement;
- re-use of successful processes;
- management through enhanced process status visibility;
- automated process guidance;
- execution as a long running process (enactment).

Understanding and communication are at the heart of all process modelling work. Although many organizations possess voluminous standards documents and procedures, there is often a lack of fidelity between official processes and actual project behaviour [6]. Such differences are often due in part to the difficulty of describing the iterative, interleaved and concurrent nature of software development using text, and in part to the difficulty of actually comprehending the intentions of the authors.

Probably the single most common objective is to improve. Implicit in this objective is the need to first understand. Improvement without prior knowledge seems a rather hazardous enterprise. Process modelling provides the opportunity to analyze and review processes, to spot the bottlenecks and the redundancy. Process modelling can also provide the opportunity for a degree of experimentation without causing disruption.

A longer term objective, once a process has been understood (and possibly improved), is dissemination of this good practice. Process models are a means of capturing and communicating this good practice. More sophisticated modelling notations and mechanisms also offer a means for customizing the process to best fit the process environment. This can be useful since there is a danger that just because a process has been successful in one situation it does not mean it will always be successful without adaptation.

Another popular objective is support for project management. The enhanced visibility of the process status can provide a manager with a much clearer idea of progress. In addition, some modellers [20] argue that process models can offer far greater control, defining what tasks must be performed and in what order.

A related application for process modelling is the provision of automated process guidance. In a sense, this could be no more than an on line procedures document in the form of a set of process models. However, there are other possibilities such as making the process guidance context sensitive and the provision of cross reference facilities. Update and configuration management of processes is more straightforward and can be carried out more reliably.

The final process modelling objective is to make process models executable (or enactable) as long running processes. This work is often associated with the development of software engineering environments and tends to assume a high degree of prescription. There is a considerable amount of activity in this area, see, for example, [1, 3, 4, 7, 19].

So far, this book has adopted a predominantly product based view of measurement. We have examined a range of products such as software architectures and specifications and have then considered how these might most usefully be measured. The underlying problem is that a product may enter into a variety of processes, to the extent that this may greatly alter the meaning of a product metric. A system architecture might be used at the initial high level design stage, when the designers are working with a 'clean sheet' and are consequently relatively unconstrained. By contrast, the very same product might be involved in an optimization process, for example to improve execution performance by collapsing module call hierarchies. Evidently, the second process is quite different from the first, resulting in the product metric having an entirely different meaning. Yet again, the self same system architecture could be modified as part of a maintenance exercise. And even maintenance may vary widely from the removal of faults to the introduction of major new functions, or, rather more occasionally, the removal of existing functions. Software engineers may use the system architecture to identify potential candidates for re-use or they might use it for a re-engineering or re-structuring exercise. Thus we are able to identify at least five quite distinct software engineering processes within which the same product participates, yet this is not explicitly recognized by workers in the area of product metrics.

The incomplete nature – in terms of the absence of process – of the models underlying product metrics is significant for three reasons. First, although the originator of a metric may have a clear notion of its intended application, there remains the likelihood of misapplication by others. Second, since differences in process can have such a substantial impact upon meaning, this renders validation inherently more difficult. Note that, even where the process appears to be essentially the same, for example software maintenance, there still remains much scope for variation. Whilst the focus of an investigation is so fixedly upon the product, there is little possibility of understanding the complex interactions between product and process. Yet, unless we come to terms with these interactions, our ability to incorporate product metrics into software engineering practice usefully will be decidedly limited. Third, the avoidance of process makes it difficult to consider issues of how the metric is intended to fit into the wider software engineering process. For instance, when during software maintenance should the system architecture be measured? How should the engineer react to these measurements? Can the metric be incorporated into any wider quality assurance procedures? These are highly pertinent questions and must be addressed in order for there to be widespread, industrial acceptance of software metrics. It is not sufficient that we are able to validate product metrics in laboratory style conditions. We must address their application as part of software engineering.

This chapter goes on to study the various notations and approaches to process modelling before describing how they can be integrated with metrics in order to provide useful, instrumented software engineering models.

8.2 Different approaches

In the preceding section we saw a very simple process model of coding and testing software. This section explores some contrasting methods for representing the process and we will consider some of their strengths and weaknesses. However, it must emphasized from the outset that choosing the most appropriate modelling notation depends to a large extent upon the modelling objective. If understanding is the chief goal, then a graphical notation will be most suitable but if we wish to enact the process, then the process notation must be automatable and will in all probability look very similar to a conventional programming language.

The approaches to representing the process fall into the following five main categories:

- life cycle models;
- executable languages;
- formal models;
- psychological models;
- graphical models.

Life cycle models, such as the waterfall model [25] and, more recently, the spiral model [2], tend to have a very coarse granularity and have not, therefore, always been considered as process models. Due to their general nature and high level, such models cannot do much towards our detailed understanding of software processes.

Executable languages, by contrast to the life cycle models are highly detailed, usually requiring a great deal of procedural and type information. Not surprisingly, Osterweil [20] has drawn a parallel between this type of modelling and software programming. There is some debate as to how appropriate this approach is for modelling the inherently non-deterministic behaviour of the human actors involved in a process. The advantage is, of course, that such models can support the development of automated software engineering environments.

As an example of an executable language we briefly review MVP-L [12, 24], which comprises three basic building blocks in the form of elementary processes, product and resource models. These can be combined to form project plans. For instance, a resource model of a software designer taken from [24] is as follows:

```
resource_model (eff_0: resource_effort) is

  resource_interface
 {designer within organization_X}
    imports
      resource_attribute_model resource_effort
    efforts
      effort: resource_effort := eff_0

  end resource_interface

  resource_body
 .
 .
 .
  end resource_body
end resource_model R_type
```

This form of process modelling is very similar to the more conventional programming as suggested by Osterweil. Rombach *et al*. propose that such programs be executed in order to help to analyze project plans and other similar processes. The program can also be used to provide a trace of historical processes and, it is claimed, support process re-use.

Related to the executable languages are the formal models of process. These are formal in the sense that they are based upon the use of mathematics. Examples are the use of OBJ by Nakagawa and Futatsugi [18] and VDM by Minkowitz [17]. Although the unambiguous semantics of such models provides the opportunity for mathematical reasoning, such models are difficult for users to understand and, as with executable languages, there remain doubts as to whether they are fully appropriate for capturing human behaviour.

A contrasting approach is the development of psychological models, often very detailed, which focus upon human decision making behaviour. Guindon and Curtis [8] developed an opportunistic model of designer behaviour obtained through studying a 'think aloud' protocol of a software engineer using JSD to solve a lift problem. A clear feature of this model is the way in which the designer jumps between different levels of abstraction and between design and requirements whilst attempting to find a solution. This contrasts somewhat with top–down, or bottom–up approaches of design text books.

The final class of process modelling notation is that of graphical models, including flow charts, data flow diagrams and state transition diagrams.

One of the most popular, and simplest, approaches to developing process models for the purposes of communication is to use dataflow diagrams (DFDs). This type of notation tends to emphasize the information requirements and outputs of each function or activity along with the process data stores.

Figure 8.2 shows a DFD for a rapid prototyping process. The bubbles represent functions, the arrows flows of data and the three-sided boxes data stores. In this diagram the overall process has been broken down into four functions: produce informal requirements, build prototype, evaluate prototype and build a 'real' system. The functions are linked by data flow output from one function becoming the input of another function. Where the flow is stored, not necessarily on a computer file, this is depicted as a data store. For example, the input to the evaluate function is the stored prototype – the function cannot occur until this is present – and the outcome, also stored, consist of change requests, which then form the input for the build prototype function.

A strength of a hierarchical notation such as DFDs is that higher level or more abstract activities can be broken down into more detail if and when it is required. This way the reader can have a set of diagrams, starting at a top level to introduce the process and subsequent diagrams to provide additional detail.

Figure 8.3 shows a refinement of the process evaluate prototype, which is depicted as a single bubble in Figure 8.2. Note that in the refinement there are now three functions, which, if combined, comprise the evaluate function of Figure 8.2. For large processes this can be a very powerful way of handling complexity and can also make the model useful to a wider range of users. For example, managers might be more interested in the top level model, whereas engineers might need the more detailed models as well. A range of CASE tools supports data flow diagrams, thereby allowing on line documentation and typically also support data dictionaries

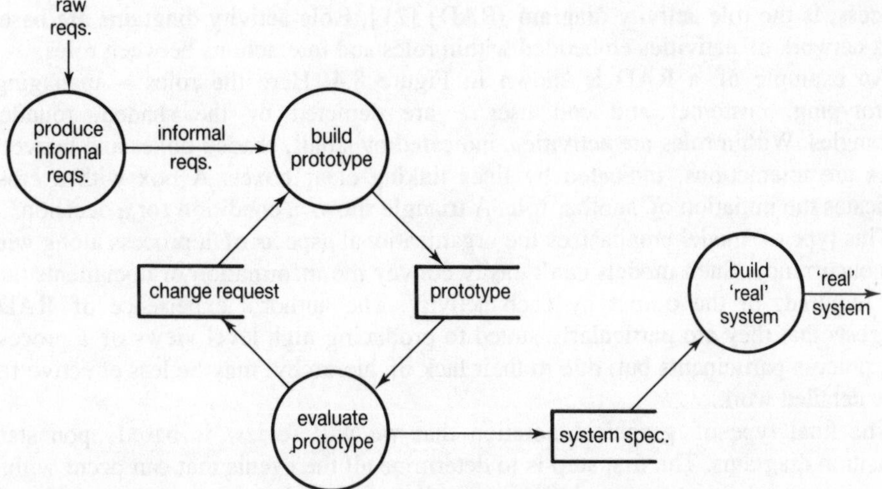

Figure 8.2 Using DFDs to model a prototyping process

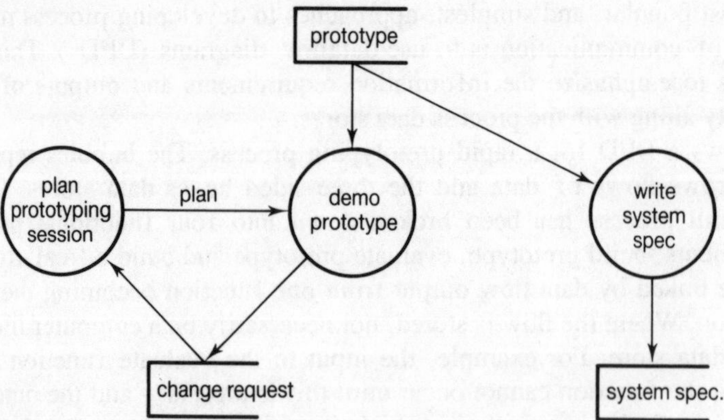

Figure 8.3 Details of evaluate prototype process

and process specifications, thus enabling powerful and detailed models to be constructed.

There are two main weakness with DFDs as a process modelling notation. First, they do not convey any control information. For example, in Figure 8.3 it would be very difficult to determine when the system requirements should be specified, or even when to stop demonstrating the prototype to users. A second disadvantage, common to most graphical notations, is that they possess very informal semantics. Without some shared understanding as to the meaning of the labels, the DFD would communicate very little information. Despite these drawbacks, this notation has been used successfully in industry, particularly where there has been an emphasis upon process communication [22].

Another graphical notation, but one that adopts a very different perspective of a process, is the role activity diagram (RAD) [21], Role activity diagrams are based on a network of activities embedded within roles and interactions between roles.

An example of a RAD is shown in Figure 8.4. Here the roles – managing, prototyping, customer and end user – are depicted by the shaded, rounded rectangles. Within roles are activities, indicated by small, shaded boxes and between roles are interactions, indicated by lines linking clear boxes. A box with a cross indicates the initiation of another role. A triangle shows a condition for a decision.

This type of model emphasizes the organizational aspects of a process along with its concurrency. Such models can't easily convey the information or documents that are required, or the output by each activity. The author's experience of RADs suggests that they are particularly suited to producing high level views of a process and process participants but, due to their lack of hierarchy, may be less effective for very detailed work.

The final type of graphical notation that we will review is based upon state transition diagrams. The first step is to determine all the events that can occur within the process and impose an ordering upon these events by means of an entity life history (ELH) chart. Consider the prototyping process; the entity of interest is the

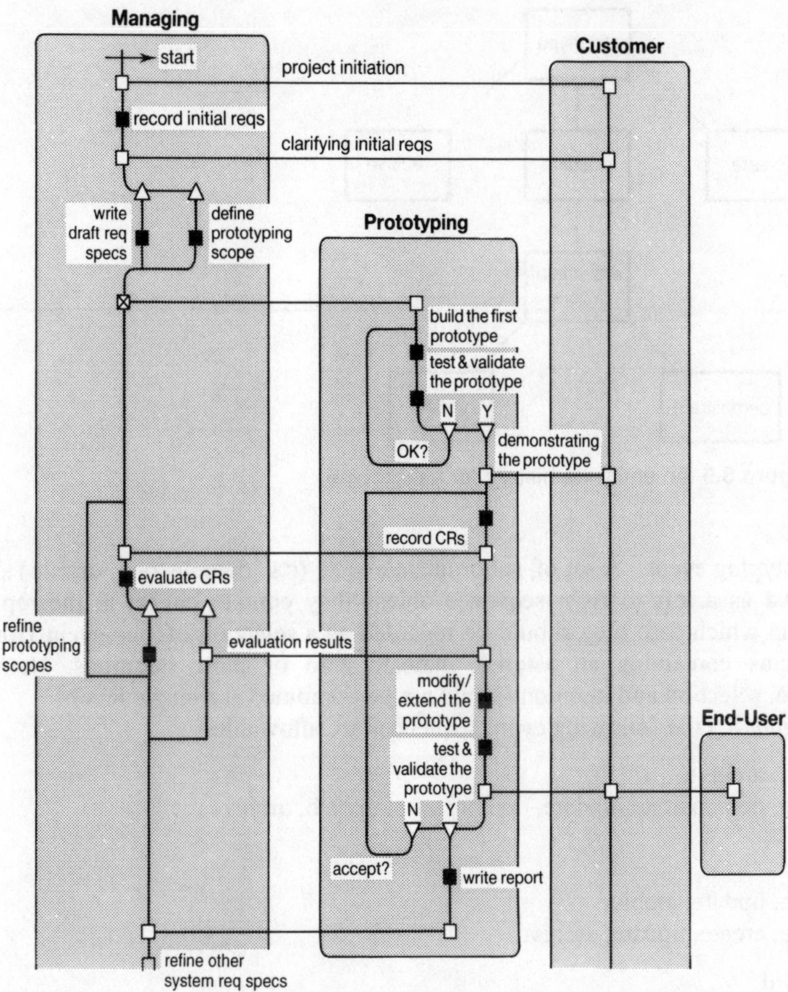

Figure 8.4 A role activity diagram of a prototyping process

prototype and the events that can occur to it are: creation, demonstration, update and archiving (when sufficient understanding of the user's requirements has been obtained, that development of the system proper can proceed).[2]

The events are shown as rectangles in the ELH chart in Figure 8.5, with the leaf events corresponding to the primitive events for a prototype that we have already identified. By analyzing the ELH chart we can determine all permissible sequences

[2] For a more elaborate model we should also consider the possibility of an abandonment event; however, for the purposes of simplicity this will be assumed to be subsumed into the archive event.

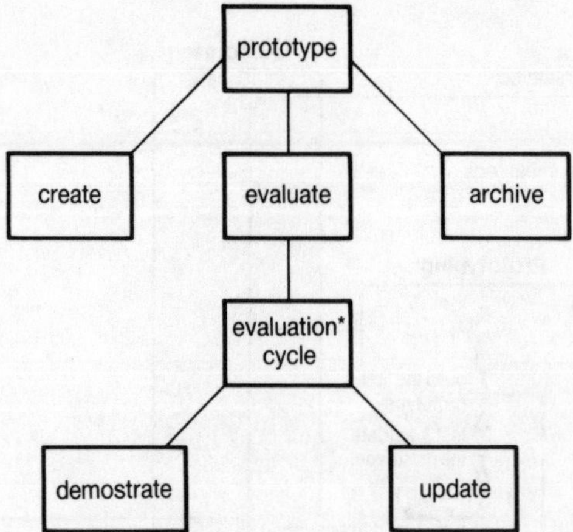

Figure 8.5 An entity life history for a prototype

of prototyping events. A set of subordinate events (e.g. demonstrate, update) should be treated as a left to right sequence unless they contain circles in the top right corner, in which case they should be regarded as a selection of one event from the set. Events containing an asterisk indicate zero or more iterations. Note that sequence, selection and iteration should not be combined at a single level.[3]

In Figure 8.5 the following event sequences are allowable:

create, archive
create, demonstrate, update, demonstrate, update, archive

whereas:

create, update, archive
create, create, update, archive

are invalid.

The next step is to use the ELH to construct STD, using the primitive or leaf events as the transitions. In our prototyping example we can derive an STD like the one in Figure 8.6. Note that we have added distinct `START` and `STOP` states in order to make the diagram unambiguous.

The STD in Figure 8.6 can be read as follows. The process is initially in a `START` state but when a create prototype event occurs it goes into a `READY FOR DEMO` state and waits until a `demonstrate to user` event happens. At this stage the process is now in a `DEMO COMPLETED` state and will wait for either an archive or an update event. The only way a `STOP` state can be achieved is via an archive event. This is a simplified form of the notation used by Kellner [11] when constructing statemate process models, and it also forms the basis of the instrumented models

[3] The notation is identical to that used by Jackson for JSP [10].

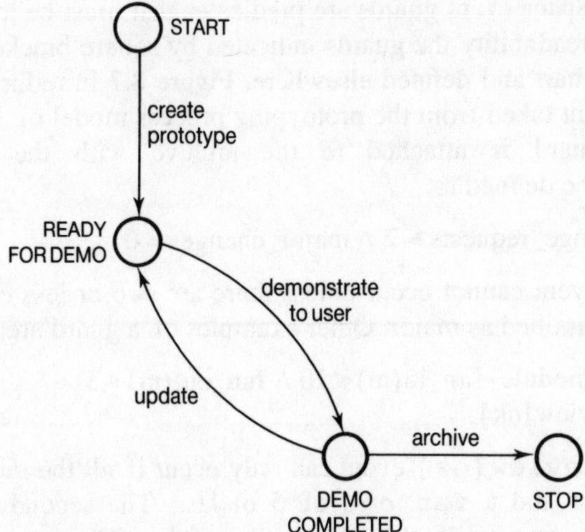

Figure 8.6 State transition model of a prototyping process

used by the author [26, 27] and described in the next section. In its unextended form, the models are clear to read but convey little information about the conditions necessary for an event to occur, for example how we can know when to archive a prototype.

This section has explored a number of contrasting approaches to the problem of depicting software processes. These approaches differ mainly because they adopt very different vantage points: we are seeing the same process but from different perspectives, such as functional, information-centred, psychological and organizational. Indeed, these techniques can be regarded as complementary. Thus the choice of technique depends to a large extent upon the modelling goals and the resources available.

8.3 Integrating process models and measurement

In this section we will address the problem of integrating measurement into process models. Despite the obvious synergy to be obtained from linking measurement and process technology, there is comparatively little work in this field. Some of the earliest models came from Radice *et al.* [23], with their entry task exit measure (ETXM) framework with its explicit use of measurement. More recently, Lott and Rombach [15] have explored the linking of the goal question metric (GQM) paradigm with their process language MVP-L. In principle, it should be possible to couple GQM with any process notation that embodies explicit measurement.

The modelling notation that we will examine is the state transition diagram (STD) that was introduced in Section 8.2, but extended to incorporate event guards, based on measurement expressions. Space event guards are predicates that must be true for a transition to take place. For readability the guards indicated by square brackets are usually given a name on the chart and defined elsewhere. Figure 8.7 introduces the notation. The STD is a fragment taken from the protoyping process model of Figure 8.6, but in this case a guard is attached to the archive with the name `prototype_ok`. This could be defined as:

$$\text{prototype\_ok} = \text{change\_requests} \geqslant 2 \wedge \text{major\_changes} = 0$$

which states that the archive event cannot occur unless there are two or less change requests, none of which are classified as major. Other examples of a guard are:

$$\text{review[ok]} = \forall \text{m:module} \cdot \text{fan\_in(m)} \leqslant 10 \wedge \text{fan\_out(m)} \leqslant 5$$
$$\text{review[fail]} = \neg \text{review[ok]}$$

The first guard states that the `review[ok]` event can only occur if all the modules have a `fan_in` of 10 or less and a `fan_out` of 5 or less. The second guard indicates that the fail guard is true when the `ok` guard is false. The next guard example demonstrates how to construct time based expressions.

$$\text{design\_inspection[ok]} = \text{YW(design)} \leqslant \text{YW(design')}$$

Here the guard states that the Yin and Winchester graph impurity metric for the current design must not exceed the value for the design prior to the last event acting upon the design. Previous values are indicated by the use of a prime.

We now show a more complex example based upon a maintenance process for a system design (see Figure 8.8). From this ELH we can create an STD complete with guards to indicate information such as when a review can be considered complete (see Figure 8.9).

The major feature of the model in Figure 8.9 over and above an ordinary process model are the guards attached to the review event. In this case we distinguish between three distinct review outcomes, using measurement as follows:

$$\text{review[ok]} = (\text{Y\&W} < \text{n}) \wedge (\text{\#chgs/mod} \leqslant 1)$$
$$\text{review[minor-errors]} = (\text{Y\&W} < \text{n}) \vee (\text{\#chgs/mod} \leqslant 1)$$
$$\text{review[major-errors]} = (\text{Y\&W} \geqslant \text{n}) \wedge (\text{\#chgs/mod} > 1)$$

where `Y&W` is the Yin and Winchester metric [29], n is an arbitrary constant to represent a trigger threshold and `#chgs/mod` is the average number of changes per

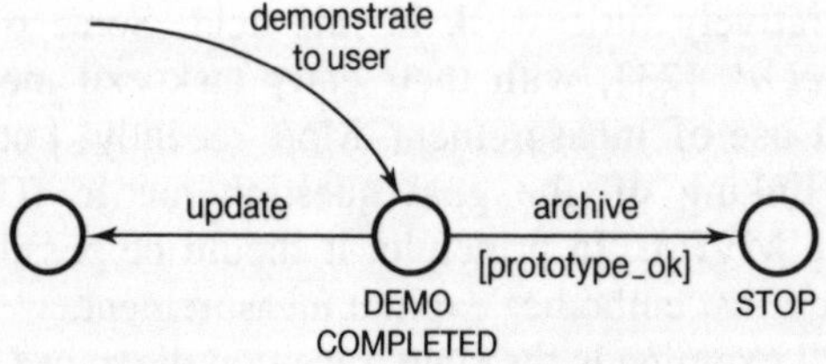

Figure 8.7 Event guards on a state transition diagram

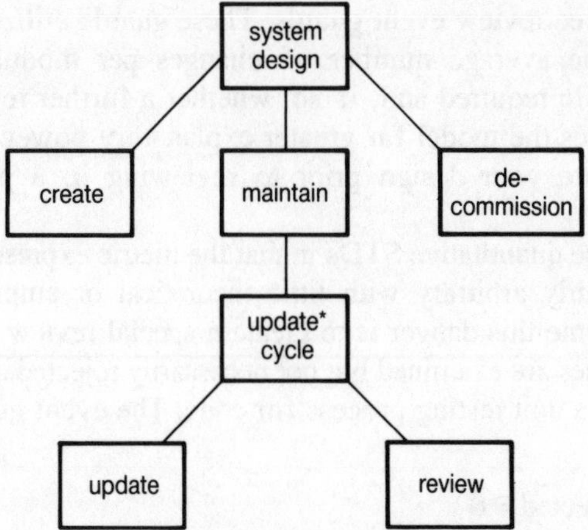

Figure 8.8 An entity life history for a system design

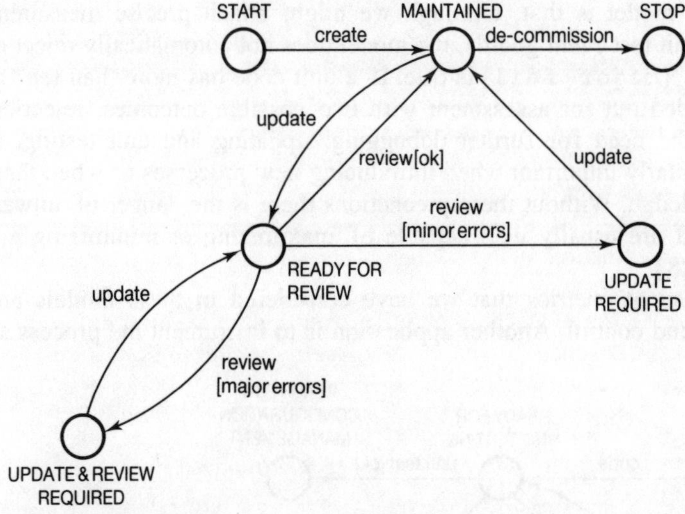

Figure 8.9 Measurements on a state transition diagram

module resulting from the review. (Note that these guards are intended to be illustrative rather than have any absolute meaning.)

Tracing through STD in Figure 8.9 we can observe a variety of scenarios. Beginning from the `START` state, we wait for a create a system design before moving to a `MAINTAIN` state. In the happy situation that no maintenance is ever required we would eventually encounter a decommission event and the model would reach the `STOP` state. More probable is that once in the `MAINTAIN` state there would be an update event, as the result of some maintenance need, and a corresponding transition to a `READY FOR REVIEW` state. At this stage there are three possible review outcomes reflected by the three review event guards. These guards utilize the Yin and Winchester metric and the average number of changes per module to determine whether further updates are required and, if so, whether a further review is called for. This is useful as it gives the model far greater explanatory power than merely stating that you must update your design prior to reviewing it: a pretty obvious statement in any case!

Clearly, there is a danger with these quantitative STDs in that the metric expressions that make up the guards can be fairly arbitrary with little theoretical or empirical foundation. One technique to overcome this danger is to create a special review state where out of the ordinary metric values are examined but not necessarily rejected.

Figure 8.10 shows a fragment of a unit testing process for code. The event guards are as follows:

$$\text{unit test[ok]} = \text{faults\_detected} = 0$$
$$\text{unit test[minor fail]} = \text{faults\_detected} > 0 \wedge \text{faults\_detected} < 10$$
$$\text{unit test[major fail]} = \text{faults\_detected} > 10$$

A feature of this model is that, although we might attach precise measurement conditions to the unit test event guards, the model does not automatically reject code for which unit test `[major fail]` is true. If a unit code has more than ten faults detected, it is singled out for assessment with two possible outcomes, rejection or acceptance, with the need for further debugging, updating and unit testing. This flexibility is particularly important when introducing new processes or when there is only limited knowledge. Without these precautions there is the danger of unwanted side effects as staff are usually well capable of maximizing or minimizing a few simple measures [28].

The types of use of metrics that we have considered in these models are to provide feedback and control. Another application is to instrument the process so as

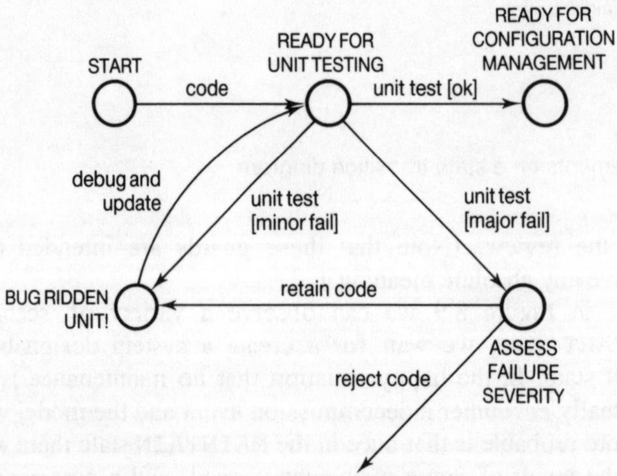

Figure 8.10 Flexible decision making in quantitative state transition diagrams

to provide better understanding. This can be accomplished by means of traces through the process model coupled with appropriate process metrics, most typically effort data.

Quantitative process models offer many benefits. First, they support dynamic processes which are controlled by quantitative feedback. Many software engineering processes are highly iterative and so it is valuable to be able to model this aspect of a process. Second, these models focus upon the objective exit criteria for each activity. For example, it is of limited use to be able to state that unit testing takes place after coding, but of great value to know when we can consider unit testing to be complete. Third, quantitative models help us to know when to collect metrics and define how to respond to metrics. This is particularly important, as throughout this book we have stressed the dangers of random data collection, hoping that it might be useful. These models force workers to consider how their metrics are to be utilized.

On the other hand, quantitative process models are not without their problems. They can be time consuming to develop, and very time consuming indeed in an organization with chaotic or immature processes, the more so where there is little experience of process modelling or metrics [11]. Second, they can be overprescriptive. The fact that it is possible to attach precise metrics values to different outcomes and decisions does not mean that it is always wise to do so. An element of flexibility is usually a sensible precaution. Last, there is a need for further experience of using this form of modelling in industry. Quantitative process modelling is still in its infancy despite the high degree of consensus over its relevance for software metrics.

8.4 Summary

In this chapter we have examined the relatively new technology of process modelling. This is concerned with representing and reasoning about processes. Although the processes under discussion have all been related to software engineering, this is not necessarily so. We have seen that there are many different perspectives of a process: behavioural, organizational, functional and information based and that the choice of perspective and modelling notation depends to a large extent upon the modelling goal.

The chapter has reviewed a number of pictorial notations that are particularly suited to the goals of understanding and communication and has studied an extension to state transition diagrams that enables measurement expressions to be incorporated as event guards.

We have argued strongly that process models and metrics are complementary technologies because without understanding of the underlying process it is difficult to know when to collect a measurement, how to use it or even what its meaning is. Measurement based process models have additional explanatory power because they can describe when and how decisions should be made in a more objective fashion.

Lastly, as a postscript, the reader might ponder the following quotation from Curtis [6]:

> *Since the payback from inserting [new software engineering] technology has been modest, greater leverage for improving project results appears to reside in better management of the software process.*

8.5 Exercises and further reading

1. Develop a graphical process model of the 'cleanroom' method. The 'cleanroom' method is so-called as it is based upon the principle of not allowing defects into the software as opposed to detecting and removing them afterwards. It was first proposed by Mills *et al.* [5, 16] and is based upon the following four techniques:

    - incremental development;
    - formal specification and design;
    - development without program execution;
    - statistical process control.

    There are three separate teams:

    - specification team;
    - development team;
    - certification team.

    The specification team is responsible for producing the:

    - external specification – understandable to user community,
    - internal specification – states the mathematical function which the system/increment will implement:
      – specify relationship between stimuli histories and response(s);
      – expected usage profiles,
      – will guide preparation of usage test sets for statistical testing.

    The development team are responsible for:

    - stepwise refinement of the specification into design (i.e. top–down design);
    - functional verification – that the design correctly implements the specification;
    - producing the code, but note that they do *not* compile or execute code.

    The certification team are independent from development team and are responsible for:

    - applying tests randomly drawn from usage test set;
    - reporting all failures to development team who fix faults as next version;
    - using all past mean time to failures (MTTFs) to predict future MTTF.

    [**Hint**: if you need further help, refer to the process model contained in [13].]

2. Develop a state transition based process model for a code inspection process using the entity life history model below. Using either metrics you consider appropriate or Table 3.2, attach measurement based event-guards to your process model.

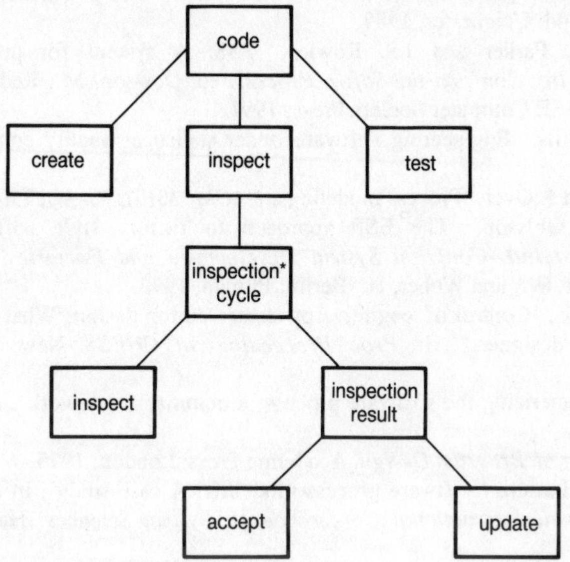

Entity life history of a code inspection process

Curtis, B., M. Kellner and J. Over, 'Process Modeling', *CACM*, **35**(9), 75–90, 1992.

An excellent tutorial introducing the process modelling that summarizes work in the many areas including that of role based modelling, rule based modelling and Statemate.

Ince, D.C. and C. Tully, eds., 'Special issue on software process modelling in practice', *Info. and Softw. Technol.*, **35**(6/7), 1993.

A collection of eleven papers representing the state of the art of software process modelling with a particular emphasis upon industrial practice. Recommended reading.

Lott, C.M. and H.D. Rombach, 'Measurement-based guidance of software projects using explicit project plans.', *Info. and Softw. Technol.*, **35**(6/7), 407–19, 1993.

An interesting account by Rombach *et al.* attempting to link the goal question metric paradigm with a process modelling approach, in this case the process language MVP-L in order to 'gain intellectual control'.

References

[1] Belkhatir, N. *et al.*, 'Adele 2: A support to large software development process', in Proc. *1st IEEE Intl. Conf. on the Softw. Process.* ed. Dowson, M., Redondo Beach, CA Oct 1991: IEE Computer Society Press, 1991.

[2] Boehm, B.W., 'A spiral model of software development and maintenance', *IEEE Computer*, **21**(5), 61–72, 1988.

[3] Bourguignon, J.P., 'The EAST Eureka project: European Software Advanced Technology', in *Software Engineering Environments: Research and practice*, K.H. Bennett, ed., Ellis Horwood: Chichester, 1989.

[4] Bruynooghe, R.F., J.M. Parker and J.S. Rowles, 'PSS: A system for process enactment', in *Proc. 1st Int. Conf. on the Softw. Process.* ed. Dowson, M., Redondo Beach, CA; Oct. 1991: IEEE Computer Society Press, 1991.

[5] Cobb, R.H. and H.D. Mills, 'Engineering software under statistical quality control', *IEEE Softw.*, **7**(6), 1990.

[6] Curtis, B., M. Kellner and J. Over, 'Process modeling', *CACM*, **35**(9), 75–90, 1992.

[7] Fernstrom, C. and L. Ohlsson, 'The ESF approach to factory style software production', in *Proc. 1st Intl. Conf. on System Development and Factories.* eds. Madhavji, N.H., Schaefer, W., and Weber, H., Berlin: Pitman, 1990.

[8] Guindon, R. and B. Curtis, 'Control of cognitive processes during design: What tools would support software designers?', in *Proc. Proceedings of CHI'88.* New York: ACM, 1988.

[9] Humphrey, W.S., 'Characterising the software process: a maturity framework', *IEEE Softw.*, **5**(2), 73–9, 1988.

[10] Jackson, M.A., *Principles of Program Design.* Academic Press: London, 1975.

[11] Kellner, M.I. and G.A. Hansen, 'Software process modeling: A case study', in *Proc. 22nd IEEE Annual Hawaii International Conference on System Sciences.* Hawaii: IEEE, 1989.

[12] Klingler, C.D. *et al.* 'A case study in process representation using MVP-L', in *Proc. 7th Annu. Conf. Computer Assurance (COMPASS 92).* 1992.

[13] Linger, R.C., 'Cleanroom process model', *IEEE Softw.*, **11**(2), 50–58, 1994.

[14] Linkman, S., L. Pickard and N. Ross, 'A practical procedure for introducing data collection (with examples from maintenance)', in *Software Engineering for Large Software Systems*, B.A. Kitchenham, ed., Elsevier Applied Science: London, 1990.

[15] Lott, C.M. and H.D. Rombach, 'Measurement-based guidance of software projects using explicit project plans', *Information and Softw. Technol.*, **35**(6/7), 407–19, 1993.

[16] Mills, H.D., M. Dyer and R. Linger, 'Cleanroom software engineering', *IEEE Softw.*, **4**(5), 19–25, 1987.

[17] Minkowitz, C., 'Formal process modelling', *Information and Softw. Technol.*, **3**(11/12), 659–68, 1993.

[18] Nakagawa, A.T. and K. Futatsugi, 'Software process a la algebra: OBJ for OBJ', *in Proc. 12th International Conference on Software Engineering.* Nice, France: 1990.

[19] Osterweil, L. 'Automated support for the enactment of rigorously described software processes', in *Proc. 4th International Software Process Workshop.* ed. Tully, C., ACM Press: Moretonhampstead, England: 1988.

[20] Osterweil, L.J., 'Software processes are software too', in *Proc. 9th International Software Engineering Conference.* IEEE Computer Society Press, Monteray, C.A. 1987.

[21] Ould, M.A. and C. Roberts, 'Modelling iteration in the software process', in *Proc. 3rd International Software Process Workshop.* Breckenridge, Colorado, USA: 1987.

[22] Phalp, K. and M.J. Shepperd, 'A pragmatic approach to process modelling', in *Proc. 3rd European Workshop on Software Process Technology.* Villard de Lans, France: Springer-Verlag, 1994.

[23] Radice, R.A. *et al.*, 'A programming process architecture', *IBM Sys. Journal*, **24**(2), 79–90, 1985.

[24] Rombach, H.D., MVP-L: A language for process modeling in the large. Technical Report No. CS-TR-2709, University of Maryland, 1991.

[25] Royce, W.W., 'Managing the development of large software systems: concepts and techniques', in *Proc. WESTCON*. San Francisco, CA: 1970.

[26] Shepperd, M.J., 'Products, processes and metrics', *Information and Softw. Technol.*, **34**(10), 674–80, 1992.

[27] Shepperd, M.J., 'Quantitative approaches to process modelling', in *Proc. Colloq. on Process Planning and Modelling*. London: IEE, 1992.

[28] Weinberg, G.M. and E.L. Schulman, 'Goals and performance in computer programming', *Human Factors*, **16**(1), 70–7, 1974.

[29] Yin, B.H. and J.W. Winchester, 'The establishment and use of measures to evaluate the quality of software designs', in *Proc. ACM Softw. Qual. Ass. Workshop*. ACM Press, 1978.

Index